DATE DUE		

D. Scott Rogo, a renowned expert on the paranormal, is the author of many books, including *Leaving the Body* and *Our Psychic Potentials,* both published by Prentice-Hall. In addition, he is a member of the graduate faculty at John F. Kennedy University in Orinda, California. He lives in Los Angeles.

The Search for Yesterday

A Critical Examination of the Evidence for Reincarnation

D. Scott Rogo

PRENTICE-HALL, Inc.
Englewood Cliffs, New Jersey 07632

Library of Congress Cataloging in Publication Data

Rogo, D. Scott.
   The search for yesterday.

   Bibliography: p.
   Includes index.
   1. Reincarnation.   I. Title.
BL515.R63   1985   133.9'01'3   84-26208
ISBN 0-13-797036-6
ISBN 0-13-797028-5 (pbk.)

This book is available at a special discount when ordered
in bulk quantities. Contact Prentice-Hall, Inc., General
Publishing Division, Special Sales, Englewood Cliffs, N.J. 07632.

10 9 8 7 6 5 4 3 2 1

ISBN 0-13-797036-6

ISBN 0-13-797028-5 {PBK}

Editorial/production supervision by Chris McMorrow
Cover design © 1985 by Jeannette Jacobs
Manufacturing buyer: Carol Bystrom

Prentice-Hall International, Inc., *London*
Prentice-Hall of Australia Pty. Limited, *Sydney*
Prentice-Hall Canada Inc., *Toronto*
Prentice-Hall Hispanoamericana, S. A., *Mexico*
Prentice-Hall of India Private Limited, *New Delhi*
Prentice-Hall of Japan, Inc., *Tokyo*
Prentice-Hall of Southeast Asia Pte. Ltd., *Singapore*
Whitehall Books Limited, *Wellington, New Zealand*
Editora Prentice-Hall do Brasil Ltda., *Rio de Janeiro*

To my father,
who taught me how to argue
both sides of any issue

Contents

Preface

Books on reincarnation have been proliferating on the already overcrowded popular occult/psychic market. Although most of them have eagerly attempted to *prove* the case for reincarnation, practically none of them has tried to evaluate this large body of evidence critically. Either basing their case on a wide and superficial view of the literature or concentrating on a specific case study, these books have basically taken a simplistic approach to the reincarnation problem.

I have designed this book as a more critical, sophisticated, scientific evaluation of the reincarnation riddle. It offers an overview of the many different kinds of evidence that serve to support this ancient doctrine—including reports of adults who have momentarily flashed back to their previous lives, children born with extracerebral memory, people who have recalled their past lives through hypnotic regression or LSD psychotherapy, and instances in which individuals have actually spoken the languages they purportedly used during their fomer lives. Cases have even been placed on record telling of patients undergoing psychotherapy who have been cured of their problems by recalling their previous existences. But this book is meant to do more than merely present all this evidence.

Interspersed with these case studies are discussions of various problems and possibilities raised by this material. These are issues most writers on reincarnation have usually failed to address. Are the past lives so many people remember historically accurate? Can such factors as fraud or genetic (inherited) memory account for past-life recall? Were these cases well investigated to begin with? These are the truly crucial issues raised by the study of past-life recall.

These cases also raise many parapsychological issues as well. How can you account for a case in which two children recall the *same* past life? Or cases in which a person recalls a previous life that has been apparently drawn from the terrestrial existences of two *different* people?

Cases such as these exist in the literature, although they are often swept under the carpet by many popular writers on psychic phenomena. *The Search for Yesterday* is therefore a different kind of book, since it not only thoroughly surveys the evidence for reincarnation but also emphasizes just how complex the evidence really is.

At the conclusion of this volume I present some explanatory models that can account for the evidence—the good, the bad, *and* the puzzling. There doesn't seem to be any doubt that some people can tap into the memories of other people, cultures, and places long removed in time. But does this phenomenon suggest reincarnation? Might it be pointing to something even more complex? My own feeling is that the evidence, taken as a whole, is impressive but that it cannot be subsumed within a simplistic reincarnation theory. I think we are, indeed, dealing with something vastly more complicated.

Because my approach to the rebirth controversy is controversial, perhaps I should preface the following chapters by explaining my own biases about what is popularly called "reincarnation."

Although I have long been interested in the problem of life after death, until a few years ago I had never been attracted to reincarnation research—either as a parapsychologist or as a person concerned with the mystery of life. I was particularly unimpressed by the evidence produced through hypnosis. Gradually though, I came to realize that my reluctance to make any detailed study of the reincarnation question was mostly a matter of personal and very unscientific prejudice. I found the idea of reincarnation distasteful, and I had allowed my bias to interfere with my objectivity. When I came to grips with my feelings, I realized that I had a personal and professional responsibility to undertake a thorough evaluation of the reincarnation controversy. I began studying the literature all over again—even those areas I had previously dismissed—hoping that perhaps I might find something that I had overlooked when I studied it years ago. Gradually I found myself changing my opinion about the value and quality of the evidence. But I also found myself thinking in less and less conventional terms about reincarnation. The problem wasn't so much with the evidence itself, but with the way in which the Western mind conceptualizes reincarnation to begin with. I needed to cast off not only my own biases about reincarnation, but even the biases about the way most of us *think* about the subject.

I have written the above comments so that you will realize just how I came to approach the reincarnation question. What I offer is a very different approach to this doctrine and its understanding from that with which you are probably familiar. It will be up to you to determine whether I have indeed cast off my old biases or have merely disguised them.

On pages 24–25 the excerpts from _Lifetimes: True Accounts of Reincarnation,_ copyright © 1979 by Frederick Lenz, are used with permission of the publisher, the Bobbs-Merrill Company, Inc.

Extracts from S. K. Pasricha and D. R. Barker, "A Case of the Reincarnation Type in India: The Case of Rakesh Gaur," are reprinted by permission of the _European Journal of Parapsychology._

A portion of "The Rosemary Case of Egyptian Xenoglossy" by William Kautz is used by permission.

Portions of Chapters, 6, 8, and 9 have been expanded from "Adventures in Make-Believe" by Scott Rogo (December 1982) and "A Psychiatrist Uncovers a Past Life" by Christopher Bloom (March 1983) and are reprinted by special permission of _Fate_ magazine.

The excerpt from Masters and Houston, _The Varieties of Psychedelic Experience,_ appearing in Chapter 10 is reprinted by permission.

Scattered quotations from _Realms of the Human Unconscious_ by Stanislav Grof, copyright © 1975 by Stanislav Grof and Joan Halifax-Grof, are reprinted by permission of Viking Penguin Inc.

On page 35 material referring to the Shafenberg case is taken from _Reincarnation: The Second Chance,_ copyright © 1974 by Sybil Leek, and is reprinted by permission of Stein and Day Publishers.

In Chapter 11, excerpts from _Death and Eternal Life_ by John H. Hick, © 1976 by John Hick, are reprinted with permission of Harper & Row, Publishers, Inc.

The
Search for
Yesterday

1

Parapsychology and the Rebirth Controversy

The case of Edward Ryall is an extraordinary one. Ryall lived a rather quiet life in Essex County, and didn't admit recalling a previous existence until he was about seventy. He had never talked about his reincarnation memories as a young child the way many Asian children are prone to do. He was quite mature when recollections of a previous life in seventeenth-century England began flooding his mind. He distinctly recalled being born in 1645 and being raised on a farm near Weston Zoyland. His name had been John Fletcher. His parents died when he was young, and by the time he was a teenager, he was responsible for the family holdings. He eventually married, settled down in Dunwear, sired two sons, and found himself involved in the British civil war of the 1680s. He died at the hands of royalist troops.

These memories emerged over the course of several years. They began welling up in his mind in the same manner that we all sometimes suddenly recall events from our past. But the case of Edward Ryall is not particularly noteworthy merely because of its reincarnationist nature, but because of the sheer mass of information he purportedly recollected. He was able to write a lengthy book about his past life, and at least one parapsychologist endorsed his claims after studying his material in depth. Dr. Ian Stevenson, a prominent psychiatrist at the University of Virginia, wrote the introduction to Ryall's *Second Time Round* after convincing himself that the author was not trying to pull a hoax. Dr. Stevenson was especially impressed by the book's rich historical detail.

Dr. Stevenson, however, may have spoken too soon. When the case

1

began to receive considerable publicity, historians as well as a few parapsychologists went on the attack. The first problem was Ryall's use of language. Experts pointed out that his accounts, often phrased in the English spoken in the seventeenth century, incorrectly used such common pronouns as *ye* and *thee*. He had also apparently used archaic words that had died out by the seventeenth century. The critics were also puzzled by a reference to a religious movement that didn't spread until half a century after "John Fletcher's" death. All this was added to the fact that some words found in the text are used in the context of their modern denotations, although they had different meanings during the 1600s.

Nor was Ryall's history all that accurate. *Second Time Round* includes a rich collection of historical names, dates, and places, but the book also contains a number of embarrassing errors. Even more damning was the fact that church records of seventeenth-century Weston Zoyland revealed no mention of a "John Fletcher," nor any names matching those of any possible relatives.

Historians of seventeenth-century English life also faulted Ryall on his understanding of the customs prevalent during the era. Renée Haynes, who is an historian as well as a British writer on the paranormal, soon became a one-woman expert on the Ryall case during the fray. Discussing the role the historian can play in the study of reincarnation cases, she points out in the August 1981 issue of *Fate* magazine that Ryall appeared to be especially shaky about the food common to seventeenth-century England. She noted that:

> It is not that the dishes of which he writes were necessarily unobtainable; it's just that he knows nothing about the circumstances under which they were eaten. French fricassees may have been popular in London circles but would surely have been regarded with contempt in rural Somerset, where he claims he lived, as infinitely inferior to the roast beef of Old England. He also "recalls" that syllabub, a froth made of cream and wine, was prepared with clotted cream—impossible since the cream has to be raw in order to combine properly with the other ingredients (wine, lemon juice and sugar) and to separate curd from whey.

Some of Miss Haynes' other criticisms were considerably more damning. She was especially critical of Ryall's (or "Fletcher's") peculiar understanding of seventeenth-century social mores, writing that:

> . . . where manners and customs are involved, Ryall has no idea of the cultural life of 17th Century Somerset. Ryall records that because his wife of those days suffered from some painful gynecological complaint, her sister, who lived with them, replaced her in his bed as a matter of hygienic convenience acceptable to all concerned. Such an arrangement would have outraged the community, which would have seen it as adulterous incest. The neighbors would have protested with "rough music" (a clattering of pans and crockery, accompanied by shouting, jeering and stone-throwing) out of fear that the presence of "notorious sinners" could bring a curse down on the whole district. During that

historical period Somerset was deeply puritanical when it came to questions of moral conduct. The threat of pregnancy would also have thwarted the plan. There was, after all, no Pill in the 17th Century.

Miss Haynes' criticisms did not go unchallenged by supporters of the case. Soon she and Dr. Stevenson were engaged in a correspondence battle over the historical merits of the case. (Their correspondence even included a spirited debate about the best way to make syllabub.)

But the death knell for the case came when Michael Green, an architectural historian from London, began investigating the case. His primary interest was in Ryall's detailed description of his home in Weston Zoyland. There seemed to be descrepancies between the architecture common to the period and Ryall's description. Ryall's house had allegedly been built in 1530, and Ryall even included a map in his book outlining the area where it stood. Green corresponded with Ryall to get him to pinpoint its exact location. By consulting maps dating from the nineteenth century, Green ultimately showed that the location in question had been open moorland when Ryall allegedly lived there.

Edward Ryall was close to seventy when he published his past-life autobiography. No one—not even his harshest critics—ever directly accused him of any falsehood. But the fact remains that Ryall was known to have read extensively, and it is likely that he began confusing his own memories with information he had come by years earlier in his studies. A reincarnation fantasy may have resulted from this process. Even the irrepressible Dr. Stevenson, who valiantly supported the importance of the case to the very end, finally began changing his mind about its merits. Writing in the February 1983 issue of the *Journal* of the Society for Psychical Research, he finally admitted that "I do not now believe that the proper names of John Fletcher and his family and friends derive from memories of a past life." He adds, however, that it is still possible that Ryall "had some memories of a previous life and these are in *Second Time Round,* perhaps even comprising most of it, but mixed—now inextricably— with later accretions from normal sources and literary invention to complete the narrative."

This is possible but doubtful. The case can probably be best explained as a complex example of cryptomnesia—the emergence into the conscious mind of information once buried in the unconscious.

The strange case of the late Edward Ryall typifies the kind of controversy that has long raged over the whole issue of reincarnation—and especially within parapsychology, which is the science that seeks to study the world of psychic phenomena. Just about every aspect of the reincarnation controversy is contained within it. The case demonstrates, on one hand, that quite normal and sane people sometimes remember having lived past lives in distant times and places. Nor is this a phenomenon that is reported only from those cultures in which reincarnation is commonly accepted. The Ryall case also demonstrates that people who recall their past lives often seem to recollect historically accurate information, at least to some degree. But most of all, the strange chronicle of Edward Ryall illustrates the maddening complexities inherent in studying cases suggestive of reincarnation.

The accurate information contained in such accounts is often mixed with inaccurate or unverifiable information. It is also hard to ascertain what information may already be buried in the mind of someone who suddenly recalls a previous incarnation. We potentially accumulate a huge unconscious reservoir of information through the books we read, movies we watch, and lectures we hear. These memories may well serve as the basis for the phenomenon of past-life recall. What often results are cases, such as Edward Ryall's, that neither prove reincarnation, but that can't be *totally* dismissed as pure fantasy. So the psychic investigator who wishes to explore the reincarnation issue cannot approach such studies simply as a parapsychologist. This was Dr. Stevenson's primary error. He must also work as a psychologist, historian, and private detective.

I wrote earlier that parapsychology is the science that critically studies psychic phenomena. This would include such phenomena as ESP and mind over matter, as well as a wide variety of phenomena suggesting that life continues after death. Such phenomena as apparitions, haunted houses, communications received through trance mediums, and recollections of past lives fall within this category.

Just how parapsychology developed as a science and originally defined its subject matter is an historical issue. Understanding a little about the history of parapsychology is also essential to understanding what scientific approaches were first directed toward the reincarnation question and will set the stage for the general theme of this book.

Parapsychology originated as an academic study during the late nineteenth century. This was one of the most complex social eras in the history of Western culture. It gave birth to a new respect for science. The great inroads of the Industrial Revolution were in full swing. The discoveries and ideas of Charles Darwin had begun turning people away from many religious conventions, and the rise of scholarly Biblical studies in Germany had begun calling into question the fundamentals of Christian literalism. Yet at the same time, the mid-nineteenth century was a time marked by a resurgence in occult beliefs and superstition. The idea that man possessed all sorts of supernatural powers was one result of the vaudeville-like displays of mesmerism (the precursor of modern hypnosis), which had swept across Europe and the United States early in the century. Also popular on both sides of the Atlantic was the cult of spiritualism, which taught that especially psychic people could bring through messages from the dead. The cult originated in the United States in 1848 and spread to Europe within a decade. The end of the nineteenth century was therefore an era of questioning: an era in which people began to expect science to provide them with the answers to questions that conventional religion could no longer handle and in which new cults and sects were originating to supplant the old conventions.

Psychical research, the precursor to modern parapsychology, was born in the hope that the study of psychic phenomena could unite science and religion. Toward the end of the nineteenth century several scholars, philosophers, scientists, and spiritualists in Great Britain began thinking that the only way to save the credibility of religious values was to place such beliefs on a scientific footing. These researchers believed that the basic validity of religion and antimaterialism could be salvaged if the existence of such phenomena as life after death, the existence of the soul, and man's spiritual nature could be scientifically documented. So in 1882 several scholars connected with Cambridge University united with some of the more critical members of the spiritualist community and established the Society for Psychical Research in London. Their goal was to investigate, expose, or document those phenomena that indicated a life after death. They were also interested in determining if man possessed psychic faculties that defied the laws of science. The primary studies undertaken by the founders of the S.P.R. focused initially on apparitions, hauntings, and telepathy. Later they turned their attention to the study of trance mediumship. The problem with these studies, however, was that they often ended up in a stalemate. The group soon learned that demonstrating the existence of a life after death was much more difficult than they had assumed. It was too easy to find alternate explanations for the phenomena under study.

For example, the S.P.R. investigators soon collected several cases in which a person had reportedly died at the same time his apparition was seen. The form usually appeared to a friend or relative who may have been living many miles away. But it was a moot point whether these ephemeral forms represented the "soul" of the deceased or whether the witnesses had created the figures unconsciously in response to a telepathic message. The early S.P.R. researchers also discovered several trance mediums who could sometimes bring through astonishingly accurate messages from the dead. But, once again, they could not determine whether these messages really came from beyond the grave. They thought it possible that the psychics could have read their sitters' minds telepathically to find out all about their deceased friends or families. The result was that parapsychology eventually focused itself more toward the study of ESP than toward the survival question.

This historical backdrop should make clear just why the study of reincarnation is intrinsically involved with the study of psychic phenomena in general. From a purely empirical perspective, any study bearing on the nature of life after death necessarily falls within the domain of parapsychology. Parapsychology is, in fact, the only academic discipline that has sought to directly accumulate scientific evidence bearing on life after death. For that reason much of the earliest evidence concerning reincarnation emerged from the infant study of psychical research.

So for the next several pages, I would like to discuss some of these early studies and case reports. This research will span approximately 1882 to 1930 and will acquaint you with how the scientific study of the reincarnation question was first approached and what types of phenomena were uncovered that most directly bear on the subject. These early studies will also suggest some clues for why reincarnation studies have been the bug-bears of psychic research; for it is a curious historical fact that reincarnation was one of the few aspects of the survival issue that was not exhaustively explored during psychical research's infancy.

Perhaps I should begin by noting that research into the reincarnation question was never popular in Great Britain, although it was actively pursued by some researchers on the continent, especially in France. The reason is simple. The first psychical researchers in Great Britain spent most of their time investigating the claims of the spiritualists—with their trance mediums, seances, table tilting, and ectoplasm. Reincarnationist beliefs played practically no role in this tradition. So the early investigators probably never were presented with any case material bearing on the subject nor were they encouraged to study what little did come to their attention. F.W.H. Myers, one of the first great thinkers of the S.P.R., even wrote in his posthumously published *Human Personality and Its Survival of Bodily Death* that ". . . for reincarnation, there is at present no valid evidence." This statement, published in 1903, pretty well summed up "official" British thinking on the subject. The situation was quite different in France and other continental areas. The spiritualism movement in France had eagerly embraced the reincarnation doctrine and actively taught it. So those psychical researchers working in France and neighboring countries probably were much more keen on studying evidence bearing on the subject even though these studies had little impact on their British confrères.

What little interest the parapsychological community afforded case material suggesting the validity of the reincarnation doctrine focused on a limited range of phenomena. These included (a) a few documented cases of people who apparently recalled their past lives; (b) the claims of psychics who communicated information bearing on their own past lives; and (c) some experimental attempts to see if mesmerized subjects could be regressed to previous incarnations.

Let's look at each of these categories in turn.

Historical Cases of Past-Life Recall

Very little material of this type emerged from "official" psychical research during the historical period between 1882 and 1930. A few cases were collected by Ralph Shirley, a British writer and publisher who was fascinated by the occult; but he drew chiefly from French source material. Also included was some information from his own files.

Shirley's research focused on reincarnation dreams, déjà-vu experiences, and a few waking vision cases. (The nature of these phenomena will be explored in the next chapter.) Little of this material was of much evidential value, although a few of his cases merit further attention. The case of Laura Raynaud is certainly one of these.

Laura Raynaud was the assistant to Dr. Gaston Durville, a prominent physician in France who was instrumental in publicizing the case. Mme. Raynaud had apparently recalled partial memories of a previous existence during the course of most of her life. These recollections chiefly focused on the house in which she felt she had once lived. Her memories were so vivid that she believed that she would instantly recognize the house if she ever were to see it. She also remembered that she had been young and consumptive and had lived in a southern climate. The upshot of the case came in March 1913, when Dr. Durville was asked to attend a patient in Genoa. He could not make the trip, so he asked his assistant to go in his stead. Mme. Raynaud consented and was continually impressed during her journey by the familiarity of the Italian countryside. She eventually became convinced that Genoa was the site of her mystery house. A mutual friend of both Dr. Durville and his assistant lived in Genoa and became intrigued with these claims, so he set about investigating Mme. Raynaud's impressions. It did not take him long to discover a house in Genoa that closely matched the detailed description given him. The most dramatic aspect of the case came when Mme. Raynaud was brought to see the house. She not only recognized it, but visiting the house caused more memories of her past life to emerge. The most significant of these concerned her curious manner of burial. Sh claimed that she was buried not in a cemetery but in a church.

By this time Dr. Durville had become so intrigued with the case that he set out to verify Mme. Raynaud's claims for himself. An investigation undertaken in Genoa on his behalf revealed that an ancestor of the family that currently owned the house had indeed died there of consumption in 1809. The young woman had been buried in the local cemetery but had later been removed and reburied in a church.

Dr. Durville published all the documents he had collected, including the official affidavits from his sources in Italy. The exact location of the house and the name of the family who once lived there were, for obvious reasons, concealed.

While the case of Laura Raynaud appeared impressive, an even more fully documented case of a spontaneous past-life recall had been reported three years earlier in Sicily. It was an extraordinary case not only because of its nature but because of the careful way the evidence documenting the case was collected and published.

The case was reported by Dr. Carmelo Samona, a prominent physician whose five-year-old daughter had died of meningitis on 15 March 1910. He explains in his reports that, three days later, his wife had a peculiar dream in which little Alexandrina appeared to her and announced that she would be reborn as a future child. This seemed unlikely since, for medical reasons, it did not seem possible that Mrs. Samona was capable of bearing any more children. The Samonas had no interest or belief in reincarnation, which also encouraged them to dismiss the dream. Yet this did not keep Mrs. Samona from having similar dreams as the weeks went by.

Despite their basic incredulity, the Samona's house soon became the scene of some minor poltergeistery. This consisted primarily of strange knockings heard in the villa. The Samonas were so impressed by the outbreak that they began sitting with a trance medium, through whom Alexandrina began communicating. Once again she announced her intent to be reborn as their daughter and further claimed that she would be born as a twin. These messages continued for three months and finally became more credible when Mrs. Samona realized in April that she might be pregnant. She still remained skeptical of Alexandrina's claim that she would be born as twin, but this claim, too, seemed possible when Mrs. Samona was informed during her fifth month of pregnancy that she would bear twins. She gave birth to two daughters on November 22.

As the girls grew, it became obvious that they were developing very different personalities. It was also obvious that the younger twin, who had been named Alexandrina, was beginning to resemble her deceased sister in both temperament and appearance. Dr. Samona noted that both Alexandrinas were marked by hyperemia of the left eye, slight subborrhea of the right ear, and a slight facial asymmetry. The new Alexandrina was also left-handed, just as her progenitor had been. The Samonas' other twin, Marie-Pace, was apparently unaffected by any of these conditions.

The remarkable similarities between the two Alexandrinas multiplied as the twins grew older. The following is an abbreviated version of a report Dr. Samona wrote in 1913, in which he outlined these parallels in detail. Note the critical tone that he adopts in discussing these comparisons, which indicates that he took a scientific as well as personal interest in the drama unfolding before him:

> I can affirm in the positive manner that in every way, except for the hair and the eyes, which are actually a little lighter than those of the first Alexandrina at the same age, the resemblance continues to be perfect. But, even more than on the physical side, the psychological similarity developing in the child gives the case in question further and greater interest. From the time that the consciousness of the twins began to enter into active relationship with the exterior world, it showed itself in two such distinct and diverse directions that we could not fail to observe two totally different natures in the two children.
>
> Alexandrina is, generally speaking, calm in temperament, quite unlike her sister in this respect, and this tranquillity of nature extends even to the manifestation of her affection which is, in spite of this, none the less tender and demonstrative. One of her principal characteristics is her way of spending the

day. She will spend it folding up and tidying and arranging any clothes or linen that she may have in her room, placing them carefully and tidily on a chair or chest. If the opportunity does not present itself to do this, her favourite occupation is to settle herself in a chair, on which she places some object of her choice or anything that serves her as a toy for the time being. In the meantime she chatters quietly to herself and constantly remains for a long time at this occupation, without apparently tiring of it.

Her sister on the contrary is always on the *qui vive* and running about and cannot remain for more than a minute at the same occupation, and always requires to have company and someone to amuse her.

It is worth noting that this calm temperament and these particular occupations were special characteristics of the first Alexandrina. . . Alexandrina is indifferent to dolls and prefers to play with children of her own age, a preference which was equally noticeable with the other Alexandrina. Like her, too, she is always anxious that her little hands should be clean and insists on having them washed if they are in the least degree dirty. Like her predecessor again, she shows a singular repugnance for cheese and will not touch soup if it has the least taste of cheese in it.

After discussing the peculiar and apparently uninherited left-handedness of his daughter, Dr. Samona goes on to report:

When she has a chance of opening the chest of drawers in the bedroom it is a great amusement to her to pull out the stockings and to play with them. This was also a passion of the other Alexandrina. We have also noticed that this one, like the others, always insists on putting one of these stockings—naturally a great deal too large for her—on her little foot and walking about the room with it on.

Another noteworthy fact is that the first Alexandrina, when about two years old, began to alter people's names, apparently out of sheer caprice. For example she turned Angelina into Angelanna or Angelona, while Caterina, the name of her aunt, became Caterana or Caterona. The second Alexandina showed the very same peculiarity at the same age, which astonished us all.

Eventually the little girl began to remember incidents from the life of the first Alexandrina. Dr. Samona described one such incident in a private letter he sent to Dr. Charles Lancelin, a noted French authority on the occult at the time. He explained that he and his wife had decided to take their twins to Monreale to see a famous Norman church and other local landmarks. Mrs. Samona was telling the children about the trip when Alexandrina suddenly remarked that she had already been to Monreale. The little girl went on to accurately describe the statue on the roof of the church, talked about "some little red priests" she had seen there, and mentioned a "lady who had horns." This information startled Mrs. Samona because she and her husband had indeed once taken the first Alexandrina to the church. There they had encountered some Greek priests outfitted in black robes decorated with red ornaments. They had been accompanied on the trip by a friend who was traveling to Palermo for a medical consultation because of the disfiguring excrescences on her forehead.

Dr. Samona was aware of the controversial nature of his claims so, in 1911, he began publishing several corroborative statements from other witnesses to properly document the case. He published these initially in *Filosofa della Scienza,* an Italian science journal. These documents fully supported his statements about his wife's dreams, the communications received during the 1910 seances, and the similarities between Alexandrina and his deceased daughter.

Because of the many details that were published on the Samona case, it is still possible to analyze it in retrospect. The only valid objection I can find to the report is that somehow Dr. and Mrs. Samona were unintentionally feeding information to the girl and molding her behavior. This is possible because the couple had already been alerted to the possibility that Alexandrina was coming back to them. Such a possibility seems unlikely, though, since Dr. Samona's careful reports indicate that he always attempted to keep his objectivity as the case developed. Nor can the "cuing" explanation account for the specific physical resemblances between the girls—especially the nongenetic similarities in their medical conditions. The information Alexandrina spontaneously remembered is also impressive. The only way that she could have known about the trip to Monreale was by hearing her parents talk about it, and while this is certainly possible, it seems unlikely that they would have discussed such details as the priests and the statue.

The Samona case is essentially similar to several other less fully documented cases reported during these early years in the history of psychical research. In some of them the children expressly claimed to remember past lives as their own relatives. These cases were chiefly reported anecdotally so it is difficult to tell in retrospect how much information these children could have picked up normally from their parents or from their other relations. Some of these cases were rather spectacular. Consider, for example, the following case reported from Rome by Capt. Floriandro Battista in 1905. Battista, who was the primary witness in the case, published his account in 1912 in an Italian magazine. His integrity was vouchsafed by the editor. The captain claimed that one day in 1905 his wife was resting in their home when an apparition of their dead daughter appeared to her and announced her coming rebirth as their next child. Mrs. Battista gave birth to a daughter in February 1906, and the girl began resembling the earlier child as she matured. The climax of the case came when the girl was six years old. One day she began singing a French lullaby that a Swiss servant had often sung to their previous child. This servant had left their employ before the birth of their new daughter.

Unfortunately, this brief report was published without any corroborative evidence, and apparently no one troubled to investigate Battista's story.

The Reincarnation Claims of Psychics and Mediums

Since the spiritualist movement in France explicitly supported the rebirth doctrine, French psychics and trance mediums often tended to claim recollections about their past existences. Few researchers took such statements seriously until the 1890s, when Catherine Elise Mueller, a trance medium in Geneva, Switzerland, came into prominence with her reincarnation claims. She received special attention when Professor Theodore Flournoy, an eminent psychologist at the University of Geneva, became actively involved in studying her purported powers and proceeded to write two books about her. (He referred to her as Mlle. Hélène Smith in all his published writings on the case). Flournoy was especially intrigued by the fact that, while entranced, Mlle. Mueller often discussed her past lives in great detail. These communications often included verifiable historical information, as well as bits and snatches of the actual languages she had spoken during her past lives. The Swiss psychologist spent years analyzing these communications, verifying some of them, and attempting to find the sources for her information. What resulted was a detective story still fascinating when read today. His first book on the case, _From India to the Planet Mars,_ was published in 1900 and has since become a classic. Just how successful Flournoy was in tracking down the psychological and literary sources for _all_ Mlle. Mueller's reincarnation claims is, however, a matter of debate. Perhaps it would be best to start from the beginning.

Catherine Elise Mueller was the daughter of a Hungarian merchant who had settled in Geneva. Born in 1861, she was introduced to the world of spiritualism in 1891 when she began reading books on the subject. Her readings encouraged her to join some friends for table tilting and soon Mlle. Mueller developed into a full-blown medium. She developed a trance state, trance speech, and automatic writing.

Mlle. Mueller first initiated trance discussions about her past lives in 1893, a year before Flournoy embarked on his study of the case. She first claimed a past life as a young woman who unfortunately turned out to be a fictional character drawn from an Alexandre Dumas novel. Soon she switched to claiming that she was the reincarnation of Marie Antoinette, a claim Flournoy was soon able to demolish, since "Marie's" communications contained appalling anachronisms and faulty history. Later communications dealt with the psychic's previous life on Mars. Included were several scripts written in an odd-looking "Martian" language. The Swiss psychologist had little difficulty showing how the construction of this language followed the rules and syntax of normal French.

The whole case could have probably been dismissed as either a fantasy or a conscious hoax were it not for some peculiar messages she communicated in 1894. These contained detailed information about the psychic's past life in

India. This information was so detailed that even Flournoy couldn't reject it out of hand.

The basic plot of Mlle. Mueller's past life in India revolved around her role as the Arab wife of a South Indian prince who had lived in the fifteenth century. The story unfolded during several sittings and included some interesting and potentially verifiable historical data, including such items as the name of a hill on which the prince had built a fortress. The communications also contained a number of proper names, such as those of the prince (Sivrouka Nayaka) and the medium herself (Simandini). She also made considerable mention of geographical locations near where they had lived. While immersed in her trance Mlle. Mueller also wrote out some brief scripts in Sanskrit and one in Arabic. Flournoy found this Indian romance challenging. It was clear to him that to get to the root of these communications, he either had to find the source of the psychic's information or properly document the names and locations she had specified. At this point in his investigation the famous psychologist ran into a series of complications that still remain partially unsolved today.

Flournoy was at first put off because he could not locate any history books on India that mentioned the people listed in Mlle. Mueller's communications. His interest in the case was piqued, however, when he consulted an obscure six-volume text by M. de Marlès on the history of India. This set, magnificently titled *General History of India, Ancient and Modern, from the Year 2,000 B.C. to our own Times,* verified much of the information he was looking for. It was a little suspicious, however, that the text was too consistent with the Mueller communications, since no other source on Indian history Flournoy had consulted mentioned *any* of the names under investigation. This suggested to him that perhaps the psychic had—consciously or unconsciously—drawn information from the book during a casual glance at the text. He was too cautious and objective an investigator to posit this as a conclusive explanation for Mlle. Mueller's information, though. Only two copies of the de Marlès' tomes could be found in Geneva, and one was hidden in a private library. The other, though publicly available, was still covered with dust when the psychologist discovered it. The set has obviously not been consulted *recently*.

In the end, Flournoy was left with no alternative explanation to account for the case, and finally opted for his original theory. He wrote in his *From India to the Planet Mars* that " . . . all allowances made for possible surprises in the future, I do not hesitate to regard as the more probable and more rational supposition, that it really was the passage of de Marlès . . .which furnished the subliminal memory of Helen Smith."

Flournoy was, however, still not yet quite prepared to let the matter go at that. He added that, "The Hindu romance, in particular, remains for those who have taken part in it a psychological enigma, not yet solved in a satisfactory manner, because it reveals and implies . . . a knowledge relative to the customs, language of the Orient, and actual sources of which it has up to the present time not been possible to discover."

In order to further evaluate Mlle. Mueller's romance in ancient India, Flournoy moved his investigations in a different direction. Since the psychic had written out some scripts in Arabic and Sanskrit, these now became the focus of his attention (This research is described both in his first volume and in his subsequent _Nouvelles Observations sur un cas de Somnambulisme avec Glossalalie_). The results of this investigation did not bear up well for Mlle. Mueller, for Flournoy showed that her sole script written in Arabic had been apparently copied or subliminally remembered from a book written by a Geneva physician. Included in the dedication was the same Arabic phrase produced by Mlle. Mueller while in trance. Her (wildly ungrammatical) automatic writings in Sanskrit fared little better. Flournoy never discovered the exact source for these scripts, but he later learned that Mlle. Mueller had once given seances in the home of a gentleman who owned a Sanskrit grammer book. The book had been left in the room where the seances were held, and Flournoy believed that the medium may have once browsed through it.

The publication of Flournoy's books in 1900 and 1902 ended his further involvement with Catherine Elise Mueller. She had already grown irritated by his skepticism and began restricting her seances just to close friends. She suffered a traumatic shock in 1915 when a close friend died, and she died (apparently insane) in 1921. It should be noted, however, that Flournoy never totally rejected the value of the Mueller case. He even admitted in some of his last writings that he had witnessed some evidence of telepathy and displays of telekinesis in her presence.

Flournoy's research made quite an impact on psychical research in general. His first book was quickly translated into English and was soon being cited by other researchers as a conclusive study of the evidence bearing on reincarnation. It was, of course, nothing of the sort, and the many researchers who cited the book were probably overlooking just how tentative many of Flournoy's explanations really were. It was certainly the most detailed investigation of a single case bearing on reincarnation but was not a thorough consideration of the evidence. Even the normally open-minded and conciliatory F.W.H. Myers only refers to the Flournoy work in his discussion on reincarnation that he included in his _Human Personality and Its Survival of Bodily Death_. Myers rejected the case as evidence for reincarnation but suggested that perhaps the psychic had borrowed material from the de Marlès' source clairvoyantly during her trances.

Perhaps the final say in the Catherine Elise Mueller case should be given to C.T.K. Chari of Madras Christian College, who is one of India's leading parapsychologists and scholars. He undertook a re-evaluation of the psychic's Hindu communications and published his findings in 1963. He, too, agrees that the psychic probably drew her information from de Marlès, whom he feels merely made up the information that served as the source for Mlle. Mueller's communications. His conclusion is that " . . . the reincarnationist and spiritualism claims of Helen's 'Hindoo cycle' can no longer be countenanced by responsible scholars."

Theodore Flournoy's investigation of Catherine Elise Mueller was probably the most detailed evaluation ever made of a psychic's past life memories. The influence it had on psychical research in general probably did much to dissuade many other researchers potentially interested in the subject. Yet it did not stop similar cases from being reported in the British Isles. These cases tended to come to light in the 1930s, and their emergence may have been due to social reasons. The 1920s and 30s were a time when the reincarnation idea was becoming more familiar to the British public. Some years earlier Helen Blavatsky, a self-proclaimed psychic and mystic, had spread her doctrines throughout England via the Theosophical Society, which she had founded in the United States in the 1870s. This movement popularized many Eastern concepts, and the idea of rebirth was prominent among them. It may be that by the 1920s and 1930s, psychics and other mystic voyagers in England began coming up with claimed memories of past lives simply because they were more familiar with the idea than their predecessors had been. This theory is not meant to deprecate the value of these reports but only to explain why the rebirth doctrine suddenly became popular in England during this period. Unfortunately, these were the years when the great golden age of psychical research had already been eclipsed. So these reports made little impact on scientists studying psychic phenomena, for these researchers were already immersed in carefully drawn lines of study and weren't prepared to undertake any new ones. So the reincarnation reports that came to light during these decades rarely found their way into the official publications of the Society for Psychical Research.

This was, in retrospect, regrettable, because at least one case was reported during this time that should have received much more attention than it did.

The case was reported in a now nearly forgotten book titled *The Soul of Nyria*. The author was Mrs. Campbell Praed and her book concerned the trance recollections of an anonymous friend. Mrs. Campbell Praed was first introduced to the case while traveling with her friend on the continent. This friend apparently underwent a spontaneous trance while they were sitting together, during which she took on a new and strange personality. This personality claimed to be a slave girl named Nyria who had lived in Rome during the early Christian years, and Mrs. Campbell Praed spent the next months recording her life story and memories. The information contained in *The Soul of Nyria* consists primarily of colorful portraits of Roman life after the birth of Christianity. The story is complete with dozens of historical references and the proper names of real but obscure people. In fact, this information was often so detailed and accurate that it would put many an historical novelist to shame.

Mrs. Campbell Praed was deeply impressed and set out to investigate the accuracy of all the names, dates, and places she had recorded. This proved no small task and she had to search through dozens of scholarly sources to properly verify her friend's utterances . . . and was constantly amazed by the accuracy of even obscure historical points.

The only outside investigation into the case was made by Ralph Shirley. Shirley was not only a keen student of the psychic field but also the head of Rider Co., the publishing house that ultimately issued *The Soul of Nyria*. He threw himself into the study of the case while preparing it for publication.

Most of his work entailed rechecking Mrs. Campbell Praed's research, since Shirley was better versed in the classics than the author apparently was. He was continually impressed not only by the almost casual mention of historical figures who actually lived in Rome after the birth of Christianity but specifically by some material concerning Pliny, the Roman philosopher. Scholars had usually maintained that Pliny married twice, but the Nyrian records indicated what appeared to be a *third* wife, who died while still quite young. Shirley was intrigued by this apparent discrepancy and threw himself into the literary works of the philosopher. There he found a single reference to a third wife in one of Pliny's letters. She had died during childbirth only a year after their marriage. Even many classical scholars were unaware of this reference.

The Soul of Nyria also contained discussions of Roman customs, and these, too, bore up well under critical scrutiny. Shirley's own personal conclusion was that the case represented either evidence for reincarnation or spirit communication.

A similar case, though not nearly as thoroughly investigated, managed to make its way into the publications of the Society for Psychical Research in 1928. It has been directly reported to the S.P.R. in March 1928 by the vicar of a parish in northern England and concerned one of his parishioners who was an "automatic" writer. The scripts referred to the chief communicator's past lives in several different countries. The S.P.R. was impressed enough by the report to ask one of its members in London, J. Arthur Hill, to look into it. Hill traveled to northern England (the actual location was never revealed) and met with the vicar and the woman. Although he took a large number of her scripts, he was unimpressed by what he discovered.

The psychic turned out to be a working-class woman in her fifties. She was a voracious reader and had apparently undergone several mystical experiences as a child. She told Hill that her automatic writing ability had developed after the death of her son in 1914. Her grief had led her to explore spiritualism and, later, Theosophy, during which time her budding mediumship further developed. Her chief "communicator" claimed to be her "soul mate" from several of her past incarnations, and, through her, he communicated the story of his past lives. These allegedly took place in ancient Germany, Scandinavia, Egypt,

Greece, and Galacia. Several proper names were given in the scripts, but for some reason Hill made no attempt to trace their historical accuracy. Hill saw the case more as a study in psychology and cryptomnesia than as anything else.

The last and most celebrated case reported from this same period was described and discussed in several books and articles by Dr. F. H. Wood, a British musicologist and amateur student of the psychic field. Sometime in the late 1920s he discovered a nonprofessional medium who he called "Rosemary" in all his published writings on the case. Several of the medium's communications dealt with her own past life in ancient Egypt, and the personalities who communicated through her often spoke in the alleged language of the ancient Nile. Dr. Wood spend years analyzing every aspect of the case; but his reports are so complicated and controversial that I shall bypass them for the present. An entire chapter will be devoted to the case later on.

Experimental Attempts to Trace Past Lives Through Mesmerism

The use of hypnotic regression to "take" an experimental subject back to a purported past life is extremely popular today, yet few students of reincarnation seem aware that this technique was actually first practiced more than half a century ago by psychical researchers in France.

Little of this early research was preserved, and much of it was obviously informal. Probably the only important text on the use of mesmerism, or hypnosis, to facilitate past-life recall was a lengthy book titled *Les vies successives,* published in 1911. The author was Col. Albert de Rochas, who was one of France's most eminent psychic investigators until his death in 1914. Sometime shortly after the turn of the century, de Rochas decided to use mesmerism to see if he could trace the past lives of his acquaintances. The practice was apparently common among the spiritualists, but de Rochas was the first to *systematically* use the technique and publish his findings in France.* He worked primarily from his home in Paris. His usual procedure was to regress his subjects through an entire series of past lives, sometimes even progressing them to their future ones.

Very little of this work was evidential, and even de Rochas never believed that it proved the existence of reincarnation. His most important finding was that his hypnotic subjects, even if they were not in the least interested in reincarnation or psychic phenomena, tended to remember past lives when requested to do so. Several of his subjects did manage to come up with potentially verifiable names and information. But de Rochas could never really verify that the people so identified ever lived. In many cases he found that the *infor-*

---

*De Rochas mentioned in an article published in 1905 that work similar to his own had been conducted in Spain, but he cites no references.

mation his subjects gave about some distant town or location panned out, while their claimed past life identities did not!

De Rochas first summarized his conclusions about his work in 1905. Sadly he had to admit that "if we could prove that the personalities 'played' by the subjects had really lived, we should have a proof of very great force in favour of the survival of the soul and of its successive reincarnations. Unfortunately that proof has not been obtained."

The pioneering French researcher was nevertheless impressed by the consistency of his results, and found himself incapable of explaining the sources or psychological dynamics of his subjects' stories.

From a purely historical perspective, the early years of psychical research contributed a great deal of solid case material to the study of reincarnation. It is therefore doubly unfortunate that little of this information had much of an impact on the field in general. Much of this neglect was probably the result of bias. Researchers then were looking for more direct approaches to the survival issue. The founders of the S.P.R. in particular were essentially out to legitimize many of the common dogmas of Christian faith, a set of beliefs to which the idea of reincarnation was alien. The topic was hardly mentioned at all in the writing of the S.P.R. founders. The exception was of course F.W.H. Myers, who at least saw nothing philosophically repulsive in the idea.

It is also unfortunate that much of the psychical research undertaken in France, Germany, and Italy during these years had so little impact on the dominant research tradition in Great Britain. In general, researchers there didn't take much of an interest in Continental research unless it bore directly on their own studies. Since parapsychology today is an outgrowth of the traditions that evolved from the early work of the Society for Psychical Research, this may help to explain why reincarnation research has never been a mainstay of parapsychology's subject matter.

But there are also other reasons why reincarnation research made little impression on the psychical research tradition. The lack of clear-cut and properly investigated case material was one problem. The S.P.R. investigators really didn't think much of *any* case they hadn't personally investigated. This prejudice was probably coupled with their bias against anything that sounded too "occult." They were very concerned about keeping their science "pure" from cult movements, occult beliefs, and any other shadows that would make their work and field appear unscientific. The idea of reincarnation was essentially non-Western, an idea imported from the East. This made it suspect in the eyes of the S.P.R. investigators, most of whom were steeped in the Western philosophical tradition. Nor did it help matters when the reincarnation doctrine became linked with the teachings of the Theosophical Society, founded to spread "occult wisdom." The S.P.R. had investigated and condemned its founder, Helen Blavatsky, as a fraud in 1885, though it technically held no corporate viewpoints. The Society wanted nothing to do with practitioners of popular occultism, so reincarnation was probably considered just a little too "unclean" to pay much attention to.

The failure of later reincarnation cases reported during the 1920-30s to make an impact on the field was presumably due to other reasons.

By the 1930s the whole area of survival research had begun to fade, so there was even less chance that reincarnation might finally emerge as a legitimate research area within psychical research. It was clear by 1930 that psychical research needed a new approach to the study of psychic phenomena; and it received just such a jolt when the young J. B. Rhine initiated his experimental studies of ESP at Duke University in Durham, North Carolina. Rhine's innovation was to show how the problems of telepathy, clairvoyance, and other psychic talents could best be studied experimentally and statistically. By adopting the methodology of experimental psychology, he showed that parapsychology could be brought forcefully to scientific attention. This bid for scientific respectability was one the old S.P.R. researchers had also made; but it was one in which they had partially failed. Rhine's basic concept was to have his subjects guess the geometric symbols stamped on ordinary cards. The phenomenal success of this work had such an impact on psychology in general that, almost over night, parapsychology left the world of psychics and mediums to become an experimental science.

The Rhinean revolution also took parapsychology out of the hands of the philosophers and the scholars. It converted it into a psychological discipline. Rhine also demonstrated that perhaps the proper place for parapsychology was within the university system and not in the hands of the old-fashioned psychical research societies. Because laboratory experimentalism became the dominant approach to parapsychology from the 1930s well into the 1960s, even the basic research questions that had so occupied the founders of the S.P.R. went by the boards. Reincarnation research had barely survived the heyday of Victorian psychical research. Now it was being suffocated by the stampede toward the laboratory.

This isn't to say that *all* survival research stopped during these years. The Society for Psychical Research still upheld the older research traditions in Great Britain. But the "new" study of experimental ESP gradually took control as the leading paradigm within the field. It still is today.

Our modern renaissance of interest in the reincarnation issue dates from 1956. By this time parapsychology was well on the road to achieving scientific acceptance. Most researchers (especially in the United States) were carefully studying ESP safely in their laboratories. Some of the more adventuresome had even begun to study psychokinesis (the technical term for mind over matter) by seeing if their subjects could influence the throw of dice. It was a period of relative quiescence in which parapsychology was carefully guarding its new-found respectability; even the conventional scientific establishment was beginning to take a friendlier attitude toward the field. Parapsychologists were slowly graphing out how ESP related to personality traits, guessing strategies, scoring patterns, and other relatively safe areas. It seemed almost as if the field had forgotten its basis in the survival controversy and the spiritualist milieu of the Victorian age. Then in 1956 came the publication of Morey Bernstein's best-selling _The Search for Bridey Murphy_. The book reported the author's allegedly successful attempts to hypnotically regress a Colorado housewife to her past life in Ireland. The colorful account fired the public's imagination and became the focus for extended comment in the press. The case was impressive. It really did look as though Mrs. Virginia Tighe, the subject of the book, had recalled detailed information about eighteenth-century Ireland. What followed was an extended debate within the press as well as among psychologists about how much Mrs. Tighe could have normally known about Ireland. Charges and counter-charges were made, and almost against its will, the parapsychological community was forced to take sides.

Since the Bridey Murphy case will be discussed in depth in a later chapter, it need only be said at this point that today, the case remains essentially unresolved and controversial. It did, however, alert some parapsychologists to the fact that reincarnation was a scientifically valid question, even though most of them were decidedly antagonistic toward it. It tended to make the field look (they felt) silly and unscientific. Nor did it help that Morey Bernstein was very familiar with parapsychology and discussed his own involvement in the field throughout the book. Nonetheless the case did have some positive impact on the field. It impressed Prof. C. Ducasse, a philosopher at Brown University and a prominent member of the American Society for Psychical Research, who spoke favorably about the case in his influential _A Critical Examination of the Belief in Life after Death_, published in 1961.

The Bridey Murphy affair "unofficially" set the stage for the first real breakthrough in the study of reincarnation, which occurred in 1960. This was the year in which Dr. Ian Stevenson, a psychiatrist at the University of Virginia, published his scholarly but eye-opening report on "The Evidence for Survival from Claimed Memories of Former Incarnations" in the staid _Journal_ of the American Society for Psychical Research. This was the first comprehensive and critical report on the reincarnation question ever published by a contemporary leading parapsychology journal. It served as a prelude to the gradual emergence of reincarnation as a topic of important concern to parapsychology as a whole.

At the time the report was issued, Dr. Stevenson was only beginning to make his mark within parapsychology. His report was actually the winning essay in a contest held by the American S.P.R. in honor of William James, the great American philosopher and psychologist. The fact that Stevenson was a psychiatrist at a major American university and displayed a creditable knowledge of parapsychology in his essay made the parapsychological community take note. Stevenson's goal in writing his essay was to establish reincarnation research squarely within the psychical research tradition, and he succeeded admirably. Stevenson ultimately dedicated his entire career to the reincarnation question and elevated the study of the subject to a respectability it had never achieved before.

It is impossible to understand the status of reincarnation research today without knowing something about Stevenson's work, for his name has now become virtually synonymous with the study of the rebirth question. He has not only brought the subject to the attention of parapsychology but has also published several papers on the issue in more academic psychiatric journals. His research is cited in virtually every scholarly book or report on reincarnation and even in religious and theologically oriented publications. The reason for these accomplishments lies in the sheer respectability he has brought to the reincarnation question, primarily through his medical training and background.

Dr. Ian Stevenson was educated at McGill University in Montreal, where he took his medical degree in 1944. Later he became an assistant professor and eventually an associate professor of psychiatry at the Louisiana State University School of Medicine, where he stayed until 1957. At that time he took over the reins as chairman of the department of psychiatry and neurology at the University of Virginia, where he has remained to this day (although he is no longer the chairman of the department). During the 1950s he made a name for himself in traditional psychiatry and authored a book on the clinical interview.

Though Dr. Stevenson's early writings had contained various references to parapsychology, it wasn't until after his move to the University of Virginia that he made his personal interest in the field explicit. During the late 1950s he began publishing a few essentially minor papers on parapsychology and then, in his 1960 essay, made his first major contribution. This was followed by several case studies, reports, and proceedings. Most of these concerned the survival problem, often focusing on the reincarnation issue in particular.

The substance and implications of Dr. Stevenson's work will be analyzed in more depth in Chapter 3, but some mention of the scope of his early work should be made now. His major contribution was in showing how the study of reincarnation could be approached from a somewhat different perspective than had been employed during parapsychology's past. Most parapsychologists knew that there were cases suggestive of reincarnation scattered in their own historical literature. Many of these reports concerned children who had begun talking about their past lives while still quite young. Few contemporary researchers had paid much attention or given much credence to this data, since most of the cases had been reported purely anecdotally. Certainly no one had ever tried to draw any meaningful conclusions from them. But this is exactly what Dr. Stevenson did in his 1960 paper.

The crux of Dr. Stevenson's seminal paper was an historical overview of several cases that directly bore on the reincarnation question. He summarized some of the cases mentioned earlier in this chapter, but he focused his essay more directly on several other cases where young children had recalled specific past-life memories. What was so surprising was the sheer volume of these cases. Stevenson cataloged forty-four reports drawn from various sources, including relatively scarce and obscure books dating back to the turn of the century. These reports were collected from India, Burma, Italy, and the United States, as well as from Belgium, Cuba, Japan, and several other countries. The majority of them came from countries in which the reincarnation doctrine is commonly accepted. Stevenson found that in twenty-eight cases the children remembered more than six specific pieces of information about their previous lives that later proved accurate. In many of these cases the children were under the age of ten. Stevenson especially noted that the children usually spoke about living in different towns or countries, and the person whose life was usually "remembered" was often totally unknown to the parents. These two factors suggested to Stevenson that the children could not have come by the information contained in their "memories" normally. Most of the reports concerned children who claimed to be reborn within the same sex, although some exceptions cropped up. The actual memories appeared to emerge spontaneously, although in a few cases they were precipitated by a period of stress or trauma in the child's life.

Some of these reports, although brief, were extremely impressive. Dr. Stevenson cited one case from Japan that he discovered in an obscure book published in 1897. The story concerned a boy named Katsugoro, who began claiming a former life in another village when he was eight years old. He gave the name of the village, his own name, and those of his wife and father, and he explained that his mother had remarried after his father's death. He further explained that he had died from smallpox a year after his father. The boy's parents were so impressed by the story that they took their son to the town in which he claimed he had lived. There they found that the names Katsugoro had given matched several people who had actually lived there. The boy was also able to lead his parents to the house in which he had lived. The source upon which Stevenson drew included affidavits from various witnesses.

Outside investigators had even taken a hand in verifying crucial information in some of the cases Stevenson unearthed. A report issued from India in 1923, cited by Stevenson with obvious relish, involved a young boy who recalled no less than thirty-six items about his past life in Bharatpur. These included several proper names, a detailed description of the house in which he had lived, and even a description of a local landmark. The boy had never been to the town, and an inquiry into the case was undertaken by officials from the local state government. They found that twenty-nine names, dates, and places communicated by the boy matched the life of a former villager who had lived in Bharatpur for several years.

Despite the large number of these cases, Stevenson—as well as any critical reader of his paper—was quite aware of the obvious problems in the material. It was impossible to tell just how these cases had been investigated, how accurate the reports were, and what opportunities the children may have had to come by the information normally. These are, of course, problems that generally cloud the investigation of spontaneous case material. But the central question posed by these cases was a rather simple one. Did they represent the result of some paranormal process at work? Or could they be explained normally? This was the main issue Stevenson addressed in the second part of his paper. Based on the corroborative evidence presented as part of the original case reports, Stevenson rejected the idea that they could be accounted for by fraud or hidden memory. This left him with a variety of psychic explanations for the cases. These included the possibility that the children may have "inherited" their memories through some sort of genetic memory; tuned in on the information telepathically; somehow psychically made contact with the past; were responding to spirit communications; were being actively possessed by the dead; or were genuinely recalling past lives. Dr. Stevenson's own predilection was toward the reincarnation explanation.

Being well aware of the basic inadequacies in the cases he had salvaged from the past, Dr. Stevenson came to the conclusion that the only really satisfactory way to approach the reincarnation question would be to search out new and still active case reports. This is exactly what he set out to do, and ten years after the appearance of his seminal report, the psychiatrist published his *Twenty Cases Suggestive of Reincarnation*. This volume included accounts of several cases he had personally studied and/or investigated. These investigations focussed on children living primarily in India, Ceylon, Brazil, Alaska, and Lebanon. It was the most detailed and scholarly study ever given the reincarnation question and was followed by several further books full of case studies published over the next several years. Several of these reports will be discussed in Chapter 3.

Looking back over the last hundred years, it certainly seems clear that while the reincarnation question has always been a scientific as well as a philosophical issue, a wealth of avenues are still waiting to be explored. Though Dr. Stevenson's work has now become the mainstay of reincarnation research, his findings must be evaluated within the context of other approaches to the rebirth question. So during the course of the next several chapters we shall be taking closer looks at many different types of case material that bear on the reincarnation question and at some of the ways in which they have been interpreted. Some of these avenues may be already familiar to you; others will undoubtedly lead through unfamiliar territory. But one thing will soon become clear: To understand the significance of the reincarnation issue, we are going to have to find some new ways of looking at the problem.

2

Far Memory

People in all walks of life sometimes remember their past lives through deeply personal, though often momentary, experiences. These are the cases with which we will be concerned in this chapter. They are not as evidential as those cases of young children who are literally born with their past-life memories intact. Nor are they as exciting as the accounts of those hypnotized subjects who have suddenly relived their lives after being regressed to a time before their births. They are often undramatic events—a dream, a vision, a momentary intuitive flash—that bring to the experiencers an indelible feeling that they have lived before.

These incidents can happen to anyone and at any time: Even people who have never heard about reincarnation report them.

My interest in spontaneous past-life recall was piqued by a curious book I read in 1981 by Dr. Frederick Lenz, a San Diego psychologist. Dr. Lenz reports in his engrossing book, *Lifetimes,* how he has collected more than 120 accounts from people who have suddenly recalled their past lives via dreams, meditation, waking visions, and other altered states. Two of Dr. Lenz's provocative findings especially struck me as impressive. The first was that most of his correspondents claimed no prior interest or belief in reincarnation. Their experiences had come spontaneously and had, of themselves, produced a strong conviction in the rebirth doctrine, even when it went against their former intellectual and/or religious training. Even more interesting was that these momentary past-life recalls had not occurred randomly but emerged from within a specific and highly structured phenomenological syndrome. I'll return to this second feature of Lenz's cases momentarily.

The following case, which has been drawn from Dr. Lenz's files, is fairly typical. The woman reporting the incident had the encounter when she was attending high school in San Diego. She intuitively linked it to her own previous incarnation, and it made a deep impression on her:

> It happened when I was just seventeen. I was at home, babysitting for my little sister. My parents had gone out to celebrate their wedding anniversary. I was in the kitchen cooking dinner when I heard a loud ringing sound in my head. It got louder and louder until I was very frightened. The sound did not come from outside me, but from within. The room began to shift and fade, and I thought I was going to pass out. The next thing I remember, I was standing on a cliff overlooking the sea. I was watching the waves roll in and break on the rocks far below me. I heard the pounding surf and smelled the salt air. I turned around and began to walk through a field that was behind me. The sun was out and I felt warm and happy. I was returning to my flock of sheep that I had left up at the pasture. As I walked I sang a favorite song until I reached the crest of the hill. I thought about many Greek towns that I would like to one day visit. I sat down near the sheep and, all alone, rocked back and forth singing. Then the vision ended, and I was back in my kitchen.
>
> I didn't know what to make of what happened to me, and I figured that I had had some kind of vivid daydream. However, several years later when I was on vacation from college, I went to Europe, and one of the countries I visited was Greece. I was very much attracted to some of the small coastal cities. One day while motoring with friends we came to a stretch of road that overlooked the sea. I was filled with a number of conflicting emotions, but one thing was clear: I wanted to get out of the car. I asked my friends to stop for a minute; they pulled over to the side of the road overlooking the sea and looked down. As I did I saw the exact scene I had seen several years before in my vision in the kitchen. I turned around and walked away from the car and my friends. I walked with a purpose, as if I knew the way. I followed a path through a field and began to ascend an embankment. When I reached the top and looked around, I recognized the spot where I had been with the sheep in my vision. It was exactly as I had remembered it. I was filled with memories of places and scenes, and I knew I had returned "home" again. Although it made no sense, I felt that I had lived there in another time. I returned to my friends in the car and explained my sensations to them. They didn't seem to understand what I was saying, and I finally gave up trying to explain to them.

The following case, which is also drawn from Dr. Lenz's book, was contributed by a middle-aged physician from Connecticut. It, too, is fairly representative of the types of cases the San Diego psychologist has collected:

> One day in late October I was outside in my yard raking leaves. I had been working hard all morning, and I felt it was time for a break. I sat down under a maple tree and was starting to relax when my whole body began to shake vio-

lently. I lost awareness of where I was, and all I could see was blackness in all directions. I felt I was plunging down a long black tunnel; I was nauseated from the falling. Then I began to see light at the end of the tunnel. I found myself sitting upright in a chair in my living room. One of my servants approached me and told me that my horse was ready for my trip into town. I followed him outside the house, mounted my horse, and rode into town. I remember that I passed a group of merchants on camels on the way to town. They were all acquaintances of mine, and each one paused for a moment of brief conversation. We discussed the weather and the state of the crops. After each encounter, I continued my journey toward the town. Arriving in town, I dismounted and entered a drinking house. There I joined several of my friends and we drank and joked for some time. The thing that stands out in my mind the most was how real everything was. I could see the crowds of people inside, feel the metal goblet in my hands, and taste the drink. I even was sexually aroused by seeing some of the women there.

A fight broke out, and there was yelling and cursing. I was thrown violently to the floor. Before I could raise myself up I was kicked in the head, and I lost consciousness. I found myself surrounded by blackness again . . . I found I had returned to the present. I was sitting up straight under the maple tree in my backyard.

Now there is more to these cases than at first meets the eye. Note how the first case is "veridical" (from the Latin word _veritas_), or "truth telling." In other words, information was communicated to the subject during the experience that was true, although the experiencer could not have had normal access to it. This is a feature that crops up several times in the accounts Dr. Lenz has collected. It is not an invariable feature, however, since most of these spontaneous revivications concern times and events too far back in recorded history to be easily documented. The fragmentary nature of many of them also reduces the possibility that they could ever be properly verified. But since both veridical and nonveridical cases seem in all other respects identical, there is really no reason to consider one group more important for study than the other.

But now let's get back to the "phenomenological syndrome" that was mentioned earlier. Note how, in both the above accounts, the emergence of the past-life recollections was heralded by some initial subjective experiences. The first correspondent heard an odd ringing in her ears, while the second seemed to undergo an out-of-body experience. In both cases the past-life recalls _emerged_ from these initial sensations, as though the sensations were an integral part of the experience itself.

Dr. Lenz explains in his book that people who remember past lives through such spontaneous imagery go through a specific series of stages before the emergence of the actual memories. During the first stage the subject begins to hear a ringing or other sound in his ears that becomes overpowering. He feels his body becoming lighter, sees vivid colors dancing before his eyes, and the room seems to vibrate. The experiencer becomes nearly ecstatic, and then finally merges with a scene from his previous life. The whole drama is, in fact, similar to the phenomenology that accompanies those near-death encounters reported by people who have undergone clinical death or who have had other close encounters with death. To be sure, not everyone goes through all these stages, since the symptoms I have just described represent only the most complete syndrome. Some people go through all the stages; others go through only one or two.

This syndrome seemed to accompany most of Lenz's cases in one form or another. The only exceptions are dream cases that emerge naturally from sleep. These, too, seem to be accompanied by their own patterns—the experiencers find the dreams especially vivid, they remain in memory permanently, and they are intuitively linked to reincarnation.

The thing that especially struck me was how Dr. Lenz's correspondents invariably had their experiences while momentarily entering altered states of consciousness. This seems to be a prominent feature of these cases.

An altered state of consciousness is any experience of mind that appreciably departs from the state of "normal" awareness that occupies us during the "regular" part of our daily lives. Many of these altered states are simply mild inner-directed alterations of awareness, such as those that occur in meditation, during daydreaming, or as a result of mild hypnosis. But they also can occur as radical disturbances in normal awareness. What are called "inwardly directed states of awareness," such as meditation and daydreaming, seem particularly associated with past-life recall.

All inwardly directed states, from simple daydreaming to intense sensory deprivation, share certain fundamental qualities. The experiencer's basic thought processes are altered; his sense of time is disturbed; he loses his self-control; his emotional expression is increased; the experiencer's mental picture of his physical body is distorted; hallucinations or mental imagery are likely to preoccupy his attention; and his subjective experiences are viewed with new meaning and significance. In other words, when an individual enters into a discrete ASC (altered state of consciousness), he or she is overwhelmed by a wide range of subjective experiences. (This is a natural outcome of an ASC, since awareness of the outside world is greatly reduced as the mind turns inward.) The mind seizes onto internal pictures and messages with the same sort of attention and vigilance usually reserved for processing information from the environment. That is why this information takes on new significance. For now the experiencer is usually paying *attention* to what is going on in his or her mind.

This rush of information may take many forms, but most of it is coded within mental imagery.

The implication all this information has for the study of past-life recall should be obvious by now. If memories of past lives genuinely exist within the structure of the brain, they must be buried deep within its storage banks. If they weren't, we would all be inundated with past-life recall all the time. It seems clear that, to make contact with these memories, we must enter into some state of mind in which these deep levels of the unconscious may be tapped. Inner directed states of awareness are the most likely choice to explore. This is why hypnosis is so commonly used to help experimental subjects make contact with purported past-life memories. Formal hypnosis is an effective method by which attention can be channelled away from the outside world, permitting the subject to enter into an active dialogue with material from the unconscious. This general model can also explain why young children are prone to recall their past-lives while adults are not. Youngsters have not yet logged enough life experiences to "clutter" their access to early and even pre-natal experiences. They may therefore also have a natural ability to tap into memories from previous lives. Access to this information may well be shut off as normal memory functions evolve and focus on "present life" information.

Most students of the reincarnation issue are, of course, aware that past-life recall is linked to hypnosis and hypnotic regression. However, relatively few students of this mystery seem aware that other altered states of consciousness may be linked to these memories as well and that these memories can surface spontaneously in everyday life.

I was very challenged by Dr. Lenz's work when I first read it, since it seemed to represent a very fruitful line of inquiry into the nature of reincarnation. It was nonetheless clear from his book that the San Diego psychologist had collected his material rather informally. He apparently compiled his accounts case by case as he heard about them and then added other cases to his files as more people heard about his work and approached him with their own accounts. There is nothing wrong with this approach, but it does open up the possibility of what social scientists call "response bias." Dr. Lenz's cases could be fitting into a consistent pattern simply because those people who had heard about his work were tailoring their accounts specifically for him.

I, on the other hand, was interested in seeing if I could replicate the "Lenz syndrome," as I began calling it, through a more random sampling. There were actually two goals to my project. I was of course hoping to find out whether people who had never heard of Dr. Lenz or his work would report similar cases, but I also wanted to determine independently the frequency with which reincarnation memories emerge from altered states of consciousness.

I began my project early in 1981, soon after first reading Dr. Lenz's book. I wrote letters to two popular psychic-oriented magazines asking interested readers to send me accounts of any reincarnation memories they had experienced that had emerged in any way _other_ than through hypnosis. My aim was to chart just which specific states of consciousness were linked to these memories and what kind of people tend to remember their past lives. My letters prompted an immediate response. I received about fifty replies, but many were unusable. Some were so eccentric that they were hardly credible, while others were so brief and offered so little detail about the experiences that the accounts were worthless for my purpose. And a few other individuals sent me hypnotic regression accounts that while interesting, were not what I was studying.

Nevertheless, the results of my survey, after I sifted through the material I received, were encouraging. I was able to collect a core of twenty credible accounts from what appeared to be stable, educated, and literate people who had experienced spontaneous reincarnation memories. Seven of these experiences came by way of dreams, while six others could be classified as "waking visions." Four cases evolved from strong déjà-vu reactions to places the percipients had visited or to material they were reading at the time. Two other reports came from people who had been meditating when the memories surfaced, and one account was of a past-life scene encountered during a vivid out-of-body episode. (This totals more than twenty accounts since some of the respondents included more than one set of recollections.) This simple survey did much to bear out my feeling that memories of past-lives, be they genuine or fantasy, are linked to altered states of mind in general and not just to hypnosis.

Now let's take a look at some of these cases in more depth.

Reincarnation "Dreams"

The dream cases were the most notable and consistent of the lot. My correspondents tended to identify them as reincarnation dreams because of their odd subjective quality. The dreams were especially vivid or repetitive, or they brought with them a strong sense that they were actual memories and not simple unconscious constructions. Also impressive was the fact that a few of them contained veridical elements. All this was in keeping with what Lenz reports about dream cases in his book.

One case was contributed by a woman in California who had been having repetitive reincarnation dreams over a number of years. I was struck by her matter-of-factness when she began her account by writing that "being a realist I did historical research on these dreams to see if [they had] any basis in fact. Many facts proved true." One such dream dealt with her terror during a volcanic eruption. Her subsequent historical research, based on details contained within the dream, led her to believe she had witnessed the eruption of Mount Vesuvius in 79 A.D.

Another of this woman's dreams also turned out to be veridical. The dream setting was a crude hut in some distant country and era. The woman found herself dressed in peasant garb sitting with her obese, reddish-haired husband:

> I am greatly worried, but my husband, my boss, keeps telling me there is nothing to worry about. He has arranged everything. I'm aware my husband was a ruler on the mainland, ruthless often in conquering of other territories; something I hated. Now, invaders had approached the mainland coming near my husband's territory. We had fled to a small, green, farming island. We had

changed into peasant garb to conceal our identity, to appear as members of a farm family. The invaders would kill my husband if they found him, and kill me too since I was his wife. There were shouts outside and we went out and saw Viking-like ships approaching the island. They were looking for my escaped husband!

The dream came to a violent climax when the woman noticed and, for no apparent reason, panicked at a ring on her husband's finger. It bore a huge rectangular stone engraved with crude carvings. It was at that moment in the dream that the door to the hut was broken down and the invaders entered. The woman woke up before re-experiencing what was most likely her imminent death:

> I thought it interesting that I had seen Viking ships, but I could not believe that anyone, with any comfort, could wear such a huge ring as I had seen on the man's finger. Nor did I catch the significance of such a ring.
>
> I went to the library to research the age and value of a beautiful cameo ring passed down in several generations in my family. It was in that ring book that I discovered the origin of the cameo—carved stone. Originally these were signet rings of rulers. The largest and most crudely carved were of ancient Scandinavians! The life-size photos of such relics matched the ring in my dream as to size and clumsiness!
>
> Then no wonder my panic in that dream. The signet my husband absentmindedly forgot to remove identified him to the Viking invaders!

Seeing or recalling such artifacts or emblems, which helps the dreamer to date the dream and its significance, cropped up in more than one case I collected. Another woman wrote about a dream she had experienced as a teenager in which she perceived herself as a man in a drafty and uncomfortable stone building. Later she realized that she had probably been wealthy, because servants had been part of the scene. But the real significance of the dream rested with a peculiar brooch the woman had seen her "wife" wearing:

> My wife wore a large silver brooch like a buckle only with no belt, under her breasts. That seemed to be very important. It was beautiful, too. I drew a picture of it then, although its design has faded and my memory [was] lost in the ensuing years.

It was not until many years later that the meaning of the brooch came back to her dramatically. She was reading about Scottish history when she saw the identical brooch illustrated in a section dealing with a particular clan. It was a family insignia. "When I saw the picture," she explained in her letter, "my stomach turned over and I started to perspire with the excitement of recognition."

The woman also dreamt of her death at the hands of marauders. The dream was so striking that, even before she verified the buckle and its design, she wrote out an account of the dream and sent it to a researcher interested in reincarnation.

This witness, now an associate professor at a well-known college, remains puzzled but intrigued by her teenage experience. In fact, she was one of two college professors at major universities who contacted me about their reincarnation recollections. Dr. Lenz likewise had found that many of his accounts came from such professional people.

A third fascinating dream case I received came from a woman in Texas. She also discovered that her nighttime reveries contained a veridical element. In this case the dreams were repetitive, which suggested to her that it was a memory and not a true dream:

> There was a suspension bridge high above a wide expanse of water. It was a narrow walkway, swaying in the wind, with nothing to hold on to and floor boards spaced so one could see the water below through the cracks. The bridge was reached by a ladder. Here my dreams varied: sometimes I would mount the ladder and turn back as soon as I reached the top; other times I would creep out onto the bridge on hands and knees and a few other times I would go out onto it a short distance walking erect. Never did I reach the other side.
>
> About 25 or 30 years ago I picked up a copy of "Life" magazine, and what should I find in it but a half page picture of *my* bridge. And what is more, it was taken from the same angle that I always approached the bridge in my dreams. The article accompanying the picture identified it as the first catwalk thrown across the East River preparatory to building the Brooklyn Bridge back in the 1870's; it also stated that a number of persons, both men and women, had fallen to their deaths from the bridge.
>
> I am convinced that I was one of those because I have never had that particular dream again.

My correspondent also mentioned that this revelation also helped her overcome her lifelong phobia that she would die by falling from a high place. Seeing and reading about the bridge in *Life* permanently and instantaneously cured the problem.

A somewhat similar case was sent to me by a homemaker and mother from Washington. She explained that her experience occurred when she was fourteen years old and living in a small town in Wyoming. The dream impressed her because of its vividness and internal consistency. "It was very vivid and not like the usual mumbo jumbo kind that I'd always had," she explained. "It stayed with me for days." My correspondent also noted that she was totally unfamiliar with the concept of reincarnation at the time but felt certain that she was somehow linked with the woman in her dream:

> The dream was in an area about 10 or 12 miles south of La Barge, Wyoming, and I could see myself in a kind of long, plain dress, and I was in front of a really rough looking small house with my three little girls (ages about 3-5).

I'm looking across this long valley toward the north. There is a lot of smoke billowing out of this mine (coal I suppose) and my heart is beating very hard and I'm terrified. I know my husband is in that mine and it seems to be just him. Like it was some private mine. Our own? I run to a small corral beside the house and get a horse and tell the little girls they have to stay there. That I had to get help. Then I'm riding at a full gallop toward La Barge and the feeling of panic is with me the full time. I can still see the smoke as I'm galloping through this valley which has tall grass and sagebrush and I seem to know that my husband is dead but I have to get help. Then I woke up, terrified and crying. The dream was in my memory for several days, very real, and at 14 I couldn't figure out why I would dream something like this.

The upshot to the dream came two years later when the woman was working on a hayranch in Fontenelle, Wyoming:

I helped a rancher's wife cook and babysat and cleaned house. They had a 14-year-old son who was interested in old buckboards and wagons. One afternoon when we had a few free hours, the lady I worked for took her son and me and her other two children and said we were going to [a neighboring ranch] because they had a bunch of old wagons and her son wanted to see if there were any he'd be interested in. The ranch is (or was then) along the highway going to La Barge. We talked to the rancher there, and he said that the wagons were at the old home place out in the hills and gave us directions. We crossed the highway, and went west. We had gone a couple of miles when we topped this rise and all of a sudden, I got goosebumps all over, because there was this same valley that had been in my dream, and my dream came back instantly. I knew I had been there before. I looked immediately to where the house and corral had been and then across the valley to where the smoke had been coming out of the mine, but there was nothing there. Just a valley with sagebrush.

Do these dreams really "prove" reincarnation, though? Not really, but what does impress me about the reincarnation dreams I collected is how they all seem to follow a consistent pattern. They are all violent and usually relate to the dreamer's death. This came as a bit of a surprise since Lenz makes no mention of this pattern in his book, although at least one of his cases fits this pattern. Now if reincarnation actually occurs, it strikes me that this is just the type of experience or information that would indeed emerge. One's death, especially if it occurred violently or tragically, might be expected to impress itself forcefully on the new life. The death of a loved one might equally be imprinted in the same way. The traumas we suffer in childhood affect us all the rest of our lives, so traumas suffered in a previous existence might make a similar impression. Dr. Ian Stevenson has found a similar pattern in his investigations of children who spontaneously recall past lives, since they, too, tend to remember lives that ended tragically.

The skeptic will of course argue that there is probably some obscure psychoanalytical reason for the predominance of the death motif in reincarnation-type dreams. But death is certainly not a prominent theme in normal dreaming. More impressive, still, were the strong veridical elements the dreams often contained. So reincarnation seems to explain these cases (especially the veridical ones) better than a contrived psychological hypothesis.

Waking Visions of Past Lives

The data I collected from people who recalled their previous lives during waking visions did not conform to as consistent a pattern, but they were no less fascinating. These were primarily cases in which the participants found themselves suddenly transported in time and momentarily *living* a scene from a past life. These reports read much like those rare instances of retrocognition that have found their way into the literature of psychical research—cases in which people become so caught up in the sights and sounds of a past time that they actually become confused between the scene and normal reality. They also conform closely to the types of cases Lenz has collected.

For example, one woman wrote how she underwent such an experience while a student listening to a lecture:

> Suddenly the room filled with intense light. It became warm, almost stuffy—I turned to see what the light was from and was startled to see that the tree [outside the lecture hall] was in full bloom, the sun was shining brightly and the windows were open. My attention focused on the students in front of the window and they were dressed in very strange clothes—the girls had on long dresses and ribbons, most of the dresses had high collars, no makeup (which was totally unusual) and the boys were dressed in cord knickers with hightop shoes or sneakers, collarless shirts and very strange haircuts. My own dress was similar to the other girls' and I was totally dumbstruck by this since I *always* wore jeans. I must have gasped because the next thing I remembered was the teacher saying something to the effect that I should pay attention and answer her question, if I could. Most startling to me was that I apparently did not miss much of the lecture since I answered the question correctly but do not remember what the question was or the fact that a question was directed to me.

A correspondent writing from Idaho contributed a similar account. She was in bed waiting to fall asleep when her eyes became affixed on a peculiar light in the room. Suddenly it appeared that, in her own words, "I seemed to shift into a completely different world than the real one in which I lived." She meant this literally and not figuratively. She found herself as a child huddled with her mother in a house hiding from German soldiers who were prepared to kill them upon discovery.

This particular correspondent had undergone a handful of such experiences during her life. These scenes tend to be so vivid that the woman actually sensed that she had been transported back in time. They don't manifest as "visions" as we normally conceptualize them, and she describes them as "switching time frames." During one such episode, for instance, she was riding in a golf cart with her husband. "We were going down a very rough cart path through the trees, very fast, when for a few seconds I felt like I had switched time frames," she wrote to me. "We were in England, clattering down a country path in a cart drawn by a horse." The scene lasted for a few moments before she was suddenly brought back to everyday reality. She told her husband about her experience immediately, hoping that he had shared some sort of analogous experience, but he hadn't.

This is not, of course, an evidential or veridical account. But it matches closely the descriptions some of my other correspondents used to describe their waking reincarnation visions, which, in turn, are identical to Lenz's cases. Compare the description of "switching time frames" to that of a middle-aged man who wrote me how his reincarnation visions occurred as "a sudden shift in consciousness" in which he "was in a different time and place." It should also be noted that neither of these correspondents, or any of the others who described waking reincarnation visions, had in any way sought their experiences. All had occurred spontaneously, often to the percipients' surprise.

Analyzing the meaning of these experiences is just as challenging as interpreting dream recollections. Such episodes could indeed be due to the revivications of past-life memories, but as suggested earlier, they could also be due to some type of retrocognition—that the percipients suddenly and paranormally tuned into a past time and place. But perhaps more to the point is whether these waking visions cases can be explained in any normal way. So before continuing any further, let's examine this issue in some depth.

The only truly cogent explanation for such incidents might be that they result from spontaneous electrical activity in the brain, especially in the temporal or frontal lobes and are then mistakenly interpreted as reincarnation experiences. It is well known that tiny seizures (which have little to do with epilepsy) sometimes occur quite spontaneously in these areas. They can happen to anyone and do not indicate any actual or permanent pathology. The episodes usually result from spontaneous neural firing, and the result is sometimes a strong déjà-vu experience in which the percipient will believe he has lived whatever he is doing or seeing before. Sometimes brief visual hallucinations may also result. If such an hallucination were to occur along with a neurologically based déjà-vu sensation, the experiencer might well relate his experience to something that occurred to him in a previous life. In other words, he might experience his hallucination as a memory. Instant reincarnation!

Epilepsy also occurs as a result of such firing, though in this case the electrical activity is much more overt and pathological. Some experiences that severe epileptics undergo may also provide a clue by which waking vision cases might conceivably be explained. Please remember that not all forms of epilepsy result in the violent seizures we normally associate with the disorder. Sometimes the result of the electrical activity storming within the epileptic's brain will be more subtle, subjective, and bizarre. During the "aura" that precedes some forms of epilepsy, the sufferer will experience sinking sensations, dizziness, and visual or auditory hallucinations. Note that this is similar to the type of sensations that herald the emergence of past-life memories typified by the "Lenz syndrome."

In the long run, though, I don't think that any simple neurological explanation can account for the reports Dr. Lenz and I have collected for the following reasons:

1. Such electrical activity in the brain does not lead to the emergence of prolonged, complex, or structured visions. A single fragmentary scene may briefly occur, but little more.

2. Experiments in which the cerebral cortex of the brain has been deliberately stimulated have caused experimental subjects to recall scenes drawn from their *own* earlier lives and are usually identified as such. New experiences or scenes do not evolve.

3. The "aura" that seems to uncannily match certain aspects of the "Lenz syndrome" usually heralds the onset of Grand Mal seizures. They do not usually appear isolated from them.

There are also other weaknesses to the seizure/epilepsy theory, and these emerge from the patterns inherent to the cases themselves. Many of the waking vision cases in my collection, for instance, revolve around the experiencer's death, just as the reincarnation-linked dream cases do. This overall thematic consistency is hard to explain as a result of simple neurophysiology. It is also obvious that simple neurophysiology cannot account for the veridical elements that are contained in so many of these cases, nor have I come across any purely neurophysiological writings on hallucinations that include or describe experiences that match those given by my correspondents.

The fact that electrical stimulation of the brain can occasionally result in delusionary déjà-vu or apparent reincarnation experiences is a good reason to treat such experiences cautiously. However, it is also possible that the emergence of deeply buried memories *causes* odd neural firings in the brain that might result in epileptiform symptoms. Thus the superficial parallels be tween the past-life memory syndrome and brain pathology *may* be the *result* of the emergence of these revivications, not the cause.

Déjà-Vu Cases

People tend to associate the term "déjà-vu" with a momentary and vague feeling that they have seen or experienced something previously. The sensation may hit the percipient as he is engaged in almost any sort of activity—from carrying on a conversation with a friend to doing the laundry. These experiences happen to all of us now and then and can usually be explaind neurophysiologically. However, some cases of déjà-vu are much more complex and strongly suggest extrasensory elements. Such experiences are not momentary. Some people have found chronic déjà-vu feelings virtually controlling their lives, and such cases bring us back to the subject of reincarnation and past-life recall.

The experiences of Ernest Shafenberg, a retired farmer living in Kingfisher, Oklahoma, are typical. A small town in Oklahoma right in the heart of the Bible belt isn't exactly the kind of place where the subject of reincarnation is often discussed or even thought about. Yet this didn't keep Shafenberg from having vivid flashbacks and déjà-vu experiences even as a child in the early 1900s. His first experience came when he was a schoolboy. Sometimes while reading history books on the West and the great Indian wars, he would have sensations that he had actually lived through them. These were not ordinary daydreams, but vivid impressions in which he saw himself fighting the Indians on the great plains of the central West. These experiences continued through adolescence and into adulthood. Based on clues contained within his "fantasies", Shafenberg began to understand exactly _who_ he had been in his past life. He came to intuitively realize that he had lived in the mid-1800s as one Billy Comstock, who had been a half-Indian scout for the U.S. Cavalry. He also came to realize that he had been reborn as a Robert Mackereth in the 1870s and had been a trumpeter with the U.S. 8th Cavalry. He felt that he had died at an early age in both lives.

It wasn't until he was in his sixties that Shafenberg was finally able to track down the source of these strange impressions, when he began traveling throughout the central West in hopes of exploring the sites of his obsessions. The climax to his search came in August 1970, when he visited the battlefield of the tragic battle of Wounded Knee, near the town of Pine Ridge in South Dakota, where hundreds of Indians who were holed up there were massacred by government troops. "As I read the names of the dead from the plaque erected there to commemorate those killed in the battle and looked around the terrain," he later told investigators, "I was overwhelmed by the feeling that I had been there before. This is the first time I positively knew I had lived before. I suddenly had a flashback as though I were carrying the feelings from an earlier lifetime over into the present. The continuity was strong, similar to returning home after a short visit elsewhere. The feelings, the knowing, the closeness seemed to increase as it all came back to me."

His déjà-vu reactions continued as he began reliving some of his lifelong flashbacks about the area. He now knew that he had participated in the massacre of 1890:

> Even the pit that had been dug to bury the dead was exactly where I had seen it in my flashbacks—just back of the church. I remembered clearly on that day of the mass burial how I had stood on the east side of that gruesome pit. A

blizzard had occurred following the battle, and it was four days before the dead could be buried, almost 150 Indian men, women, and children.

After visiting the site of this great battle, Shafenberg began delving into old U.S. Cavalry records. There he found the name of Robert Mackereth. He had joined the 8th Cavalry on 31 March 1890.

He was able to document the life of Bill Comstock as well. This occurred during a visit he was making to Analarko, Oklahoma, on the advice of a psychic who had told him that he had died there by a bridge near a ravine. His death, he was told, had come during a battle. Shafenberg was able to find a bridge matching the psychic's description after talking with some local residents. It was situated some eight miles west of the town itself, so he rushed to the site. Merely seeing the bridge ignited yet another déjà-vu experience. "I knew that I had been there before," he later reported. "I knew every rock and tree in the area." He even recalled how he had died there–from an arrow wound while he was hiding under the bridge. Later he was able to find an old photograph of Comstock and identify it.

Ernest Shafenberg is still retired. He still lives in Kingfisher and has erected a sign across the roadside by his property, testifying to his belief in reincarnation.

None of the cases I collected during my 1981 project was as exciting as Shafenberg's life-long involvement with his déjà-vu experiences. But several of them were impressive and point to some type of reincarnation experience. Space limitations will permit me to cite only two of the more evidential ones, but notice how they both resemble Shafenberg's experiences rather uncannily.

A particularly impressive déjà-vu case occurred to one of my correspondents while she was driving with a friend through New Jersey:

We were driving down the New Jersey Turnpike, and I felt very strange, all this landscape was very familiar to me. . . . I turned to Joanne, and said, "You know, I have never been here before, but I believe about a mile or so down the road, is a house I used to live in."

As we went down the turnpike, (heading North), everything was familiar . . . . the older houses, and I began describing *what* we would see before we came to it.

Approximately three miles or so passed, and I told my friend, that around the bend, we would come to a small town, it was set very close to the turnpike. I told her that the houses would be white frame, two storey homes, rather close together . . . and that I felt that I lived there when I was six years old or so, and that I used to sit with my "granny" on the front porch. The memories overwhelmed me, and I could remember sitting on the swing, on the front porch, and my grandmother buttoning up my high-topped shoes. I could not do it myself. When we got to the town, I recognized the house immediately, only the front porch swing was not there . . . however, at the time I lived there with my Granny, there were also wicker furniture on the porch with green cloth cushions. I told my friend I *remembered* sitting there, and also that my granny used to walk two blocks down the street with me, to a drug store, and there was a high marble counter, white, and we used to get lemonade from the drug store, and I liked to go there. As we drove down the little street, I took her to the drug store, or where it _used_ to be. It was still there, or rather, the building was still there, much the same as it used to look, but it was boarded up, and we could not look inside. As we stood there , I "knew" that I had died when I was about 6 or 7 years old . . . and I tried to get Joanne to let me direct her to the cemetery where "I" was buried, but she was so frightened that she would not take the drive. As we were leaving the town I told her, "In about three blocks there is a small hill, rolling, and the cemetery is _there,_ and that is where they buried me." It was true . . . the cemetery _was_ there and as I had described it.

We got on the turnpike again, and went on to Paterson . . . and I still know that once, round the early 1900's that I lived there, and died there.

Probably the most curious déjà-vu case I received was from a man in Michigan who had experienced a long-lived fascination with the career and death of General Custer, although he had never taken the time to research the cavalryman's life. His actual reincarnation experience came while he was reading a book about Custer to see if some of his "impressions" and intuitive feelings about the man's life and career—especially his death—were correct:

While reading I suddenly realized I was actually living some part of the real action. My heart was pounding like I was riding among the Indians and I found my hands sweating so bad I could hardly hold the book! I was in real terror when the sudden realization hit me that I was simply holding the book in my hands and was not riding and fighting for my life. I was shocked!

This experience led my correspondent to believe that he probably rode with Custer during his last and famous stand. His recollections also seemed to tie in with the fact that, as a young child playing cowboys and Indians, he had developed the notion that an Indian fighter should save one bullet for himself in case he was caught. He later learned that this was a widespread custom among nineteenth-century Indian fighters, who considered suicide a better option than death by torture should they be taken captive.

Much more could be said about the phenomenon of spontaneous past-life recall, and the cases reported above are only a sample of what is actually a large body of fascinating case material. The real puzzle does not rest with this material itself but with why so few researchers interested in reincarnation have ever bothered to study this body of literature. The so-called serious or scientific parapsychological literature on reincarnation has focused almost exclusively on two types of cases—children who have recalled their past lives from birth and those recollections elicited through hypnotic regression. Yet these spontaneous cases represent a formidable range of material that is potentially just as valuable.

In conclusion, then, just how did my attempt to replicate the Lenz effect fare? It was actually a mixture of success and failure. My data indicate that the *types* of cases Dr. Lenz has collected seem to be fairly common. People with no prior interest in reincarnation are being led to accept its reality because of their personal experiences with dreams, waking visions, and déjà-vu encounters. I was not, however, able to confirm the universality of the "Lenz syndrome." While some of my correspondents reported odd subjective experiences during the initial stages of their encounters, I found no widespread mention of the floating sensations, vivid colors, or vibrations that Lenz has noted. In fact, not a single case in my collection showed any conformity to the *specific* syndrome Lenz outlines in his book.

But how can we account for this disparity? One possible explanation might be that, in collecting his data, Lenz somehow cued his correspondents and witnesses about the type of material he was collecting and expected them to come up with. If, for example, he had described the syndrome he was isolating during a television appearance, some of his viewers could have tailored their reports to conform to this pattern before making contact with him. Or perhaps only people whose experiences closely matched what Lenz was known to be collecting tended to get in touch with him. The results of my own work leads me to believe that the "Lenz effect" is not as universal, structured, or consistent as he believes it to be, nor does it necessarily appear to be an integral part of the reincarnation experience. On the other hand, it is only fair to note tht Dr. Lenz was working from a much larger data base than I had to work with. A more consistent effect might have shown up had I been able to work with more cases.

Despite the fact that I wasn't able to establish the existence of a universal "Lenz syndrome," this fact in no way deprecates the value of the cases he and I have (now) independently collected. One goal of my project was to see if I could find cases resembling Lenz's that point directly to reincarnation. The result of this endeavor must be considered a success. There seems no doubt that many people undergo intense and spontaneous reincarnation-like experiences every day. These experiences appear accidental; certainly they are not sought out. But their frequent occurrence strikes me as significant.

Of course, the most obvious question the critic might raise at this point is a rather simple one. Just how good a case for reincarnation do these reports actually represent? Do they represent a valid case at all?

There are several possible answers to this question. The most obvious is to point to those cases in which the past-life memories contained veridical information. The cases I was able to collect indicate that some people, while momentarily reliving their past lives, come up with information about people they had never met and places they had never visited. No pedestrian explanation for spontaneous past-life memory derived from psychology, psychoanalysis, or neurology can explain these cases. Now the skeptic might counter by pointing out that these veridical cases are rare. Perhaps, it could be argued, they should only be considered as unexplained anomalies within a great mass of cases that are worthless from an evidential standpoint. But this would, I think, be a totally invalid point. It seems to me significant that there is so much similarity between those cases that contain veridical elements and those that do not. The two classes of cases follow the same patterns, especially the dream cases. The experiencers all noted that the dreams were intensely vivid, stayed with them longer than normal dreams do, and were intuitively linked to reincarnation. Waking visions follow their own patterns as well. It seems clear to me that we are dealing here with a phenomenological syndrome—self-consistent and unique—that does not conform to any perceptual anomaly known to conventional psychiatry.

This is certainly true of the waking visions cases. Certain elements of these reports—the odd sensations that initiate them, reliving mental pictures, and the emotional reactions the percipient usually has to the experience—can all be explained rather piecemeal by drawing on bits and pieces of neurological data. But no findings in neurology can explain this _entire and consistent sequence of related phenomena._

Finally, there remains the fact that, no matter how these memories surfaced, they were intuitively linked to reincarnation. While some researchers might eschew placing any value on this type of subjective evaluation, I think this fact is more important than you might believe. Even conventional psychology is beginning to realize that only the individual himself can legitimately evaluate his subjective experiences. This is true, for example, in the case of dream interpretation. The old psychoanalytical practice whereby the therapist dictatorially explained a dream to his patient is now out of vogue with more enlightened therapists. The problem with this approach was that the patients often didn't believe what they were told, and no two analysts could ever seem to interpret a dream the same way. Psychologists interested in dream interpretation have now come to realize that the best way to proceed is to offer alternative suggestions to the dreamer until one of them seems to "click." Then the psychologist knows he is on the right track. There now exists a whole school of therapy called "focusing" that teaches the patient to go inside himself, focus on a problem in a state of detachment, and consider ways of dealing with it until something "clicks" within his mind and body. There is a great deal of experimental evidence that focusing works and is a very cogent form of self-therapy. Note again how it is the experiencer himself whose insights are considered all-important.*

The critical point I am trying to emphasize here is that in dealing with data such as "reincarnation memory," intuitive judgment is just as valid as scientific assessment . . . _so long as no obvious normal explanation fits the data._ The fact that the people whose experiences have been reported here intuitively linked their encounters to reincarnation may be in itself evidential.

But couldn't these individuals be simply self-deluded, nonetheless?

*_Focusing_ by Eugene T. Gendlin, Ph.D.(New York, Everest House, 1978.).

This is possible in some cases. I am especially skeptical of those cases in which people who have had a long history of interest in the metaphysical and the occult claim memories of past lives. But the fact remains that the people who so often report past-life recollections were not usually inclined to believe in reincarnation—or, at any rate, not *until* they had their experiences. Many had their experiences as children and before they had ever heard of the doctrine.

The results of any case collection of the nature reported in this chapter are bound to be inconclusive in the long run. No matter how suggestive these reports appear to be, they fall short of formal proof. The memories these people have experienced through their dreams and visions are fragmentary and ephemeral. Not enough information is contained in most of them that *can* be documented. So to build a really strong case for reincarnation, we need cases of people who can recall a great deal of specific information about their past lives—including names, dates, and places. This search naturally leads us to our next point of inquiry, for there exists a large body of reports centering on children who seem literally "born" with memories about their pervious lives. But even this data is more complicated than you might think.

Conclusions

There seems little doubt that many people experience vivid memories of their purported "past lives" during the course of their daily lives. These may occur via dreams, or more dramatically, in the form of striking waking experiences. The value of these cases is that they seem to follow certain patterns, often contain veridical elements, and cannot be explained as the result of normal though perhaps anomalous brain activity. They represent a strong line of inferential evidence favoring the reincarnation theory. Certainly this explanation can account for these experiences better than any other so far proposed.

3

In Search of Past Lives I: Selected Cases

Cases of spontaneous past-life recall serve only as intimations of reincarnation. They cannot serve as particularly strong evidence of and by themselves. The information contained in these accounts is often too fragmented and/or unverifiable to analyze. A more revealing approach to the reincarnation question would be to track down those lucky individuals who remember a great deal of specific information about their past lives. But do such people even exist? The answer is yes.

Back in 1917 a newspaper in Puerto Rico published just such an account. It told a strange story about a little boy who lived with his parents at No. 33, Rue San José in Havana, Cuba. Eduardo Esplugus-Cabrera apparently began talking about his past life almost from the time he could speak. His parents first realized there was something unusual about their son when he spontaneously told his mother that he had previously lived across town at 69 Rue Campanairo. It soon became clear that the boy was talking about a past life. Mr. Esplugus-Cabrera was a local businessman and was anything but a believer in the psychic or occult, but he was nonetheless impresed by the adamancy with which his son talked about his previous life. This prompted him to ask the boy a series of test questions about his recollections. Eduardo explained that his name had been Pancho, said his parents had been Pierre and Amparo Seco, and once again mentioned the address of his previous home. He added that his two brothers were named Jean and Mercedes. He described his "past life" mother as being a hat maker and having a dark complexion. No particular memories about the nature of his death were forthcoming, but little Eduardo did recall leaving his parents' house on 28 February 1903, when he was thirteen years old. He recalled driving his bicycle over to a chemist's shop run by an American to buy some drugs.

This list of information was so detailed that Mr. and Mrs. Cabreras took their son to the house where he claimed to have lived. They were sure he had never been to that part of town before. Eduardo immediately recognized his former home when he spotted it from the street, so his parents decided to investigate the history of the house. Their investigation uncovered a remarkable set of facts that fully substantiated their son's claims. The house had been occupied until the early part of 1903 by Antonio (not Pierre) and Amparo Saco (not Seco), who had left Havana after the death of their youngest son, Pancho. They had taken their two other sons, Jean and Mercedes, with them. The Cabreras also located the druggist's shop that had played such a prominent role in their son's recollections. It was close by and had indeed been run by an American.

Does this case, then, serve as the "perfect" case of reincarnation?

Investigating these "cases of the reincarnation type" can be very difficult. The case of Eduardo Esplugus-Cabrera is impressive since his parents made a written record of the boy's claims before they attempted to verify them. But could the boy have heard, or learned normally about the Saco family, through local gossip perhaps? This certainly seems unlikely, yet his confusion over the name Saco (which he gave as Seco) is just the sort of error that would seem based on something he had heard.

So is it even possible to set forth what criteria would constitute the "perfect" proof of reincarnation? Perhaps. The truly perfect case of reincarnation memory would have to entail the following extraordinary characteristics:

1. The subject under investigation should be able to recall his past life in considerable detail.

2. Someone should have made a written record of these claims before any attempt at verification is undertaken.

3. This information should turn out to be accurate upon investigation.

4. The adult or child whose memories are being investigated should display certain behavioral traits apparently inherited from the "donor" personality from whom he claims to have been reborn.

5. He or she should bear a birthmark inherited from a mark or wound on the donor's body.

6. The subject should be able to speak the language (if foreign) spoken by the previous personality during his/her lifetime.

This list of features characterizing the "perfect" reincarnation case is not my own. It was first presented by Dr. Ian Stevenson during a presentation he made in the summer of 1972 at a conference on parapsychology at the University of Edinburgh. He was using the occasion to present the criteria for the magic case he felt would "prove" the reality of reincarnation once and for all. A year later he again broached the subject of the "perfect" case at a similar conference and alluded to his 1972 presentation. He pointed out that "in outlining this theoretically perfect case I said that I did not expect to find such a case and I still do not." But he added that "there are, however, some less-than-perfect cases that should have considerable persuasive power if we can find and investigate them more often." This is exactly what Dr. Stevenson has been doing since 1955 and, to date, he has catalogued close to 1,900 cases. Most of them focus on children who have allegedly recalled their previous lives.

As I have already said, Dr. Stevenson has almost single-handedly elevated the status of reincarnation research within parapsychology. He has taken it out of the realm of simple storytelling by actively investigating new cases and reinvestigating some of the older cases he has found in the literature. His success at elevating the scientific credibility of reincarnation research was primarily accomplished by restricting the focus of his interest. Instead of pursuing many lines of evidence, he concentrated his attention on cases in which children seem literally "born" with memories inherited from their previous existences. Dr. Stevenson rightly believes that these children are too young and naive to be either lying about their experiences or responding to normally acquired memories buried in their unconscious minds. These reports also struck Stevenson as particularly persuasive since, in some cases, the parents of the children had witnessed the emergence of the memories. Sometimes they had even made written notes before trying to verify what they were being told.

Dr. Stevenson had realized all this when he undertook his historical examination of the evidence bearing on the reincarnation question, which culminated with the publication of his "The Evidence for Survival from Claimed Memories of Former Incarnations" in 1960. This essay not only served as a masterful summary of the evidence, but ended with Stevenson's announcement that he was interested in collecting and investigating new cases himself.

Since the publication of his 1960 report, Dr. Stevenson has issued a series of books on his further case studies. Most of his reports derive from India, Sri Lanka, Turkey, Lebanon, and among the Tlingit eskimos of southeastern Alaska. He has also written a plethora of papers on the implications that can be drawn from his studies. These have appeared not only in publications normally devoted to parapsychology, but also in psychiatric and sociology journals.

Dr. Stevenson's basic approach has been to work from the "case study" method. This approach is characterized by making an all out investigation of any case coming to his attention that seems worth following up. The problem inherent in much of the older literature on extracerebral memory cases was that they were presented anecdotally and informally. Dr. Stevenson rejects the idea that any reincarnation report should be taken at such face value and has established a well-defined "research tradition" for how new cases should be investigated. His procedure consists of (a) going to the town from which the case is being reported; (b) making contact with the child and family involved in the story; (c) interviewing any and all witnesses who can help document what the child originally said about his past life; (d) and then independently corroborating the accuracy of this informtion. He then attempts to determine any way the child may have come by the information normally.

This has not, of course, been an easy task. Language barriers have made the investigation of several cases extremely difficult. It is also very hard to work successfully in cultures that have customs different from our own. To deal with these problems, Dr. Stevenson has sometimes employed proxy investigators to carry out his probes. He has also attempted to reinvestigate older cases he has learned about to see if they withstand critical scrutiny. Unfortunately, only rarely has Dr. Stevenson been able to learn about a case while it is still active.

Before we look at some of Dr. Stevenson's more extraordinary cases, keep in mind just how difficult investigating cases of extra-cerebral memory can be. It is rare not to find what appears to be a very impressive case contaminated by ways in which the child could have come by his or her "memories" normally. The following famous story and its unsatisfactory resolution will give you a good idea of the problems Dr. Stevenson and his colleagues have been up against during the course of their field work. This case will also alert you to the pitfalls for which you should be on the lookout as you evaluate some of the other cases outlined later in this chapter.

Shanti Devi began talking about her past life in 1933. She was born in 1926 in Delhi, India, so was seven years old when her past-life recollections first emerged. Her claims revolved around her life in the town of Mathura, which is located about a hundred miles away. She also claimed that her name had been Ludgi, that she had been born in 1902, that she had married, and that she had given birth to three children. Her death, she also recollected, resulted from the birth of her third child in 1925. Shanti's parents were surprised by these revelations. Even though reincarnation is a commonly accepted belief in India, it is nonetheless relatively rare for children there to talk about their purported last lives. The parents of these gifted children usually try to stifle the talk, since it is considered a bad omen for a child to remember a past life. Yet children who seem to recall their past incarnations inevitably tend to become local celebrities. Shanti's parents made no attempt to verify their daughter's claims when she first started remembering her past life. But the case came to a climax in 1935 when a cousin of the girl's past-life husband visited their house on business. Shanti immediately recognized him, and the startled man was able to verify much of the information she was remembering. He told the family that Shanti's memories fit the life of his cousin's wife, who had died about a year before Shanti's birth. Her name had been Ludgi.

Ludgi's husband was Kedarnath (or Kedar Nath) Chaubey, who still lived in Mathura. He was, of course, intrigued when he heard news of his wife's rebirth in Delhi; so he made the long trip to Shanti's home to see if the girl could recognize him. He wasn't disappointed. Shanti took one look at the visitor and ran to him, addressing him by name. Later the girl was even taken to Mathura where she recognized several other relatives, spoke intelligently with many of the people who had known Ludgi, and even walked through the streets of the city with obvious ease. She was apparently familiar with the neighborhood. She also correctly explained that her previous home had been repainted and pointed out where a well had once been dug on her mother's property but was covered over.

Despite the fact that this case is cited in most popular books on reincarnation, it falls apart when critically examined. There were a number of ways that Shanti could have come by the information that pertained to her past life. It was only later discovered that Kedarnath was a frequent visitor to Delhi, where he often bought sweets from a shop next to the Devi home. It is very possible that Shanti could have met the man during one of his trips and/or overheard him talking about his wife. It is also difficult to ascertain just what information Shanti could have picked up from Kedarnath's cousin, Sri Lal, during his first visit to her home. Lal's visit had not been an acccident. Shanti's grand-uncle had written to Mathura to see if he could locate some one there matching Ludgi's description. Kedarnath Chaubey heard about the case through these inquiries and had deliberately sent Sri Lal, who lived in Delhi, to visit Shanti and investigate her claims. We have no record of just what Sri Lal said to Shanti, but there is reason to suspect that he fed all sorts of information to the girl about his cousin and his deceased wife. They spoke, after all, at some length.

But what about her familiarity with the streets and people of Mathura?

By the time a trip to Mathura was planned, the local newspapers were running stories on the case, which had become something of a *cause célèbre*. Shanti, her parents, and several investigators made the trip to Mathura by train. There they were met at the depot by a crowd of well-wishers and curiosity seekers who had heard about the case. The crowd was excited and noisy, and quite a bit of talk must have gone on about Kedarnath and Ludgi in the girl's immediate presence. This is especially likely because some of Ludgi's surviving relations were included. Shanti made all her recognitions and walked through the streets of the town while accompanied by the crowd. It is not hard to believe that they provided her with all sorts of information, cues, and hints upon which she relied as she made her identifications and walked unerringly through the streets of Mathura.

This is not to say that Shanti was merely a clever trickster. She may have really believed that she was the reincarnation of Chaubey's wife. Perhaps she really *did* somehow recall her past life in accurate detail, but the case is a washout as strong evidence pointing toward reincarnation. It is not so much that the case itself was poor, but that the investigation that went into it was flawed. During his probes of several contemporary cases, Dr. Stevenson has attempted to continually refine his field work. He was very aware of the traps into which earlier researchers had fallen. He has, therefore, been especially interested in those rare cases in which some sort of written record was made of the child's statements before any attempt was made to verify them. Unfortunately, only about a dozen or so cases meeting this criteria have been uncovered. These cases might be considered the *axis mundi* of Dr. Stevenson's case load. They certainly constitute the strongest cases in his files.

For convenience I will divide these cases into three general categories: (1) simple cases of past-life recall in which the evidence revolves primarily around the information remembered by the child; (2) birthmark cases in which the child has apparently inherited a skin defect from the donor personality; and (3) anomalous cases that include extraordinary details that do *not* suggest reincarnation as it is normally understood. Before drawing any conclusions from the phenomenon of extra-cerebral memory, some representative examples from each of these categories will be outlined. This will give you some idea of the pattern into which these cases fall, as well as some insight into the complexities that sometimes characterize them.

Simple Cases of the Reincarnation Type

The children in these cases can usually identify just "who" they were during their prior incarnations. They often produce several pieces of information about their past lives that usually prove reasonably accurate. In all three of the following cases, some sort of written record was made before the case was actively investigated. Two of the cases were reported from India, while the third was filed from Sri Lanka.

The story of Jagdish Chandra's rebirth memories was originally reported in 1927 in a book titled *Reincarnation: Verified cases of rebirth after death* by K. K. N. Sahay, the father of the boy in question. Dr. Stevenson reinvestigated it during the 1960s. Jagdish Chandra was born on 4 March 1923 in Uttar Pradesh, a district in northern India. His parents were the aforementioned K. K. N. Sahay and his wife, Jamina. The child was only about three and a half years old when he started talking about his previous life in Benares. Sahay was a lawyer by training and was familiar with the value of making a written record of his son's statements, so it wasn't long before a log of the boy's memories was being carefully kept. Jagdish first claimed to be from Benares in June 1926, when he started demanding that his father procure "his" car for him. Sahay didn't understand at first what his son meant, but it soon became clear that he was talking about a past life. The boy went on to insist that "his" car was in Benares at the home of his "father," whom he called Babu or Babuji. During the course of the next five days, Sahay and several of his friends queried the boy and elicited further information about his apparent past life. Included were the facts that his previous home had a guarded gate outside and that a safe was located on a wall in a underground room. He also described a ghat (a stairway leading down to the Ganges river) by his home, and specified that it was called the Dash Ashwamadh. He said that his "real" father's family name was Pandey, that the man had a wife who had died and two sons, and that he owned a car. (Automobiles were not commonly owned by the locals at this time.)

This information was detailed enough to enable Sahay to dispatch a letter to the *Leader,* an English language newspaper published in northern India, about his son's claims. The letter detailed the story of the boy's emerging memories and invited any reader who could shed light on the case to contact him. Sahay didn't have to wait long. Soon after his letter was published, Sahay received a note from a municipal employee in Benares who knew Babuji Pandey and could verify the accuracy of Jagdish's memories. The only minor inconsistency was that Babuji had not actually owned an automobile but had been in the habit of renting one so that his son could be driven around the city. (This actually represented no true inconsistency, since the boy had been too young at the time to appreciate the difference between owning and merely leasing a car.) Sahay also learned from his contact in Benares that Babuji's young son, Jai Gopal, had died as a child a few years before. As Sahay began looking into the case more closely, his son gradually recalled even more details about his life as Jai Gopal. Sahay once again carefully made a written record of these claims before investigating them. Much of this information concerned Babuji's home life, his mother, and some of his other relatives. Most of this data later proved to be correct.

Sahay eventually realized that he could perhaps best document the case by taking Jagdish directly to Benares. The trip was undertaken on 13 August 1926, and the boy and his father arrived there the next day. News of the case had leaked out by this time and Sahay found himself besieged by crowds of curiosity seekers. They literally stormed the house where he and his son were staying. Sahay explains in his booklet that, despite all the confusion, his son was able to recognize and properly identify several of Jai Gopal's surviving relations when they came to visit him. To further test his son's recollections, he and Jagdish walked through the streets of Benares and the boy was able to direct them to Babuji's house. This was no mean feat since they had to traverse a maze of streets. Sahay also took his son to the Dash Ashwanadh Ghat the next day. Not only did Jagdish recognize the area, he also seemed uncannily familiar with the customs of the local residents who regularly bathe in the Ganges.

To quote from Sahay's report:

> The boy was taken to the Dash Ashwamadh Ghat which he recognized from a distance. He took his bath twice with great pleasure in the arms of a panda [an aid at the ghat] whom he recognized at first sight. He was not at all upset with the sight of the swelled volume of the Ganges in August which flowed so violently, making a terrific noise. The volume of the Ganges in August did not bother him and he behaved as one who was very familiar with this site. The panda offered him a betel [a leaf commonly chewed in India] which Jagdish

refused, saying that he being a bigger panda [i.e., of higher status] could not accept from one who was a small panda.

That the boy knew about these customs was extraordinary since there was no major river in the town where he had been raised.

The only unfortunate aspect of the case was that Babuji Pandey refused to cooperate in the investigation. His reticence long remained a mystery until Dr. Stevenson reinvestigated the case on one of his several field trips to India in the 1960s. Stevenson was able to discover that Jagdish also claimed that his (past-life) father had once killed a man for his money and had hidden the body in an old well. The truth or fiction of this story was never explored, but it seems logical that Pandey would have refused to cooperate in an investigation that might have led to a murder charge against him.

There were other aspects of the Jagdish case that were also somewhat evidential. These might be called the "behavioral" features of the case—small points of evidence that young Jagdish had inherited not only memories from Jai Gopal, but also certain of his behavioral traits. From his earliest years Jagdish preferred food prepared according to the custom of the Brahmin class, even though he himself came from a lower caste. He also often asked to drink bhang (an intoxicant popular in India) as a young child. (This would be tantamount to a three-year-old in the United States demanding a scotch and water.) But most notable was his repeated request for his car, which obviously related to the luxury Jai Gopal most have felt while being chauffered around Benares in the vehicle his father often rented.

Jagdish Chandra is still alive and well in India, where he works as a lawyer in his home town of Bareilly. He ceased talking about his past life when he was six or seven, although the memories of his existence as Jai Gopal apparently did not fade with time. He told Dr. Stevenson in both 1964 and 1969 that he still recalls the previous incarnation he had lived in Benares.

The Jagdish Chandra case may be *the* most evidential that has so far come to light; certainly it is one of Stevenson's best. The fact that the boy's father made such detailed notes as the case unfolded, and that so many witnesses were involved, elevates it well above most reincarnation stories. Stevenson has himself pointed out that "the great physical distance between the families, their separation through membership in different castes, and the close surveillance of Jagdish Chandra when he was a child made it virtually impossible that he could have picked up all the detailed information he showed about Babu Pandey and his family without someone being aware of the person who was [allegedly] passing such information on to the child."

So if one were to rank this case according to Stevenson's hypothetical "perfect" case of reincarnation, it would probably score highly. The case was replete with written records, proper documentation, as well as behavioral features. It was even reported that Jagdish was born with odd markings on his ears, designating the very locations where the pandas in Benares commonly wear earrings. Dr. Stevenson was, unfortunately, unable to verify this feature of the case.

The case of Kumkum Verma, which Stevenson looked into in 1964, is also impressive because written records were made about the child's claims before they were investigated. Sindmuja (Kumkum) Verma was born on 14 March 1955 in the town of Bahera, which is also located in northern India. Her parents were Dr. B. K. Verma and his wife, Subhadra, who were apparently very intelligent witnesses to the case. Kumkum began talking about her past life when she was about three and a half years old, explaining initially that she had lived in the neighboring town of Urdu Bazar. She maintained that she had died as a result of having been poisoned by one of her daughters-in-law. Her past-life memories were so clear that she offered the proper name of her son (Misri Lal) and grandson (Gouri Shankar). She recalled that she had married into a family of the blacksmith caste and preferred to be called "Sunnary," which roughly translates as "beautiful." Despite the wealth of details she recalled about her past life, Kumkum's parents were at first inclined to dismiss their daughter's claims. Luckily, this disinterest was not shared by some of the girl's older relatives. Swarna Probha Verma was Kumkum's paternal uncle's wife, and she began making a written record of the girl's claims about six months before any attempt was made to verify them. These notes make it clear that Kumkum was recalling her past life in vivid detail. These past-life memories were specific and included a description of a pond near her home and her claims that there was an iron safe at the house; that a pet cobra had been kept by it; that a river or other body of water stretched between her home and her father's; that her father lived in the town of Bajitpur; that there were mango orchards near his home; and that she had had two daughters-in-law.

Swarna Probha Verma also took notes on the process by which her niece was recalling her past life. Sometimes the information would be spontaneously imparted during her talks with relatives, but the older woman noted that sometimes the girl would reminisce about her past life after falling into curious trances. Kumkum would suddenly become oblivious to her surroundings and would begin talking about her past life in the present tense. The little girl sometimes entered these trances when she thought she was alone. The spells seemed to resemble a form of delirium.

Another curious feature of the case was that, being so young, Kumkum sometimes lacked the vocabulary to express her memories. She had to convey what she was trying to say by gestures. For example, she did not know the correct word for "blacksmith" when she tried to describe her son's occupation. She was only able to mimic how he had worked with a hammer and bellows. This feature strikes me as significant, for if the girl had picked up her information normally, perhaps through some local gossip, presumably she would have picked up the relevant vocabulary as well.

Kumkum frequently asked to be taken back to Urdu Bazar when her memories first began surfacing, but her parents were wary of undertaking the trip. They were especially fearful that their daughter might become ill or die if she were to confront the scene of her past life, for her identification with her previous life had become very intense. So the case remained unresolved until 1959 when Dr. Verma happened to tell a friend about his daughter's memories. The gentleman decided to look into the matter and had one of his employees check in Urdu Bazar to see if a "Gouri Shankar" lived there. (Remember that this was the alleged name of Kumkum's "past-life" grandson.) This search was successful and Gouri Shankar's father, Misri Lal Mistry, was eventually located and was able to verify much of the information that Kumkum was recalling. Misri Lal Mistry had no difficulty ascertaining that the little girl's memories focused on his mother, Sunnary, who had died in the nearby city of Darbhanga in 1950.

The case was reported in the press for the first time in March 1961. This prompted Professor P. Pal, a local Indian savant, to look into the i ncident. He was able to procure a copy of the notes that Kumkum's aunt had originally kept and he later turned the investigation over to Dr. Stevenson. Stevenson visited the scene in 1964 and further documented the original claims emanating from the 1950s. He made additional inquiries in 1965, 1966, and 1969.

This case is perhaps not as strong as Jagdish Chandra's, because the distance between Bihar and Darbhanga is only about forty kilometers. But Dr. Verma insisted that he had never visited Urdu Bazar before his attempt to verify his daughter's account. But even if his daughter had somehow learned about Sunnary's death, it is hard to explain all the detailed information she had acquired about the woman.

Sunnary had been born in 1900 in Bajitpur where her father's home had been located. Totally consistent with Kumkum's claims were the pertinent facts that Sunnary had married into a family of the blacksmith caste and had given birth to two sons. One had indeed been named Misri Lal. Her first husband died around 1926, leaving the young widow and her family in a financially precarious situation. She was initially able to manage a living by selling some of her jewelry and by hiring an assistant to operate the family smithy; but this attempt at self-support was apparently not enough to sustain her. So a few years later she married a distant cousin of her former husband. Her marriage to Jhapu Mistry was not a happy one, and she was bitterly resentful when he began selling her former husband's property and dismantling his house so that he could re-use the bricks. The tension between Sunnary and her second husband reached a climax some years later when Misri Lal—who by this time was living on his own with his wife—decided that his stepfather had misappropriated his father's ownings. He proceeded to institute a lawsuit and Sunnary soon became his leading witness.

Sunnary had become more and more estranged from her husband by this time and sided with her son in the suit, though she was still living with her husband. Unfortunately, she never lived to see the case resolved. One day she suddenly fell ill. Neither her son nor her daughter-in-law assumed that the illness was very serious, and they were naturally shocked when they learned the next day that she had died. Misri Lal's first suspicion was that his mother might have been poisoned, but his relatives dissuaded him from having an autopsy performed and Sunnary's body was duly cremated. Local gossips speculated that perhaps Misri Lal's mistress had murdered her because the two had never gotten along.

What was also truly unusual about the case was little Kumkum's attitude toward snakes and toward cobras in particular. It was true that Sunnary had kept a cobra as a pet, and even from early childhood Kumkum had no fear of these poisonous creatures. On one occasion she even approached and stroked one that had fallen from a tree.

Dr. Stevenson's role in the Kumkum Verma case was marginal and his investigation was hardly more than a formal post-mortem. He took no real role in the active documentation of the case, but was at least able to substantiate the accuracy of its earlier phases. The crux of the case was, of course, the carefully written records that Kumkum's aunt had the foresight to make. The evidentiality of the case pivots on these notes. So this case, too, would probably score highly if matched against Stevenson's hypothetical "perfect" case of the reincarnation type. And while Kumkum did not inherit any odd birthmarks from Sunnary, she did inherit some of the woman's behavioral dispositions. Kumkum's family noted that the girl often behaved very maturely for her age, often acting precociously compassionate and devoted to those around her. Sunnary had been well known for her generosity and probity. It also appears that Kumkum's speech might have been affected by her rebirth memories. Stevenson points out in his report that the dialect spoken in Bihari is Maithili, but the lower classes speak a vulgarized version of the language. Dr. Verma told Stevenson that his daughter often used lower-class jargon as a young child instead of the proper speech she was being taught.

Whether the little girl could have picked up this language off the street is a moot point, however.

Like most young children who suddenly begin recalling their past lives, Kumkum forgot about her life as Sunnary as she grew older. She eventually married and gave birth to her first child in 1973. She still lives near Bihar.

Lest it be thought that the best of Stevenson's cases are *only* ones that he has investigated post-hoc, the last report in this section will be devoted to a veridical case he investigated himself in Sri Lanka.

The subject of the report was a boy named Indika Guneratne, who was born near Pilyandala on 26 July 1962. He was the second son of G.D. Guneratne and his wife. The family lived on a rubber plantation near the village of Gonopola, and Indika was one of three children. He began talking when he was two years old, but another year and a half went by before he began speaking about a past life. He claimed to have lived in Matara, a town located on the southern coast of Sri Lanka. Among his other assertions were that he had been wealthy, that he had owned a more luxurious home than the one in which he found himself currently living, that he had owned estates, and that he had kept elephants. He further insisted that he had owned a Mercedes-Benz, and even remembered its license plate number. The young boy especially harped on the differences between the social class of his past life and his current and, to his mind, shabby living conditions. Indika's parents were intrigued by their son's claims and made some initial attempts to investigate them. They eventually learned that a man had lived in Matara who matched the description their son had given, but for some reason they did not pursue the matter.

Dr. Stevenson learned of the case in January 1968 and visited Sri Lanka along with a colleague two months later. They took this opportunity to meet with the Guneratnes and made a list of the boy's statements about his past life before setting about to verify them. Their first course of action was to take the boy to Matara to see if he could recognize any people or places there, but the results of the trip were mixed. Indika didn't seem familiar with the city, but Stevenson was successful at tracking down the source for some of the boy's memories. He discovered that a wealthy lumber merchant named K.G.J. Weerasinghe had died in Matara in 1960, and that some of Indika's memories could have applied to him. Many of Indika's statements were subsequently verified by the man's widow and adopted daughter. More light was shed on the case about two years later when Indika's father discovered that he knew a man who had looked after Weerasinghe during a hospital stay in Colombo. This was a city in which Indika claimed to have shopped in his prior incarnation.

But the case was still weak, especially since Indika had never offered the name by which he was called in his past life. By 1973, however, Dr. Stevenson had codified thirty specific statements Indika had made about his past life. Chief among these were that he had a friend or servant named Premdasa, and he continued to claim that he had owned elephants. He also recalled a railway station near his home, that his house had had electric lighting, that he had bought gifts for his wife and child in Colombo, and that he had been involved in a serious altercation with his brother-in-law during which he had broken the man's legs. He especially recalled that an elephant got loose on one occasion. Stevenson was still not sure that he had properly traced Indika's memories, even at this point in the investigation, and still harbored doubts whether Weerasinghe had been correctly identified as the likeliest donor of the alleged rebirth. So when he returned to Sri Lanka in 1973, he decided to start from scratch. He proceeded this time by locating all records of elephant owners in Matara who might fit the information Indika had given him. By engaging in a considerable amount of leg work, Dr. Stevenson discovered two elephant owners whose lives vaguely matched the content of Indika's memories. The most likely candidate was, once again, K.G.J. Weerasinghe.

Weerasinghe had been born around 1888 in a village near Matara. He had been functionally illiterate but was shrewd enough to have built up a successful business as a contractor and lumber merchant. He died a wealthy man.

His marriage had not been particularly happy. His wife objected to his gambling and drinking, and he, in turn, disliked her relatives. Sometimes he wouldn't even admit them into his house. He harbored an intense dislike for his brother-in-law, but—inconsistent with Indika's recollection—never ended up beating him or breaking his legs. Weerasinghe had at one point ordered his wife out of his house, but she later returned to him before his death from diabetes mellitus.

Stevenson was able to demonstrate that the greater part of Indika's memories fit actual incidents drawn from the life of K.G.J. Weerasinghe. It was true, for example, that his elephant once had escaped its chain and had killed a man while on a rampage. The person named Premdasa, who had played a conspicuous role in some of Indika's earlier memories, turned out to have been Weerasinghe's servant.

On the other hand, some of Indika's statements were demonstrably wrong. His memory of beating his brother-in-law was an exaggeration, nor had the elder man ever worn trousers and a coat as Indika claimed. In fact, he always wore a sarong and would tease anyone who came to his home dressed in more Western attire. The most unusual mistake Indika made, however, pertained to the claim that he had owned a Mercedes-Benz with the license plate SRI 600. It turned out that Weerasinghe had never owned a Mercedes. He had at one time bought one, but had cancelled the order when the dealer raised the price. The license number Indika remembered didn't relate to a Mercedes, but Stevenson was able to ascertain that such a number had once been issued and assigned to an Opel owned by a man who lived in a city near Colombo, where Weerasinghe had often shopped.

I find this confusion over the license number one of the most bothersome aspects of the case, even though Stevenson treats it very casually in his report. How could the boy have come up with a license number that was assigned to a man who lived so close to where Weerasinghe shopped? Could it indicate some form of paranormal cognition on Indika's part but one not linked to his reincarnation claims? It is too bad that Dr. Stevenson does not explain in his report just when this license number was assigned. If the license number had been assigned *before* Weerasinghe's death, perhaps the elderly man might have seen it and transferred this information to Indika. But if the number had been assigned *after* Weerasinghe's death, it is probable that Indika had himself seen it. He may have forgotten it until the time it surfaced in the form of a reincarnation "memory." This possibility would suggest that the boy was prone to displays of cryptomnesia, a potential source for his reincarnation memories in general.

Before going on to our consideration of birthmark cases, it should be pointed out that the documentation of some extracerebral memory cases does not rely solely on their informational aspects. The behavioral characteristics featured in some of them are sometimes just as evidential. Dr. Stevenson was able to investigate one such case in 1973 during a field trip he made to Sri

Lanka. There he investigated the case of Sujith Lakmal Jayaratne, who had been born on 7 August 1969 in a town near Colombo. Even as a baby he would become agitated when the word "lorry" was spoken in his presence. (This British word for truck was adopted into the Sinhalese language long ago.) The sight or sound of a truck also disturbed him. The boy began to talk abut his past life when he was two years old. He communicated a great deal about his past life as "Gorakana Sammy," whom he claimed had lived in the city of that name. He also vividly recalled being run over by a truck and dying from his injuries. This information was all later verified, since a Sammy Fernando had been killed in just such an accident in Gorakana on 29 January 1969. Sujith retained his fear of trucks as he grew older, although he exhibited no similar phobia toward automobiles. Even the sound of a truck passing by would cause him to cover his ears. The case is especially provocative because Sammy Fernando was killed three months *after* Sujith's conception.

The whole area of inherited past-life "phobias" will be dealt with in more detail in Chapter 8. These cases crop up now and then in several of Stevenson's records and have been reported from many different cultures.

Birthmark Cases of the Reincarnation Type

The cases that fall under this heading are a little more complicated than the relatively simple ones summarized before. They include not only informational and behavioral aspects that link the child's past and present lives, but suggest that a child can inherit a birthmark or wound from a previous life. These cases tend to be quite dramatic. Sometimes the birthmarks are only slight skin discolorations, but sometimes represent large and obtrusive skin defects. Three cases will be presented in this section. The first is a relatively simple case reported from Lebanon, while the other two are much more complicated.

Mounzer Haïdar was born in the village of Choueifate, Lebanon, on 17 February 1960. His father, Kamal Salim Haïdar, was a bus driver for the ministry of agriculture and Mounzer was his fourth child. The boy started talking about his past life when he was between three and four years old and asserted that his name had been Jamil Souki. The manner in which he first made this claim was in itself interesting. The custom among the Druse sect in Lebanon is to publicly announce deaths, even from neighboring towns, by calling them from the roof tops. It was an announcement of a death in the distant town of Aley that first prompted Mounzer to speak about his life there as Jamil. From that day forward, he began identifying more and more with the personality of Jamil Souki and offered several details about his (past-life) part in Lebanon's bloody civil war of 1958, in which he had been killed. Mounzer's parents paid little attention at first since they knew of no family named Souki in Aley. But the Haïdars gradually became more interested in their son's claims when an aunt from Beirut came to visit them. It seems that this woman had a friend whose cousin had been named Jamil Souki. He had lived in Aley and, what's more, had died in the civil war on 4 July 1958. The aunt was even able to obtain a photograph of Jamil and his mother. The boy immediately claimed to recognize himself when he was shown it.

This recognition cannot, however, be given much evidential weight. The woman who showed it to him probably also leaked considerable information. Mounzer could easily have inferred whom the picture depicted as well.

News of Jamil Souki's apparent rebirth soon spread to Aley, and the surviving members of his family subsequently made two visits to Choueifate to meet and interview Mounzer. Ian Stevenson followed up the case in 1969, 1970, and 1972 by interviewing everyone previously associated with it.

This is not as strong a case as many in Dr. Stevenson's collection for a number of reasons. The two towns of Choueifate and Aley are located in close proximity to Beirut, and there is some evidence that there may even have been some casual acquaintance between the two families involved. It is unlikely that such a casual connection could have been at the root of all of Mounzer's memories, but it is possible that he had heard stories about Jamil's death at some time in his infancy. It is also hard to determine from Dr. Stevenson's report just what Mounzer had said about his pevious life _before_ he met the Souki family. He eventually offered about seventy-five bits of information about his past life, but only a handful of them had (apparently) been made during the uncontaminated phase of the case. These remarks primarily revolved around the proper names of Jamil's relations, which strikes me as just the sort of information one might pick up through casual gossip.

The most graphic aspects of the case were Mounzer's vivid recollection of his death as Jamil and the curious birthmark he may have inherited from him. Mounzer offered a colorful description of how he had died during a mountain battle when a bullet ricocheted and struck him in the abdomen. Now it was true that Jamil died from a bullet wound. In the summer of 1958 Jamil had joined with a Druse party that supported the existing political regime in Lebanon and was killed during a battle with the rebels. He was killed either by a wound to his chest or stomach, although Jamil's mother told Dr. Stevenson that the bullet had lodged near the umbilicus. Dr. Stevenson was interested in whether Mounzer had any birthmark that reflected the wound he had suffered in his past life. Mounzer's parents denied any knowledge of such a mark, but Stevenson found one nonetheless.

In his report, Dr. Stevenson explains how he decided to examine Mounzer's body himself during one of his field trips to Choueifate. He was able to find ". . . an almost perfectly round area of pigmentation to the right of the umbilicus and a little above it. It was about 7/8 millimeters in diameter." Dr. Stevenson goes on to note that "Mounzer had indicated this place as the site where he had been shot in the previous life. Moreover, he had from time to time complained of pain in the abdomen." The psychiatrist was rather surprised that his parents had never noticed the pigmented area.

Dr. Stevenson also set about to formally link Mounzer's birthmark to the wound on Jamil's body, but here he blundered badly. After carefully sketching out the position of Mounzer's birthmark he went to Aley and interviewed Jamil's mother. He was hoping that she could verify the proper location where the bullet had entered her son's body. "She spontaneously pointed to the right side of the abdomen," explains Dr. Stevenson. "I then showed her the sketch I had made of the pigmented area on Mounzer's abdomen. She said the wound in Jamil's body was in the same location as that indicated for Mounzer's birthmark on the sketch."

The passage suggests that Stevenson may have been leading and cueing the witness. Any unbiased investigator would have asked Mrs. Souki to sketch out the place the bullet had entered without providing any hints beforehand. This sketch could then have been matched to the one taken of Mounzer's abdomen. Mrs. Souki could easily have been influenced by her own hope that her son had been reborn and by the sketch she had just been shown. This sketch alerted her to the exact position Dr. Stevenson was hoping to fix the wound. It is hard to escape the conclusion that here Stevenson was using Mrs. Souki's testimony merely to corroborate his own conclusions about Mounzer's pigmentation. This all contrived to make an already weak case weaker. Though this is not typical of the way Dr. Stevenson conducts his investigations, it is, unfortunately, a good example of the damage that poor procedure can do.

Dr. Stevenson reported a more impressive birthmark case in his *Twenty Cases Suggestive of Reincarnation*. He uncovered this case during his investigation of rebirth reports among the Tlingit eskimos of southeastern Alaska. The Tlingits accept reincarnation as a matter of course and Stevenson included several reports in his first book. This case of Corliss Chotkin, Jr., is the most dramatic. The case actually revolves around the donor personality, Victor Vincent, as much as it does Corliss, for the elder man actually "planned" the reincarnation.

Victor Vincent was a full-blooded Tlingit who lived on the islands adjacent to Alaska's southern coast. Toward the end of his life in 1946 he became very close to his niece, Mrs. Corliss Chotkin, Sr. He even predicted that he would be reborn as her next son, claiming that she would know him by two scars the child would inherit from him. Vincent had a distinct scar on his back, the result of a surgical incision, as well as another at the base of his nose. He vowed that he would imprint these onto the body of his next incarnation and apparently made good on his claim. Mrs. Chotkin gave birth to a son on 15 December 1947, a year and a half after her uncle died. The baby was born with two birthmarks that matched exactly those that had marked Vincent's body. The scar by the child's nose eventually altered position as the boy grew older and became less noticeable. But the scar on his back was not only pronounced, but striking in appearance. It didn't look like a normal scar, but more like the result of a healed-over surgical incision. Dr. Stevenson notes in his report that "it was located about eight inches below the shoulder line and two inches to the right of the midline. It was heavily pigmented and raised. It extended about one inch in length and a quarter-inch in width. Along its margin one could still easily discern several small round marks outside the main scar. Four of these on one side lined up like stitch wounds of surgical operations." Unlike simple skin pigmentation, the mark itched.

The first informational aspects of the case emerged when Corliss was a year old. One day, while his mother was encouraging him to speak, he spontaneously said, "Don't you know me. I'm Kahkody." This was Victor Vincent's tribal name. Equally surprising was that the infant spoke these words clearly without any babyish lisp. More and more memories of his life as Victor Vincent flooded Corliss's mind as he grew older. Sometimes Mrs. Corliss would take the boy for strolls along the streets of Sitki, where they lived, and Corliss would spontaneously recognize people on the street whom he had known in his past life. He also began relating incidents from the life of Victor Vincent that his parents were sure they had never told him about. He described, in great detail, for instance, how Vincent had gone on a fishing trip that ended in a minor crisis when his (Vincent's) engine broke down. This left him stranded in the hazardous channels of southern Alaska's many small islands. He went on to relate how he had put on a Salvation Army uniform before rowing out into the channel in a small boat in hopes that a ship passing by would notice his strange attire and rescue him. He eventually was rescued by the _North Star_.

Mrs. Chotkin had heard this story from her uncle's own lips and she was astonished when her son repeated it. She was also strongly affected by an incident that transpired when she and Corliss were visiting a home where she had lived during Vincent's lifetime. Corliss spontaneously identified the room in which Vincent had slept during his visits, which was all the more surprising because the building had been renovated. None of the former bedrooms were recognizable as such.

Unfortunately, young Corliss spoke less and less about his past life as he grew older. He had forgotten most of his memories by the time he was a teenager.

There were also other aspects of the case that warrant notice. It seems that Corliss shared several behavioral characteristics with his late grand-uncle. Corliss was born with a bad stutter that had to be treated with speech therapy. Vincent had suffered from a similar problem all his life. He had even once told his niece that he hoped to be reborn without the handicap. Corliss also displayed a precocious affinity not only for handling boats, but for repairing their engines as well, though he had never been given any formal training. Some of these behavioral traits were still evident when Dr. Stevenson made a return trip to Alaska in 1972 to meet with the Chotkins. By this time Corliss was in his twenties, a veteran of the Vietnam war, and had forgotten about his life as Victor Vincent. But he still seemed to retain some of the personality characteristics he had allegedly inherited from his relative. He still harbored a keen fascination for engines and until recently had maintained a lively interest in religion—a trait also characteristic of Victor Vincent. He even still occasionally stuttered. The birthmark on his back was no longer so pronounced: Corliss explained that it had continued to itch, so in 1969 he had undergone surgery to have it removed.

Of course, it could be debated whether the odd mark on Corliss's back was really a birthmark at all. Dr. Stevenson suggests that either Mrs. Chotkin had somehow imprinted the marks on her unborn child, or that Victor Vincent's surviving mind had orchestrated their appearance. The fact that the birthmark closely resembled a wound or surgical incision implies some sort of abnormal or paranormal causative factor in its development.

Stevenson includes other birthmark cases in his *Twenty Cases Suggestive of Reincarnation,* but space limitations do not permit any extended discussion of most of them in this chapter. Some mention should be made of the Ravi Shankar case, however, since it resembles the Chotkin case in one major respect: Ravi's birthmark, too, resembled a knife wound more than a simple discoloration.

Ravi Shankar was born in Kanauj in the Uttar Pradesh area of India in 1951. From the time he first began to speak he claimed that he had lived a past life as the son of a man named Jageshwar, whom he identified as a barber who lived in the Chhipatti district of Kanauj. The boy maintained that he had been murdered. Ravi talked so incessantly about his past life that his father repeatedly beat him to make him stop. Despite the beatings, the boy's memories continued to emerge, and his identification with the murdered boy grew even more strong. He became so obsessed with his past-life memories that he began to fear that those who had murdered him in his past life were out to do him harm in his present one as well. Ravi was also born with an unusual birthmark. It appeared as a two-inch long serrated mark under his chin somewhat resembling a knife wound. This peculiar mark was even most prominent when he was an infant.

Ravi's memories and birthmark were easily traceable to a horrible event that had shaken Uttar Pradesh six months before his birth. On 19 July 1951, the young son of Sri Jageshwar Prasad was murdered while playing near his home. The murderer was apparently a relative who wished to inherit the barber's estate, and he had killed the boy by slashing him with a knife and then decapitating him. The man and his accomplice were arrested and one of them allegedly confessed, but they were later released on a legal technicality. No one was ever convicted of the crime.

Jageshwar Prasad eventually heard stories about the boy in Kanauj who was the apparent reincarnation of his son and decided to visit the Shankar family to investigate the claims. Prasad had a long talk with Ravi during which the boy gradually recognized who he was and narrated the story of his murder. The details of the story closely matched what Prasad had himself concluded on the basis of the police report and the unofficial confession made by one of the murderers.

The Ravi Shankar case is very dramatic but certainly not as evidential as many other cases Stevenson has collected. The story about the murder in Chhipatti was common knowledge, and Ravi's parents may have unintentionally fed their son all sorts of information after first noticing his odd birthmark. Of course, this line of speculation does not explain how Ravi came to be born with his unusual birthmark in the first place. It didn't resemble any type of acquired congenital mole or pigmentation. It actually *looked* like a knife wound. So once again, it appears that either (1) Ravi's mother imprinted the mark on her unborn son when she read or heard about the case, or (2) the boy's mind had been somehow linked with the mind and memory of the murdered boy from birth.

Birthmark cases in general tend to be less evidential than the simpler cases Dr. Stevenson has collected. Most of the examples the University of Virginia psychiatrist has published highlight cases in which the child was allegedly reborn within his own family. The Corliss Chotkin case is very representative of a number of cases among the Tlingits. Such cases are inherently weak, since, by the time the child begins to speak, the parents usually suspect from whom their child has been reborn. This could easily lead them to feed information to the child. It would be more evidential if these birthmarks cropped up in many different cultures, but to date Dr. Stevenson has not published any data on this aspect of his work. We simply do not know how widespread these birthmark cases are, although they crop up in Turkey as well. Stevenson considers his Turkish cases to be the best in his files, though he has not yet published many of them. *Twenty Cases Suggestive of Reincarnation* only includes a handful of birthmark cases, but other than the Ravi Shankar incident, all of them represent interfamily rebirth and are drawn from Alaskan reports.

The fact that birthmark cases tend to be less evidential than many cases of the reincarnation type does not mean, however, that they can be easily dismissed. There is still the problem of just *how* these bizarre marks are formed in the first place. They certainly seem to go beyond anything modern genetics or biology can explain.

The skeptical reader might suggest that these birthmark cases arise from some type of interuterine conditioning, as I suggested in the Corliss and Ravi Shankar cases. Perhaps the mothers of these children somehow produced the marks on their developing babies. The information that later becomes the blueprint for the reincarnation "fantasy" may simply be cued to them or perhaps also genetically transferred. While conventional psychology rejects the existence of such a phenomenon, there is some strong anecdotal and experimental evidence that children can pick up some information prenatally.* This idea gains some guarded support from the fact that children born in India some-

---

*For more information on this subject, please refer to *The Secret Life of the Unborn Child* by Thomas Verny, M.D., with John Kelly (New York: Simon and Schuster, 1981).

times claim (from early childhood) to be reincarnated gods. These cases could be summarily dismissed as fantasies, except that they are sometimes born with curious birthmarks. These marks usually correspond to markings found on publicly venerated statues of the same gods. The children also tend to be intellectually precocious. In these cases, it would seem that some sort of bizarre but "normal" interuterine learning, conditioning, and genetic molding might have taken place. It might be argued then, that birthmark cases are not true cases of reincarnation at all, even granting that they could conceivably contain some paranormal elements.

It is nonetheless hard to apply this kind of explanation across the board. There are certainly cases on record in which birthmarks have appeared on children born to women who knew nothing about the lives of the donor personalities—the Mounzer Haïdar case, for example. (It is therefore doubly unfortunate that the verification of this birthmark was bungled by Dr. Stevenson.) It is possible, too, that the apparently strong relationship between birthmark cases and interfamily rebirth is an artifact arising from Stevenson's work. As I pointed out earlier, most of his birthmark cases were uncovered during his field work among the Tlingits. These natives specifically look for such marks and interfamily rebirths are conspicuously common in their culture. These factors may have simply led to the *discovery* of such cases more commonly during his field work in Alaska, than in India, Turkey, or Lebanon. Birthmark cases have been reported in Turkey, though. Stevenson has even written of these cases that many of the markings " . . . cannot be distinguished, at least by me, from scars of acquired wounds with which they would be compared except for the strong affirmations of parents that the marks in question existed at birth . . . "

Dr. Stevenson has been withholding publication of what may be his best birthmark cases since he plans to write a separate volume on them. Unfortunately, this volume will probably not be ready until at least 1988.

Anomalous Cases of the Reincarnation Type

The cases summarized in the first two sections of this chapter might appear to be evidence strongly favoring reincarnation. The veridical memories of the children involved, their curious behavioral dispositions, and their sometimes dramatic birthmarks might be best explained by taking the cases at face value. But remember that all of these cases of extracerebral memory fall within a *phenomenological syndrome*. Any theory posited to account for one specific case must also be applicable to *all* cases of extracerebral memory. It would be risky to draw any conclusions from merely a limited body of evidence. And it is here that we run into the most challenging aspect of Stevenson's case studies. For included in Stevenson's collection are one or two cases of extracerebral memory that cannot be subsumed under or explained by any simple application of the reincarnation doctrine.

The case of Jasbir Lal Jat appears in *Twenty Cases Suggestive of Reincarnation* and is one of the most bizarre in the literature. Jasbir was the three-year-old son of Sri Girdhari Lal Jat, who lived in Rasulpur, which is located in the Uttar Pradesh district of India where rebirth cases abound. In the spring of 1954 the little boy contracted smallpox and apparently died. His breathing stopped and his body became cold. His father was so sure that his son was dead that he initiated plans to bury him the next day. Girdhari Lal Jat was stunned when his boy showed signs of life the next day, and Jasbir eventually recovered completely. But the illness had taken a considerable toll, and the boy couldn't talk or express himself coherently for several weeks. His recovery was also characterized by sudden changes in his personality. He now claimed that he was not Lal Jat's son but that he was from Vehedi (another village in India), where he was the son of a local resident. He also refused to eat any food in his parents' house since he considered himself to be a member of a higher caste. His refusal to eat was so adamant that a neighbor had to specially prepare meals for him. She continued to help prepare Jasbir's food for more than a year, at which time the boy became more tolerant of his father's "lower" class. Jasbir talked regularly about his past life and especially about the way in which he had died. He claimed that he had become ill after eating some sweets and had fallen from a chariot during a wedding procession. The fall had caused an injury to his head, which resulted in his death shortly thereafter. He believed that the sweets had been poisoned and he identified the malefactor as a man to whom he had lent some money.

The climax to the case came a year later when the story of Jasbir's claims eventually reached Vehedi, where a former resident from Rasulpur decided to look into the matter. It didn't take him long to discover that Jasbir's story matched several incidents in the life of one Sobha Ram, a former resident of Vehedi who had died in an accident similar to the one described by Jasbir. Sobha Ram's surviving relatives knew nothing about the alleged poisoning, but they knew all about his chariot accident. It had occurred during a wedding procession, just as Jasbir had asserted.

Further links between Sobha Ram and little Jasbir became evident when the former's father and several of his family members traveled to Rasulpur to meet the boy. Jasbir immediately recognized them when they showed up at his door. His memories were further tested when he was taken to Vehedi a few weeks later. His current father took him to the local railway station, where he was asked to lead the way to a specific place in the village where the male members of Sobha Ram's family had often gathered to socialize. Although this location was separate from the family home, Jasbir was able to do so without difficulty. Jasbir meanwhile was being increasingly taken over by the personality and emotions of Sobha Ram. He began visiting Vehedi often and had no difficulty engaging in meaningful conversations with members of his previous family and friends. He related several trivial but evidential incidents from the life of Sobha Ram during these trips, such as being bitten by a dog while visiting a house to borrow a coat for a wedding party. He even cried bitterly when he was forced to return to Rasulpur.

The case of Jasbir Lal Jat reads almost like a text book of extracerebral memory, except for one detail: *Sobha Ram died in May 1954, when Jasbir Lal Jat was fully three years old.* It would seem that Sobha Ram's personality somehow merged with Jasbir's during the time the boy was ill with smallpox. So "simple" reincarnation, as commonly understood, cannot explain the case.

It might be argued that perhaps the Jasbir Lal Jat incident represents a case of spirit possession.* But this theory ignores the fact that the characteristics of the Lal Jat case conform to more clear-cut cases of the reincarnation type. But if the Jasbir Lal Jat case can only be explained as the result of spirit possession, then we face the prospect that many, perhaps all, extracerebral memory cases could be caused by a similar phenomenon.

Nor is the strange case of Jasbir Lal Jat the only report that serves up such exotic food for thought. A case reported from Lebanon and investigated by Dr. Stevenson in 1964 ranks as one of the most complex and enigmatic field studies in the annals of psychical research. It is so complicated, in fact, that only a brief summary can be offered in this chapter. (The original report takes up an entire chapter in Stevenson's *Twenty Cases Suggestive of Reincarnation,* which should be consulted for all the original details of the case.) It is even more baffling and challenging than the story of little Jasbir.

The case first came to Dr. Stevenson's attention during a field trip to Lebanon in 1964 and revolved around the death of Said Bouhamzy, a Druse who had lived in Khriby—a town twenty miles from Beirut. Bouhamzy was fatally injured on 8 June 1943, in a trucking accident that broke both his legs and caused severe injury to the rest of his body. He survived long enough to be taken to a hospital, where he called for his wife and son; but there was little the doctors could do for him. Even an emergency operation couldn't save him.

Bouhamzy had been very found of his sister, who was living in Syria at the time. She delivered a son on December 3, and almost as soon as he could

---

*This case is very similar to a fascinating and well-documented report issued from Watseka, Illinois, in 1877. This report revolves around a teenaged girl, Lurancy Vennum, who began suffering a series of fits when she was fourteen years old. When she emerged from one of her seizures, she explained that she was no longer Lurancy, but a girl named Mary Roff. This was the name of an eighteen-year-old girl who had died during a similar fit when Lurancy was only nine months old. "Mary Roff" possessed Lurancy for about four months, during which she proved her identity by discussing many details of her earthly life with her surviving family members. The case was reported in some detail in the *Religio-Philosophical Journal* by the Vennum's family doctor and was later discussed in some depth by F.W.H. Myers in his *Human Personality and Its Survival of Bodily Death.*

talk, young Sleimann Bouhamzy began describing his previous life as his uncle. Some of the first words he spoke as an infant were the names of Said's children. More characteristic memories began to surface when he was traveling between Lebanon and Syria. Especially vivid was his recollection of the truck accident that had resulted in his death. He even recalled such specific details as his last request to see his family when he was dying in the hospital, and his refusal to express any malice toward the man who caused the accident. Sleimann also suffered from a curious phobia as he grew a bit older. He was unusually frightened of automobiles or other motor vehicles, and he maintained a strong aversion to the sight of blood all his life. Sleimann also visited Khriby when he was about six years old and was able to point out the boundaries that separated the lands owned by several villagers who had known Said. Nor did he display any difficulties finding his way to Said's house once he arrived in Khriby. The boy's memories of his life as Said Bouhamzy were so stunningly accurate that his former uncle's relations soon accepted him as the reincarnation of the older man.

Stevenson was unacquainted with the story when he made his first visit to Lebanon. At that time he was more concerned with another case. He was focusing his attention on the case of Imad Elawar, not then realizing that it would lead him back to the older story of Sleimann Bouhamzy's claims. Imad lived in Kornayel, a town more than ten miles from Khriby. He had been born in 1958 and began talking about his past-life when he was one and a half years old . . . _as a man named Bouhamzy who lived in Khriby and who had been killed when a truck crushed his legs and caused his death._*

It began to look as if Said Bouhamzy had reincarnated twice—once in 1943 and again in 1958.

The case became even more complex when Imad also began recalling his past life in some detail. Because the case was still active at the time Dr. Stevenson was making his field trips to Lebanon, he was able to play a pivotal role in verifying some of the boy's memories.

Stevenson first met Imad's parents in March. No attempt had so far been made to check out the accuracy of what the boy was saying. Stevenson was therefore able to make a list of just what the boy was remembering. Imad's memories were somewhat fragmented, but he claimed to belong to the Bouhamzy family now living in Khriby, a town about fifteen miles away and separated by mountains. He also talked a great deal about a woman named Jamileh, for whom he had often bought clothes. He also mentioned a man named Mahmoud. Imad's parents had already inferred much about their son's past life from these statements. They believed that he was the reincarnation of

---

*It is unclear from Stevenson's report whether Imad at first claimed that the truck accident caused his own death or was merely the memory of something he knew about but which had killed someone known to him. Imad gradually (?) adopted the memory as his own, since he later commented on how happy he was to walk again.

a man named Mahmoud Bouhamzy, whose wife had been named Jamileh. They also assumed that the many other names the boy had mentioned related to his children and more distant family members.

Dr. Stevenson drove over to Khriby the next day along with Imad, the boy's father, and an interpreter in hopes of shedding new light on the case. The drive provoked the boy into remembering several more details about his past life, and he offered a description of the house in which he had lived and the slope that led to it. He also spoke of two wells on his former property. This gave the psychiatrist a list of fifty-seven specific statements that he hoped to match to some member of the Bouhamzy family who had died in Khriby.

What they found was even more baffling than what they had expected. A little detective work revealed that a Mahmoud Bouhamzy really did exist in Khriby, but he was alive and well. But interviews with several of the local townsfolk ultimately led Stevenson to the story of Said Bouhamzy's death in 1943. It was at this point in the investigation that Stevenson came up against the next problem in his analysis of the case. It was true that Imad's memories of Said's death were accurate enough, but many of his other recollections were not. Few of the names he had previously given related to Said's family, nor was the description of his house correct.

Additional light was shed on the case, however, when Dr. Stevenson revisited Khriby the next day. The psychiatrist was able to track down Said Bouhamzy's son and tell him about Imad's claims. The man was surprised by the revelations and immediately told Stevenson that many of the boy's remarks pertained to Said's cousin Ibrahim. Ibrahim Bouhamzy had also been one of Said's neighbors and had died from tuberculosis some years earlier. He had never married but his mistress had been a woman named Jamileh. Even the description of the home Imad had given while en route to Khriby matched the one in which Ibrahim had lived. It also turned out that many of the names Imad had mentioned to his parents in Kornayel designated several of Ibrahim's relatives. Mahmoud was the name of his uncle.

The only conclusion one can reach about this case is that somehow Imad had amalgamated information about both Ibrahim and Said Bouhamzy—who had already been "reborn" some years earlier—when constructing the scenario of his past life. So if we cannot find a normal explanation for Imad's memories, we would be forced to conclude that the boy experienced a "shared" reincarnation. Whether such a phenomenon could possibly exist or not is not really the crucial issue. The important point to keep in mind is that the case of Imad Elawar suggests that we are dealing with a phenomenon more complex than simple reincarnation.

I cannot emphasize enough how important it is to keep the cases of Imad Elawar and Jasbir Lal Jat in mind as you consider the evidence for reincarnation. It would be improper to propose any theory for only the strongest cases of extracerebral memory which ignores these anomalous and mind-boggling ones.

When you spend your life studying the strange by-ways of psychic phenomena, you gradually learn that nothing is as simple as it first appears. This is almost parapsychology's golden rule. This was certainly the uncomfortable lesson even the very first psychical researchers had to face as they searched for some piece of evidence that would prove the immortality of the soul. Parapsychologists have learned that you can make your most important discoveries by focusing on the exceptions rather than the rule. The founders of the Society for Psychical Research learned this lesson when they first began collecting cases of crisis apparitions.* It was easy to assume that these figures represented the "souls" of those that had just passed on. But sometimes an apparition would appear fully dressed, perhaps even carrying a walking stick. So these researchers began to realize that they had to expand their thinking on the subject. Walking sticks, after all, couldn't possess "souls." It was then that they began to realize that "apparitions" might be the product of telepathically triggered hallucinations.

This same problem arose when the early parapsychologists started visiting trance mediums who could allegedly bring through spirits of the dead. Some of the gifted psychics they discovered could do so with obvious ease. But then in January 1922, S.G. Soal—a prominent investigator, S.P.R. member, and later a mathematician at the University of London—visited a medium in London who brought through an old school chum of his. They reminisced together and the "communicator" mentioned several accurate details concerning his life. Soal only learned later that the man with whom he had "communicated" was still alive and well. Once again those pioneers of the new science of parapsychology had to expand their thinking. Perhaps the phenomenon of spirit communication wasn't quite what it seemed to be.

If it turns out that the Imad Elawar and Jasbir Lal Jat cases are genuine examples of extracerebral memory, parapsychologists investigating the evidence for reincarnation will also have to expand their thinking as well. We are obviously not dealing with reincarnation as it is normally conceptualized here in the West.

So do the several cases we have been examining in this chapter point to something akin to reincarnation or not?

To answer this question, we shall have to begin by positing several explanations for the phenomenon of extracerebral memory and then see which one fits _all_ the facts the best. Let me reiterate that most cases of extracerebral memory conform in pattern to a phenomenological syndrome. The features that characterize cases reported from India conform to the general pattern of similar cases that crop up in Turkey and Alaska. It certainly _appears_ that we are dealing with a cross-cultural phenomenon. Extracerebral memory is apparently a phenomenon that has been occurring for many years independent of both culture and era. So our job is therefore to find a universal explanation for

---

*A crisis apparition is defined as an "apparition resembling a person who has died at approximately the same time."

these cases. These explanations actually break down into three main categories:

1. That cases of extracerebral memory represent the literal rebirth of the soul.
2. That these cases are the product of lying, honest faults of memory, cryptomnesia, cultural artifacts, and bungled investigations.
3. That what we refer to as "reincarnation" is actually a very different process from what we have come to conceptualize.

I think it is fairly evident that I am tempted to reject the first of these theories for obvious reasons. Simple reincarnation cannot account for how two people can be reborn from the same donor personality. Nor would it predict that two people could be reborn as the *same* child, so I think we will have to choose between the two other lines of speculation. Either these cases are bogus and can be normally explained, or we are dealing with a psychic phenomenon of enormous psychic complexity. But how can we decide between the two? There are two ways. The first would be to take a closer look at the classic cases Stevenson and his colleagues have investigated and then determine if they were properly documented. If it can be shown that these cases were poorly reported or investigated, we can automatically dismiss extracerebral memory cases as evidence pointing toward reincarnation. We might also take a look at a large number of cases drawn from the literature to determine if cultural factors do, indeed, play a role in the way these cases manifest. If cultural factors have been influencing the way they emerge around the world, this would also indicate that these cases could be arising either from error or delusion.

The next chapter will be devoted to exploring these very issues.

Conclusions

The best evidence supporting the rebirth doctrine comes from those cases in which young children seem literally "born" with memories of their past lives. Cases in which the child has inherited birthmarks or behavioral dispositions from his or her past life serve as especially strong evidence. Many such cases have been unearthed, investigated, and documented. But a few cases have been reported that cannot be easily explained as the result of simple reincarnation. We must understand the cause of these anomalous cases before we can draw any conclusion about the nature of extracerebral memory. Determining the value of these cases is also contingent on discovering how well they were investigated in the first place and whether cultural factors may be playing a role in their expression.

In Search of Past Lives II: Culture, Bias, and Reincarnation

Before drawing any conclusions from Dr. Ian Stevenson's case studies, we have to face a very touchy question. Just how well has he investigated his cases? Did he proceed cautiously while trying to track down instances of extracerebral memory, or did he engage in his field studies simply to prove the validity of the reincarnation doctrine? Certainly it is no disparagement to suggest that Dr. Stevenson has a vested interest in documenting the existence of reincarnation. He has openly admitted that his interest in the question was prompted by his dissatisfaction with traditional psychiatric theories about personality. But then, every scientist has a vested interest in the research that will potentially substantiate his or her pet theories.

This self-evident fact has not kept several skeptics from suggesting that Dr. Stevenson's personal bias has clouded his ability to objectively study the many cases that have come to his attention. This criticism deserves considerable attention if only because Dr. Stevenson is virtually the only scientist who had made an in-depth study of extracerebral memory.* Some students of the field believe that the case for or against reincarnation stands or falls on the basis of his research.

*Some research along similar lines has been carried out in Brazil by Hernani Andrade and by Dr. Inacio Ferreira, two very competent and skilled investigators. Little of their work has been translated into English, although summaries can be found in *The Unknown Power* by Guy L. Playfair (New York: Warner, 1975) and passingly in *Every Wall or Door* by Ann Dooley (London: Abelard-Schumann, 1979). Dr. Ferreira has written a book about some of his work, but it is not available in this country.

Probably the most serious attack on Stevenson's case studies and personal objectivity has been made by Ian Wilson, a British writer and member of the Society for Psychical Research. His book *All in the Mind* (published originally in Great Britain in 1981 as *Mind Out of Time?*) is possibly the most comprehensive critical (and negative) examination of the evidence for reincarnation ever undertaken. An entire chapter is devoted to Stevenson's research, which represents the most serious attack he has probably ever had to face.

The basic approach Wilson takes to Stevenson's cases revolves around a content analysis he has made of the latter's published reports. Wilson argues that if reincarnation represents a cosmic law, then all of Stevenson's cases should conform to general patterns. The failure of such patterns to emerge, he goes on to posit, would suggest that cases of the reincarnation type are probably bogus and caused by fraud or childhood fantasy. This all-or-nothing argument is obviously simplistic, but it is the premise for all of Wilson's subsequent arguments. He begins, for example, by pointing out that there doesn't seem to be any law governing the interval that passes between the previous deaths and rebirths of the children in Stevenson's reports. Years have passed between the two events in some of Stevenson's cases, yet the very opposite exists in some of the others. Wilson reasons that if rebirth is a universal law, a consistent interincarnation time period should be exhibited in all extracerebral cases. The British author also points out that while some allegedly "reincarnated" children are born hundreds of miles away from the sites of their previous deaths, others are born very close to the towns or areas of their "previous lives." He also interprets this inconsistency to be the result of fraud, cryptomnesia, or cultural expectation.

These points are well made, and certainly Wilson's observations are valid. But whether these observations are really critical to the question of reincarnation is another issue altogether.

My own feeling is that Wilson's line of argumentation is not only hopelessly naive, but also surprisingly presumptuous. If rebirth is in fact a reality, the process governing it might very well be incredibily complicated. Certainly no one has the right to arbitrarily second-guess what principles would underlie such a process. Not even Stevenson would suggest that we know enough about reincarnation to second-guess its laws. This is why it is so important to approach these cases openly and judge them solely on the basis of the empirical evidence substantiating them. It would be fallacious to decide arbitrarily what laws might govern ultimate reality and then to reject reincarnation evidence for being inconsistent with them.

Ian Wilson also reveals through his line of argumentation just how naive he is about the whole concept of reincarnation. The term "reincarnation" has various meanings in different cultures. (It is true that in Sri Lanka, for example, the Buddhists do teach that the process of death and subsequent rebirth is separated by a set period of time. But this type of inculcation is not endorsed by many other cultures that teach the rebirth doctrine.) The whole idea of rebirth is conceptualized very differently in different cultures. Even within Hinduism two very different schools of thought exist, and both vary in many respects from how rebirth is conceptualized in Buddhism. Since the collective wisdom of world culture has been unable to discern just what laws guide the rebirth process, it seems silly for Wilson to claim he understands the process.

Probably one of the most interesting findings Wilson has made while reviewing Stevenson's case studies bears on the social status of the children involved. He points out that children "born" with extracerebral memory invariably remember previous lives among families of greater wealth or social class. "When we analyze the economic and social backgrounds of all thirty of Stevenson's most fully published Indian and Sri Lankan cases," he comments, "it is quite apparent that in no less than twenty of these the past life individual concerned was either wealthy or from a higher caste than the family of the present day child."

This pattern indicates to Wilson that rebirth cases represent nothing more than a wish-fulfillment fantasy on the part of the child. It is fun to pretend that we were once wealthy, and perhaps this natural tendency to daydream is sometimes expressed in a reincarnation fantasy. Wilson suggests that the paucity of cases in which the child remembered "a former life of grinding poverty" is a damning indictment of extracerebral memory cases.

A glance at Wilson's tabulations (which he provides on page 59 of his book) bears out his charge. There is only one case reported from India and Sri Lanka in which a wealthy child remembered living a past-life existence under socially inferior conditions. India is a land of dire poverty, so one might expect more children who remember their past lives to recall correspondingly wretched previous existences.

Certainly Wilson's observations here are accurate and cogent, but are they really as damning as he thinks? I don't think so. To begin with, it is clear that the pattern Wilson has uncovered only applies to the cases Dr. Stevenson has collected from Sri Lanka and India. There is no evidence that a similar pattern crops up among Tlingit or Middle Eastern peoples. It is common for Tlingit children to remember their past lives as their own relatives and therefore within their same social class. So the pattern Wilson outlined cannot be considered universal. It may not even be a meaningful finding at all. It is risky to come to _any_ conclusion from data that have been derived from such a small sample. The fact that twenty out of Stevenson's thirty Indian and Sri Lankan cases represent rebirth to a socially inferior status could easily be the result of chance variation within the cases. Only if this pattern were to emerge from the study of, say, two hundred cases, might we risk such a generalization.*

*Stevenson and his colleague Satwant Pasricha published three new evidential cases of the reincarnation type in 1977 in the _Indian Journal of Psychiatry_. Two out of the three concerned children who remember living their past lives under much poorer social and economic conditions.

But even if Wilson has discovered a genuine pattern within Indian and Sri Lankan rebirth cases, there are several reasons why such a pattern might naturally emerge from genuine examples of past-life recall. Two lines of speculation seem particularly pertinent:

1. We don't understand the principles that govern just who will, or who will not, remember a past life. It is possible that some crucial factor or factors catalyze these memories. Perhaps the psychological stress and indignity of finding oneself living under poor social conditions somehow *prompts* the emergence of past-life recall, especially in India where the caste system is so ingrained.

2. Perhaps we are contending with nothing more than a reporting artifact. Cases in which children recall lives as wealthy or prominent individuals may simply come to light more often. Children who recall such lives may receive more local attention and publicity than children who remember more wretched past existences. Since wealthy people are also usually prominent or well-known, it is also more likely that these cases are eventually "solved"* and reported in the press. Remember that Dr. Stevenson has learned about many of his cases through local press stories, so they may not represent a random sampling.

Now I am not claiming that either of the above explanations is necessarily correct. They are proposed only to illustrate that there are many ways the social patterns Wilson has found buried in Stevenson's cases can be interpreted. The basic validity of these cases need not be rejected on those grounds.

It is also true that at least some of Stevenson's cases were the result of hoaxes, and more than one skeptic has pointed out that the University of Virginia psychiatrist seems to sidestep this issue. Stevenson admitted during an interview he granted in 1970 that this "collapse" factor entails about five percent of his cases. Wilson obviously believes that Stevenson has underestimated the situation. However, his line of reasoning—that the children invariably fake their rebirth memories for prestige or for some other sort of personal gain—is shaky. Children in India are specifically discouraged from talking about their past lives because such recall is considered a bad omen. Reading through some of the cases Stevenson has placed on record can be rather painful, since many of his subjects were beaten, scolded, or ostracized for talking about their rebirth memories. It is doubtful that such children would pursue their fraud—if they were hoaxing to begin with—in the face of such reprisal. The age at which a typical child remembers his or her past life

*Dr. Stevenson uses the term "solved" to signify those cases in which the family or an investigator has been able to identify the person to whom the child's memory relates.

must also be taken into consideration. Some children begin to discuss their past lives at such a young age that a hoax seems unlikely. Some were hardly more than infants and the average age for most of them is between three and four. It would seem unlikely that a child of that age would have the experience or psychological resources to plan and execute elaborate hoaxes.

It is true, as Wilson claims, that the parents of a few of these children have tried to exploit the situation. But human nature is, after all, human nature. Even in these rare cases the exploitation probably began long after the child's rebirth memories first surfaced.

The only direct evidence for fraud that Wilson has been able to uncover stems from only five of Dr. Stevenson's cases. In each of these instances, neighbors claimed that the children had been coached about their past-life memories by their parents. But it really isn't necessary to take these allegations seriously. It must be remembered that we are dealing only with accusations, not with proof. These charges smack more of envy and petty jealousy than anything else. Nor can these few cases account for the many reports in which written records were made of the child's statements before they were verified. And even _if_ some parental coaching went on behind the scenes in some of Stevenson's cases, such a situation would not necessarily invalidate them. The parents in these particular instances often found themselves and their children the center of local attention. Such public exposure might easily have tempted the parents into making sure their son or daughter put on a good performance for the press or for the many curiosity-seekers who are drawn to these cases. But once again it seems that this coaching must have occurred _after_ the child's memories first emerged.

In short, I think that Wilson's argument against the validity of extracerebral memory falls apart when it is critically scrutinized. While he raises some valid objections to Dr. Stevenson's work, his findings are often inconsequential. But Mr. Wilson has not been content with merely criticizing Stevenson's research. This is only the first part of his case against the evidence for reincarnation. Besides outlining the problems with Stevenson's case studies, Wilson also offers a broadsided attack on the motivations of those who seek out and document these reports.

At the beginning of this chapter, I suggested that it is important to determine if Dr. Stevenson and his co-workers are dedicated scientists or religious zealots. It is Wilson's relief that the latter is probably more the case. He rightly argues that when dealing with a subject as controversial as reincarnation, the investigator must take pains to remain as objective as humanly possible. Pains must be taken to avoid bias. For if it can be shown that an investigator has relied on biased sources of information, his evidence is worthless.

These are the criteria Wilson uses to undermine his readers' confidence in Dr. Stevenson's work. He points out that Stevenson has long relied upon collaborators in the East to help him track down and investigate cases of reincarnation. This is true, since Dr. Stevenson often engaged the services of Francis Story, an Englishman who was also an avowed Buddhist, and Dr. Jamuna Prasad, an educational psychologist from the Uttar Pradesh district of India. It is Wilson's contention that these gentlemen were so obviously biased that the field work they undertook on Stevenson's behalf can be rejected out of hand. Since both men were thoroughgoing believers in reincarnation, Wilson argues, both their observations and their conclusions *must* have been distorted.* He even goes on to suggest that perhaps Dr. Stevenson chose these men *because* they would soft-pedal any negative evidence they uncovered.

This whole line of reasoning strikes me as unsound. Any scientist is going to have a vested interest in the work he carries out. The work and views of Dr. Stevenson, Jamuna Prasad, and the late Francis Story can be considered no less biased because of their beliefs than Wilson's would be by virtue of his skepticism. I broached just such a point when I originally reviewed Wilson's book for *Fate* magazine, on whose staff I serve as consulting editor. Tongue firmly in cheek, I pointed out to our readers that Ian Wilson is a convert to Roman Catholicism. Since the Roman Catholic church rejects belief in reincarnation, I suggested that Wilson is therefore not competent to assess the evidence for reincarnation because of his *own* religious bias. My review prompted an angry reply from Wilson, who obviously missed the point that I was playing his own game of foolish reasoning.

The point I am trying to make is that the only valid way to criticize Dr. Stevenson's research would be by examining his cases. His research can be rejected only if we can *find* signs of bias or examples of sloppy investigative procedures within the reports themselves. They cannot be called into question on the basis of unfounded attribution of bias on the part of the investigators. This is a fallacy that logicians call "poisoning the well."

Mr. Wilson's views have been discussed in some depth to show just how invalid much of the criticism leveled at Dr. Stevenson's research has been. But while I tend to reject most of Wilson's charges against Dr. Stevenson's work, I nevertheless think that some genuine criticisms can be leveled against it. Some of his investigations *have* been flawed.

It would be much too time consuming to offer a detailed examination of the sixty-five or so cases the University of Virginia psychiatrist has placed in the literature. So for the time being, our focus of attention will be directed to four of his cases that reveal clear signs of either sloppy research or misrepresentation.

---

*Wilson's attack of Francis Story's credibility is based on a single discrepancy concerning the birthdate recorded in one of the cases. No mention is made that Stevenson has repeatedly shown that birthdates are not systematically recorded in India and that such mistakes are very common.

The Case of Mounzer Haïdar and His Curious Birthmark

The crucial aspect of this case, as pointed out in the last chapter, was Mounzer's birthmark. This mark may have related to the gunshot wound by which he was supposedly killed in his past life as Jamil Souki. This case is not one of Stevenson's stronger ones and it was weakened even more by the way in which the psychiatrist led his key witness, thus increasing his chances of documenting the case. Evidence that Dr. Stevenson sometimes leads his witnesses is evident by his description of his meeting with Jamil Souki's mother. If you recall, Dr. Stevenson did not objectively determine that the wound on Jamil's body corresponded to the site of Mounzer's birthmark. He only asked the young man's mother to show him where her deceased son's wound was located _after_ he showed her his diagram of Mounzer's abdomen and birthmark. Dr. Stevenson reports that when he _first_ asked Mrs. Souki about the wound, she "spontaneously pointed to the right side of the abdomen". But this could have designated a large and unfocalized area.

The Case of Little Mallika and Her Past-Life Identifications

The whole story of this case, which is included in _Twenty Cases Suggestive of Reincarnation,_ reveals that Dr. Stevenson sometimes deletes important information when writing his reports. This case revolved around the death of Kumari Devi Sabapthy, who lived in the city of Vellore. She died from typhoid fever in 1949, when she was twenty-eight. She had never married. One of the woman's surviving sisters later moved to the town of Pondicherry with her husband, Sri S. Mourougassigamany, who worked there as a city librarian. In July 1956 he rented part of his home to a gentlemen, his wife, and their little daughter Mallika, who had been born in 1955. The little girl developed a strong attraction to Mourougassigamany and eventually began speaking as if she were the reincarnation of his wife's deceased sister. As she grew older, Mallika displayed many behavioral idiosyncracies typical of the deceased. She also allegedly identified her past-life relations while looking at a photograph of them and eventually displayed some vestigial memories of her life as Kumari Devi. Stevenson reinvestigated the case during one of his field trips and considered it at least suggestive of reincarnation.

Dr. Stevenson admits that the case is not a very strong one; but inquiries I was able to make into the case through contacts in India revealed that even the _Twenty Cases_ account is biased.

During the time Dr. Stevenson was studying the case, an independent investigation of little Mallika's claims was being undertakin by Professor C. T. K. Chari, a professor at Madras Christian College. Chari learned that Mallika's father and grandfather were publicly denying the claims being made about Mallika's behavior. They even published a refutation in the local paper. Certainly Dr. Stevenson must have known about these refutations before his *Twenty Cases* was published in 1966 and certainly before its revised version came out in 1974. Yet no mention is made of these negative aspects of the case in his summation.

This is not the time or place to argue the relative merits or demerits of this particular case. The critical point is not whether the case is good or bad but whether Dr. Stevenson may have misrepresented it when he wrote it up for his book. This possibility becomes even more credible when we examine just how he investigated the case. Stevenson writes that his investigation (in the summer of 1961) included interviews with Mallika's father and some of her other relatives. In his prefatory remarks to his *Twenty Cases,* Dr. Stevenson points out that he spoke French with two of the witnesses who could not speak English and that one of these" . . .interpreted for a Tamil-speaking witness who could not speak English or French." This may all sound very innocent, but it really isn't.

I learned from my contacts in India that Dr. Stevenson had originally spoken to Mourougassigamany, who was enthusiastically endorsing the case. He later went to interview Sri Aroumougam, the father of the girl in question, whom we now know was skeptical of the whole affair. He was the witness who could not speak English or French, and Dr. Stevenson asked Mourougassigamany to serve as translator. Naturally the gentleman was inclined to give Dr. Stevenson little hint that this ostensibly "corroborating witness" was skeptical of the whole matter. Mourougassigamany probably framed his translation of Sri Aroumougam's responses to make them correspond to his own views on the affair, possibly quite unintentionally. But the point remains that Dr. Stevenson would have had no idea whether Aroumougan was supporting or criticizing the case on the basis of Mourougassigamany's translations. Dr. Stevenson certainly used questionable judgment in employing his principle witness as his translator when interviewing the one man who could either make or break the case. He used even poorer judgment by not mentioning the fact when he drafted his *Twenty Cases.* I even wrote to Dr. Stevenson in January 1980, specifically asking him why this flaw had been covered up. His reply (dated January 14) was that it should be obvious to the readers of his book who the translator had been. This is simply not true.

To be fair, Dr. Stevenson did point out to me that he could have done a better job of camouflage were he deliberately trying to conceal the faults in his investigation. He could have simply deleted the comment about using one of the witnesses as his translator. Perhaps, but the fact remains that it is manifestly impossible for the reader of _Twenty Cases_ to figure out just who the translator was and the important role he played in the case in general.

The Case of Imad Elawar and the Memory of His Past-Life Death

Since this was one of Dr. Stevenson's most complicated cases it is understandable that there was so much confusion over it. The primary investigations, as we saw in the last chapter, took place in March and April 1964. Stevenson's goal was to discover if Imad's memories related to Said Bouhamzy, who had died in 1943, or to his cousin Ibrahim, who had died of tuberculosis at the age of twenty-five in 1949. Most of the boy's memories apparently pertained to Ibrahim, but there was some contamination from Said's life story. For the case to conform to standard reincarnation doctrine, Imad's memories should have been attributable to only one of these individuals. A careful reading of the report indeed suggests that the psychiatrist might have misrepresented some of Imad's memories to make them more applicable to Ibrahim than to Said.

If you recall, Imad spoke about a truck accident that had crushed his legs and ultimately killed him in his past life. It would appear that Imad claimed that this was his _own_ memory and not a recollection of something he had heard about. We know this because Imad later expressed how wonderful it was to walk again. When Stevenson first visited Khriby on March 17, he set about to document this particular memory. According to his report, identifying a man in Khriby who had died after being crushed by a truck was his first order of business.* This certainly implies that Stevenson was attempting to verify this incident as an important past-life memory Imad was claiming.

Yet this incident is curiously transformed in the tabulation Stevenson charts out of Imad's first fifty-seven statements about his previous life. This chart is included in _Twenty Cases_ on page 262, and attempts to show the relative merits of applying Imad's memories to Said or Ibrahim. Here it is stated that Imad remembered only that "a truck ran over a man, broke both his legs, and crushed his trunk." It appears that Dr. Stevenson has depersonalized this memory so that the case looks more clear-cut, especially since most of Imad's other memories referred to Ibrahim. Dr. Stevenson makes it appear that Imad never claimed this memory as his own. I wrote in the last chapter (see the

*See page 279 of the revised edition of _Twenty Cases Suggestive of Reincarnation_. The very first sentences Dr. Stevenson writes about his trip read: "On my first visit to Khriby on March 17, I interviewed two informants of the village. . . .They had some acquaintance with the Bouhamzy family and verified that one Said Bouhamzy of Khriby had in fact died (in June 1943) after being run over by a truck."

footnote on page 63) that there was some confusion over whether Imad's memory of the truck incident was derived from his own past life or whether it was a more impersonal memory. This obfuscation seems exaggerated to make the case fit the reincarnation mold without any procrustean limbs hanging out.

The Case of Uttara and Her Responsive Xenoglossy

This case represent one of the more recent ones Dr. Stevenson has placed in the literature. The entire story of this young woman and her past-life trances as a nineteenth-century Bengali woman will be told in Chapter 7, so it will not be summarized here in any depth. The primary features of the case revolve around the woman's ability to trace her past-life family history and to speak in Bengali, a dialect distinct from the one normally spoken in her own district.

Uttara Huddar was born in 1941 and started exhibiting her trances in 1973, during which she is totally taken over by a past-life identity. These trances have been frequent, thus giving several researchers considerable opportunity to investigate her ability to speak Bengali when "possessed." Stevenson and his colleague, Dr. Satwant Pasricha, issued reports on the case both in the *American Journal of Psychiatry* (1979) and the *Journal of the American Society for Psychical Research* (1980). The two investigators stated in their first report that Uttara's ability to speak Bengali "constitutes, in our opinion, a paranormally acquired skill." Yet in their later report they had to add a footnote that Uttara had once taken some lessons in written Bengali script. They weaken this finding by pointing out that all of their informants agreed "that she attained only a rudimentary knowledge of it and that when she terminated the lessons she could read a few words of Bengali at most."

It was fortunate that, at the time Stevenson and Dr. Pasricha issued their reports, I had already received a private dossier on the case. Professor V. V. Akolkar of Poona, India, had been investigating the case at the same time Drs. Stevenson and Pasricha were looking into it. He, too, had been able to trace down some informants who knew about Uttara's lessons in Bengali, and he cited considerable evidence in his report that she had learned the language well enough to read a primer. He even took down testimony to this effect from one of her classmates. Now this certainly constitutes more than, according to Stevenson and Pasricha, "a few words of Bengali at best."

So here again we find an important discrepancy not only between the findings of two different investigations into one of Dr. Stevenson's reports, but even between his own two reports on the case. Drs. Stevenson and Pasricha sent their report to the *American Journal of Psychiatry* in June 1979, and it was published a month later. Their report to the A.S.P.R. must have been written about the same time, since it takes several months before material submitted to its quarterly journal finds its way into print. The more skeptical reader might suggest that Drs. Stevenson and Pasricha omitted the information they had uncovered about Uttara's familiarity with written Bengali script in the first report, and then played it down as much as possible in their report to the A.S.P.R. Even if they had been misinformed about Uttara's familiarity with Bengali, the report circulated by Akolkar would at least indicate that Drs. Stevenson and Pasricha were superficial in their investigation of the matter.

It might be objected that the four examples I have cited above are all very trivial. Maybe they are, but they indicate that a systematic bias may be pervading all of Dr. Stevenson's work. It is difficult to tell just how pervasive this bias has been, and it may well be a much more serious problem than can be derived from the clues I have been able to discover. The flaws in his handling of the Mallika and Uttara Huddar cases only came to light because I was able to cross-check his reports through my own contacts in India. The flaws that existed in his presentation of the Mounzer Haïdar and Imad Elawar cases are ones that only a careful scrutiny of the reports would reveal. So the question arises whether other flaws, omissions, and camouflaging may be plaguing his published work in general.

This issue is complicated even further by Dr. Stevenson's curious response to criticism. He often doesn't reply at all to it but tries to stifle it. I learned this hard lesson myself in 1975 when I was actively re-evaluating the Mallika case. It was becoming much clearer to me that I should make the results of my inquiries known. So in January 1976 I wrote to the late J.B. Rhine at the Institute for Parapsychology in Durham, North Carolina, who had considerable editorial control over the _Journal of Parapsychology_ at the time. After advising him of my findings, I suggested that I prepare a report for publication as a letter to the editor. I also insisted that Dr. Stevenson be given the right to reply to my letter in the same issue. Dr. Rhine and the editors of the _Journal of Parapsychology_ agreed.

Dr. Stevenson prepared his rebuttal, but our little controversy never saw the light of day. When the editors requested that he remove some of the personal remarks contained in his rejoindre, Dr. Stevenson withdrew his reply. The _Journal of Parapsychology_, Dr. Rhine, and I all received letters from Dr. Stevenson's attorney shortly thereafter, threatening a lawsuit for libel if we proceeded with publication. The tactic worked, and the _J.P._ bowed to the pressure over the strong objections of both me and my attorney.*

I have not brought up this incident to embarrass Dr. Stevenson, but to show how he engages in questionable tactics when responding to criticism of his work. It is therefore impossible to determine how many other researchers have confronted similar problems when trying to publish criticisms of

---

*Despite a formal request I made to Dr. Stevenson in 1982, he has refused to show me a copy of his rejoindre to these criticisms. While preparing this chapter, I advised Dr. Stevenson that I would be criticizing his research. I invited him to read and reply to the above criticisms. He declined the invitation, though I promised to include his comments in this book.

Stevenson's work. I know of at least one other similar incident. So the public has really little way of objectively evaluating his research, since his critics may have been pressured from speaking.

Very little effort has been exerted to follow up most of Dr. Stevenson's cases. The only information we can evaluate is contained in his own reports or those filed by his proxy investigators. It is impossible to determine whether a follow-up study would support the value of many of his cases. The Mallika case seems reasonably impressive at first glance, but Chari's investigation throws considerable doubt on its validity. Now I am not implying that all, or even most, of Dr. Stevenson's cases would fall apart if they were impartially investigated. V.V. Akolkar's report actually substantiated the basic validity of the Uttara Huddar case. But it is unfortunate that more unbiased investigators aren't pursuing the study of extracerebral memory cases. If several researchers working in the same countries Dr. Stevenson has visited were also to report the discovery of veridical rebirth cases, the inherent credibility of both the phenomenon and Dr. Stevenson's case studies would be greatly enhanced. His research could then be placed in proper perspective.

The situation is actually not as barren as I have made it out to be, since a few semi-independent researchers *have* attempted to replicate Dr. Stevenson's work both in India and in Lebanon. They have come up, by and large, empty handed. The fact remains that Dr. Stevenson is just about the only researcher who has been coming across veridical cases.*

It may appear from the last chapter that veridical rebirth cases are quite common. This would be a mistaken impression. In fact, cases of extracerebral memory that include paranormally derived information are very rare. The sixty-five or so cases Dr. Stevenson has published are actually a careful selection of cases drawn from a large body of unverified cases, worthless ones, and some that were the result of obvious lying or fantasy. Even some of Dr. Stevenson's own research associates have been unable to uncover veridical cases of reincarnation memory. For example, during the 1970s Dr. Stevenson employed a young anthropologist to look into extracerebral memory cases in India. Dr. David Read Barker was a perfect choice because he had conducted his doctoral research in India. He eventually investigated several cases for his employer but was unable to find a single case that he felt implied some sort of paranormal process at work. Dr. Barker never published an official report on his studies but did briefly comment on his failure in a letter he published in the September 1979 issue of the *Journal of Parapsychology*. (He told me in August 1978 that Stevenson was pressuring him to keep silent about the barren nature of his findings.)

Dr. Stevenson's current research assistant is Emily Williams Cook, a young doctoral student in religious studies at the University of Virginia. Ms.

---

*With the important exceptions noted in the footnote appearing on the first page of this chapter.

Cook recently admitted at a parapsychology conference held on the campus of Duke University in Durham, North Carolina, that she has looked into thirty-five new rebirth cases reported from Lebanon. In twenty-eight of them the parents of the children had already "solved" them by the time she arrived on the scene. Ms. Cook had to admit, however, that in the majority of them she was unsatisfied that any paranormal factors had entered the cases.

So why should Dr. Stevenson be coming up with so many impressive cases, while other researchers come up with so few? Could this again be indicating a highly pervasive bias in his investigations? This is a possibility even his own co-workers have raised. Before hiring Dr. Barker to work with him, Dr. Stevenson employed a lawyer to help analyze his reincarnation cases. Champe Ransom worked on these cases for quite some time before he became dissatisfied with the way his employer was conducting his investigations. He wrote a detailed report of his objections, which Stevenson asked him not to circulate or publish. (I spent some time trying to obtain a copy of this report but was unable to locate one. But in 1973 I was able to talk with a colleague who had read it.)

The basic approach Ransom took to the study of Stevenson's cases was quite simple. He believed that the best way to examine each individual incident was by grouping all the statements the child had made into two categories. The first included those containing information the child could normally have learned about; the second would contain the statements purportedly containing paranormally derived information. Ransom found that the witnesses to a specific case usually or often agreed among themselves about the claims placed in the first category. But when it came to analyzing those statements that implied paranormal cognition on the part of the child, the witnesses were often confused about what was said and when it was communicated. Eventually this led Ransom to become skeptical of the cases and about extracerebral memory in general.

Ransom's analytical technique was also employed by Dr. Barker during his field investigations. It was this procedure, he later told me, that served as the basis for his own skepticism. It is also interesting that Emily Williams Cook specifically recommended this method during her 1983 presentation in Durham.

The fact that extracerebral memory cases are rarely clear-cut is, of course, the major problem the researcher faces when studying the evidence for reincarnation. It is quite obvious that the investigator's bias can often cloud the way he or she evaluates the evidence, which may be why Stevenson has been able to discover so many "strong" cases of the reincarnation type. I mentioned earlier that an independent verification of Dr. Stevenson's strongest cases is in order. It is doubtful whether such a project will ever be undertaken. However, in November 1976 two of Dr. Stevenson's co-workers jointly investigated a case of the reincarnation type reported from India. They conducted their investigation of this promising case by, according to their own words, following Dr. Stevenson's methods "as closely as we could." The result was that the two researchers came to almost diametrically opposing conclusions about it. These investigators were Dr. David Read Barker and Dr. Satwant Pasricha, who has been collaborating with Dr. Stevenson for a number of years now.

The subject of this investigation was a boy named Rakesh Gaur, who was born in Fateh Nagar (Kajasthan, India) on 15 March 1969. He was the fifth son of a Brahmin postal worker who settled in Kankroli in 1975. Rakesh began talking about his past life in the Chhippa neighborhood of Tonk (which is also in Kajasthan) as a member of the carpenter caste. He mentioned the name of his wife and added that he had been electrocuted. He also apparently mentioned that his past-life name had been Bithal Das, though there is some confusion among the witnesses about this point. Rakesh's past-life recollections were so strong that he often urged his parents to take him to Tonk. He also exhibited a marked interest in carpentry. The most dramatic upshot in the case came in the summer of 1976, when a bus driver from Tonk, Chittar Mal, stopped by in Kankroli. As he passed by Rakesh on the street, the young man recognized him by name and spontaneously started talking about his past life in Kankroli. Chittar Mal was so impressed by the conversation that he told the surviving members of the Bithal Das family in Tonk, whom he apparently knew, about his encounter.

Rakesh's parents finally took their son to Tonk in October 1976 to better investigate the information he was recalling. They arrived by bus, and Rakesh almost immediately pointed out the electrical pole on which he had been working when he was killed. Since Gaur didn't know anyone in Tonk, he first went to the local post office to recruit some one to help him document his son's claims. Several employees volunteered, and soon a large crowd was accompanying the Gaurs as they searched the city in hopes of finding the house where Bithal Das had lived. A member of the crowd volunteered that he recalled a carpenter named Bithal Das who had been electrocuted and set his date of death as 1955. Later that day, Rakesh saw and apparently recognized Bithal Das' son as well as his widow. Unfortunately, Gaur took his son back to Kankroli that night, but the investigation was hardly at an end. Bithal Das' son visited Gaur two days later, and other former relatives soon followed. They were all impressed by the boy's apparent knowledge about their deceased relative, and especially by his description of Bithal Das' house. Drs. Barker and Pasricha learned about the case in November 1976 and visited the towns in question that same month. They were able to talk to several of the key witnesses, and they conducted a follow-up in 1978.

There is ample evidence that Rakesh was somehow tapping into the life and times of Bithal Das, who had been born in Tonk sometime in the early 1920s. He lived there sporadically between 1942 and his death, and he did, in fact, work as a carpenter. He died on 15 August 1955 when he accidentally touched a live wire in the courtyard of his house. Bithal Das enjoyed fiddling with electrical work but was never an employee of any electric company.

This case history reads much like many of the cases Dr. Stevenson has collected. It seems clear-cut enough, but as their investigation proceeded Drs. Barker and Pasricha came to very different conclusions about its value. Dr. Barker eventually rejected it totally as evidence of reincarnation. He points out in his analysis which he published in the May 1981 issue of the _European Journal of Parapsychology,_ that no written record of the boy's statements had been made before Gaur began to investigate them. The evidence in the case, Barker goes on to argue, rests solely on the testimony and memories of the witnesses, many of whom were emotionally involved. Dr. Barker was dismayed by how often the testimony of the witnesses varied, especially concerning Rakesh's initial memories. All of the witnesses agreed about Rakesh's claims concerning his past life as a carpenter in Tonk. They also agreed that he asserted that his death was the result of electrocution. There also seems no doubt but that Rakesh recognized Chitter Mal when he first saw him in Kankroli. But this is where agreement among the witnesses ended. They specifically disagreed whether Rakesh had identified his past-life name as Bithal Das. Some of the witnesses claimed that this was one of his original memories, while several others believed he didn't mention the name until his journey to Tonk. It is Dr. Barker's position that the boy probably did not offer the name before undertaking his trip. Dr. Barker points out that Gaur and his son searched all over Tonk before finding Bithal Das' house, to which any one at the post office could have directed them had they inquired about the family by name.

There is also considerable evidence that many of Rakesh's memories were curiously inaccurate. He supplied the wrong name for his wife, designated the wrong neighborhood in Tonk as his community, and was wrong about dying while working on an electrical pole. Dr. Barker also found some evidence that Rakesh modified his recollections as the case progressed and as he possibily gained more access to information about Bithal Das.

There is also an important discrepancy over whether the boy spontaneously recognized Bithal Das' widow when she arrived at the Tonk post office. Gaur claimed that his son pointed to the woman, saying, "She is my wife." Yet according to another witness who was at the post office that day, the boy did not recognize the woman when she first arrived but only identified her when some one specifically _asked_ him whether the woman had been his past-life wife.

Based on these problems and discrepancies in the testimony, Dr. Barker believes that the case tells us more about cultural psychology than reincarnation. He concludes that:

> As I reconstruct this case, Rakesh as a young child repeatedly made a few general statements about a "previous life." He was taken to Tonk in order to "confirm" these statements by leading his father to the family of his previous life. He could not do this because many of his statements and recognitions did not correspond to anyone known to have existed. After two or three hours of

searching, a large crowd gathered. A person in the crowd thought of Bithal Das, a man who matched enough of Rakesh's statements to satisfy nearly everyone that Rakesh had been talking about this man from the beginning. From that moment Rakesh was provided with abundant cues for appropriate behavior, and Rakesh, an unusually intelligent and observant child, quickly learned to become Bithal Das. Equally important, everyone who was personally involved in the case became convinced that Rakesh actually was Bithal Das, and they treated him accordingly. In consequence, all the people directly involved with Bithal Das and Rakesh rapidly created a reality that is deeply rooted in Indian psychology. Rakesh became the reincarnation of Bithal Das because he identified himself fully with Bithal Das's life and because other people supported him and rewarded him in this identification.

Dr. Barker admits, however, that he can find no explanation for Rakesh's sudden recognition of Chittar Mal while still in Kankroli. Nor can his scenario (by his own admission) explain why Rakesh's revelations to the bus driver led Chittar Mal to immediately identify the boy with Bithal Das.

Dr. Pasricha, on the other hand, has taken strong exception to her colleague's conclusions. It is her opinion that the discrepancies in the case deal primarily with unimportant details that do not seriously undermine its basic validity. She points out that both S.N. Gaur and Chittar Mal heard the boy claim that his past-life name had been Bithal Das, and she believes their corroborative testimony should be taken at face value. There was even some evidence that Gaur specifically mentioned this name when he made inquiries about his son's claims to the power company in Tonk. These inquiries were made through the mail before he ever visited the city. Dr. Pasricha also rejects Barker's opinion that Rakesh only made some vague statements about his past life during the early stages of the case. Based upon her own analysis, she argues that the witnesses agreed that Rakesh made about seventeen correct claims about his past life before going to Tonk. She also points out that the boy described the interior of Bithal Das' house to the man's son before he (Rakesh) had any opportunity to visit it. In fact, the psychologist argues, Rakesh made no less than twenty-seven statements about Bithal Das before the two families ever met. Only four of them were wrong and this confusion could have been caused by normal errors of memory.

Nor has Dr. Pasricha been daunted by the fact that Gaur and his son took so long to find Bithal Das' house. This confusion may have resulted when Rakesh made his false identification of the electrical pole. The boy and his father may have begun their search in the wrong part of town, she explains, thus wasting valuble time. In fact, Dr. Pasricha admits that she and Dr. Barker really should have spent more time investigating just what transpired between the time the Gaurs arrived in Tonk and the time Bithal Das' relatives were located. This was a flaw in their investigation, and she states it openly. She concludes:

Despite the occurrence of some discrepancies in the testimonies the informants have convinced me that Rakesh knew a substantial body of detailed information about Bithal Das before the families concerned exchanged information. If we accept, as I do, the informants' firm statements that they had had no acquaintance whatsoever before the development of the case, we seem led to suppose that Rakesh had somehow obtained his information about Bithal Das through some paranormal process.

Whether the Rakesh Gaur case holds up a particularly strong one for reincarnation is in one respect inconsequential. The crucial point is how two investigators can approach the same case and evidence and still come to a dramatic disagreement about its value. I personally believe that Dr. Pasricha makes the slightly stronger case, but it also seems clear that the *interpretation* of any particular case of the reincarnation type rests on the biases and predilections of the investigator.

It might also be noted that Drs. Barker and Pasricha chose the Rakesh Gaur case because it represented the strongest report they had uncovered. So the problems they had while investigating it should also give you an idea of the confusion that may have existed in many of Dr. Stevenson's cases.

On the other hand, the fact that (in my opinion) Dr. Pasricha makes a stronger case than Barker serves as some tentative vindication of Dr. Stevenson's work.

The confusion over what value can be derived from cases of the reincarnation type is compounded by the cultural artifacts contained in them. Although cases of extracerebral memory follow general patterns, several important variations emerge from case to case, and many of these seem to be culturally linked. It wasn't long after Dr. Stevenson started reporting his cases that his critics began pointing out these differences, which suggest that cases of extracerebral memory are perhaps fantasies based on local traditions and folklore. Professor C.T.K. Chari, a philosopher now retired from Madras Christian College in India, was one of the first to criticize Dr. Stevenson's cases on these grounds. Years ago he pointed out that practically all of the cases were being reported from northern India (especially Uttar Pradesh), while very few reports were emanating from the southern states. Dr. Chari rightly argues that reincarnation is a doctrine accepted all over the country, so this reporting pattern is generally puzzling. The eminent scholar does not feel he has an explanation for this reporting effect, although he believes that we should be skeptical of extracerebral memory cases because of it.

It is interesting to note, however, that Dr. Chari does not deny that some cases of veridical past-life memory exist in the literature. His view is that these cases may essentially be rebirth fantasies. But he goes on to argue that a child may sometimes telepathically tap into a reservoir of information about a genuinely deceased individual as the fantasy develops.

The most conspicuous cultural differences that emerge from Dr. Stevenson's case studies only become apparent when we analyze data drawn from several different cultures. Then it really does begin to look as though the extracerebral memory syndrome is influenced by cultural settings and expectations. Dr. Stevenson originally pointed out some of these differences in 1970, when he published a comparative analysis of his Turkish, Tlingit, and Sri Lankan cases in the *International Journal of Comparative Sociology*. He showed in his fascinating paper that the "laws" that seem to govern reincarnation cases differ from country to country. If we extend Stevenson's analysis to the data he has collected from India and Lebanon, several more cultural differences emerge. Many of them are challenging, while others are simply puzzling:

1. The cause of death seems to be a predictable pattern in Turkish extracerebral memory cases. It is a local belief that only people who meet with a violent death will be reborn or will recall their past lives. This feature crops up in roughly 75 percent of Stevenson's Turkish cases. A similar feature is obvious in those cases reported among the Druse of Syria and Lebanon. Yet it is not prominent in the cases collected from Sri Lanka or Alaska.

2. Rebirth cases in which the personality has changed sex usually only occur in those cases in which this possibility is accepted. They are unheard of in Turkey and among the Tlingits, but they do crop up now and then in cases reported from southeast Asia and Sri Lanka.

3. Cases of interfamily rebirth are very common among the Tlingits and are also recorded from Burma. Yet this peculiarity is rarely reported from Turkey. This pattern may reflect the fact that the Tlingits are very concerned with family prestige and social standing.

4. The interval between death and subsequent rebirth tends to vary from culture to culture, often corresponding to the cultural and religious beliefs common to the local area. Tlingit eskimos tend to claim long intervals between their deaths and subsequent rebirths, while the mean interval is much shorter among the Druse.

5. Birthmark cases are very common in Turkey and among the Tlingits, but play practically no role in Sri Lankan cases. This pattern may reflect the beliefs held by many Turks that death by violence leads to rebirth, while the Tlingits culturally emphasize the reappearance of such birthmarks.

6. Cases in which the pregnant mother had a dream about the past-life identity of her forthcoming child are very common in Turkey and among the Tlingits. Similar reports are relatively rare in Sri Lanka and other Asian countries.

Several additional patterns could be documented, and I don't think anyone who studies the evidence could deny the important role cultures play in the expression of extracerebral memory.

But whether these cultural artifacts really subvert the value of extracerebral memory cases is a moot point. Cultural effects can arise in any body of data for several reasons, and Dr. Stevenson's data are no exception. The cultural differences I have outlined above can actually be interpreted along several different lines. Chari is able to accept the validity of some extracerebral memory cases while still appreciating how cultural factors might be influencing their expression. But perhaps the best reply to the critics has come from Dr. Stevenson himself, when he argues that a person who has died and is seeking rebirth might be actively guided by his own expectancies. When planning and executing a rebirth, he or she may design it to conform to his/her religious and culturally derived beliefs. Such a process would invariably lead to cultural differences in cases reported from divergent cultures.

There is nothing illogical in this viewpoint. It may well be _the_ definitive explanation for these cultural differences if one wishes to entertain the possibility of reincarnation seriously (which I certainly do).

I said at the beginning of this chapter that the value of Dr. Stevenson's case studies could only be evaluated after considering two factors. We have now looked in some detail at how culture influences rebirth cases and at the manner in which Dr. Stevenson investigates his cases. So in consequence, just where do we stand?

The data outlined over the last several pages indicate that building a case for reincarnation solely on cases of extracerebral memory would be risky. There are several problems with Dr. Stevenson's pioneering research, of which some are inherent to the cases themselves. There is also a strong likelihood that many of the psychiatrist's cases are not nearly as strong as he has presented them. The fact that attempted replications of his work by independent investigators have basically failed also calls his research into some question. Yet despite all these formidable obstacles, it would not be fair to summarily reject the value of extracerebral memory cases or Dr. Stevenson's work as evidence for reincarnation. The evidence that some (probably weak) extracerebral memory cases have been polished up before publication should not detract from the value contributed by the stronger ones.

Despite the way (I feel) Dr. Stevenson has beautified some of his reports, several of the cases he has uncovered are very compelling. Try as I might, I can see no way that a normal explanation can be found for Jagdish Chandra's rebirth memories as Jai Gopal. K.K.N. Sahay's report on his son is clear and unambiguous and suffers from few of the weaknesses I have found in some of Dr. Stevenson's original investigations. Nor could any amount of local gossip have contributed to Kumkum Verma's literal transformation into Sunnary, especially during her trances. The same can be said for Jasbir Lal Jat's "rebirth" or "possession," which represents a psychological as well as a parapsychological mystery. The Rakesh Gaur case represents the only one presented in the literature in which we can fairly examine both the pros and cons of a particular case. It is my feeling, along with Dr. Pasricha, that some paranormal cognition was displayed by the boy, thus essentially validating

Stevenson's work. I have also long been impressed by birthmark cases. No matter what access to normal sources of information some of these children may have had, the simple fact remains that they have been born with biologically inexplicable birthmarks.

So while Dr. Stevenson's research can be seriously challenged in general, some of his best cases tend to hold up well. But we must once again ask whether we are dealing with reincarnation, genetic memory, telepathically triggered fantasies, or what? This is the one question Dr. Stevenson's research has not been able to answer. It appears that a paranormal influence sometimes pervades reports of extracerebral memory, but this does not necessarily mean that we have to accept the reincarnation doctrine by virtue of the fact.

As I pointed out before, a few reported cases of extracerebral memory point away from reincarnation. Just as C.T.K. Chari is able to accept the validity of some rebirth memory cases without endorsing belief in reincarnation, several other students of the literature have also suggested alternate explanations for this strange phenomenon. Several parapsychologists have posited that we are dealing with the reappearance of memory patterns or constellations and not really the rebirth of the soul. W.G. Roll, who is the project director for the Psychical Research Foundation in Chapel Hill, North Carolina, came to a similar conclusion after making a detailed study of Dr. Stevenson's cases. He recently proposed that these cases " . . . suggest not so much the survival of any unitary personality or self as the continuation of clusters of associated memories." Theories that argue along these lines will be explored in further depth in the concluding chapter. There I hope to make a little sense out of the many complexities with which the literature on extracerebral memory provides us.

For now, just let me say that Chari, W.G. Roll, myself, and others share some common ground in our beliefs. We all recognize that the phenomenon of extracerebral memory is pointing to something very important. But we are not quite sure just what.

Conclusions

Cases of extracerebral memory have been subject to their share of criticism. Much of it has been invalid, and it is true that Dr. Stevenson's research, in particular, can be attacked on several grounds. There is evidence that many of his cases may have been more ambiguous than they appear in their published form. Dr. Stevenson's bias may also have influenced the way he conducts his investigations. And it is clear that cultural factors greatly influence the expression of extracerebral memory cases. Yet despite these findings and problems, extracerebral memory holds up reasonably well as a genuine form of paranormal phenomenon. Whether it serves as definitive proof of reincarnation is debatable, however. Several alternate explanations for these cases have been proposed, and some of them are just as viable as reincarnation.

5

Hypnosis, Regression, and Reincarnation

Writing in their skeptically toned book, *Anomalistic Psychology*, Dr. Leonard Zusne and Dr. Warren H. Jones state:

> . . . because suggestion is part of hypnosis, suggesting that the subject go back beyond the point of his or her own birth and examine his or her previous lives achieves precisely that result—the subject all too willingly proceeds to do just that. This, however, is no proof of reincarnation. The cases that have been thoroughly investigated show beyond the shadow of a doubt that one is dealing with hypnotic hypermnesia [improved recall] coupled with the subject's unconscious wish for exhibition, for romance to liven up a drab life, for fantasy as an ego defense mechanism, and similar psychological needs, all reinforced by the hypnotist's own beliefs in the reincarnation doctrine.

Students of the psychic field who believe in reincarnation will no doubt take issue with the opinion of these two University of Tulsa psychologists. Nonetheless, their view echoes the verdict mainline psychology passed on the phenomenon of past-life hypnotic regression years ago. There is probably no area of "new-age" psychology that has become as popular as past-life regression. Literally thousands of people have flocked to "reincarnation" therapists, Aquarian Age psychologists, and amateur hypnotists to trace their previous lives. There is also possibly no area of popular metaphysics that has been so roundly criticized and held in contempt not only by conventional psychology and psychiatry but even by some authorities on reincarnation. The whole area of hypnosis is inherently tied to the role-playing fantasy life of the unconscious mind. So it isn't difficult to dismiss the accounts of people who have "remembered" their past lives while hypnotized as simply fantasy.

Despite this fact, it is another matter whether *all* cases of hypnotically evoked past-life memory can be invariably traced to "hypermnesia coupled with the subject's unconscious wish . . . for fantasy." While it is true that some subjects will spin out fabulous tales of adventure and excitement while under hypnosis, some scattered evidence shows that the practice can sometimes be used as a tool in reincarnation research as long as it isn't abused.

To put it bluntly, Drs. Jones and Zusne are not correct when they state that *all* cases of hypnotically induced past-life recall can be traced to unconscious fantasy. It is also uncircumspect to argue that hypnotized subjects reel out their tales of past incarnations to liven up their "drab" lives. Sometimes a subject's hypnotically remembered past life will be even drabber than his or her present! The long, complex story of hypnotic regression and reincarnation is an involved one, and no simple and facile approach to the subject could ever do it justice.

The whole controversy over the phenomenon of hypnotic past-life recall goes back to 1956 when Morey Bernstein, a businessman and hypnotist in Pueblo, Colorado, published his *The Search for Bridey Murphy*. No single book has ever ignited as much debate about both hypnosis and reincarnation.

Today the case probably represents little more than a curious footnote in the history of psychic research, since so much criticism was leveled against the case when the book was first published. This does not mean, however, that the case is valueless. For despite all the furor the case caused in the 1950s, no one would dare say that it was ever really solved or explained away. History has also been somewhat unfair to Bernstein, the chief protagonist of the case. Bernstein proceeded with care when he undertook his investigations into past-life recall. He was no wild-eyed amateur hypnotist wallowing in his own naivete, a view of him many skeptics and debunkers tried to promote. He was a serious student of hypnosis, parapsychology, and reincarnation, and he took a sophisticated and intellectual interest in all three of these subjects. It was intellectual hunger and not idle curiosity that led him to initiate his regression experiments with Virginia Tighe, a young Colorado housewife, in 1952.

Before undertaking his experiments, Bernstein had nurtured a long-lived sophisticated interest in metaphysical subjects. He had also spent considerable time in Durham, North Carolina, with J. B. Rhine and his staff at Duke University. It is important to remember this point, for his decision to consult with Rhine revealed that Bernstein appreciated the problems of experimental design and the scientific method. A less mature student of the psychic field would have simply rushed off to visit every psychic and medium in Colorado to quench his or her thirst for occult knowledge. Bernstein's interest in the art of hypnosis was similarly sophisticated, despite his amateur status, and he had been a highly regarded practitioner for several years before he undertook the Bridey Murphy experiments.

Mrs. Virginia Tighe (whom he called Ruth Simmons in his book) was an otherwise unassuming housewife when Bernstein began working with her. He had hypnotized her once sometime before he became interested in hypnotic regression. Mrs. Tighe was twenty-nine years old at the time of the "Bridey Murphy" experiments, with a year and a half of college behind her.

It is not totally clear just why Bernstein recruited her for his reincarnation research. He maintains in his book only that when he decided to experiment with hypnotic regression, he recalled how easily she had responded to hypnosis. This encouraged him to invite her and her husband to cooperate in some further sessions. The first of these was conducted in Bernstein's home on 29 November 1952. Regressing the subject was no easy matter, but by the end of the session, Mrs. Tighe was actively remembering a past life in County Cork, Ireland, as "Bridey Murphy." Several more regressions were held over the next months, during which Mrs. Tighe filled in the gaps of her initial memories. What was so impressive was how Virginia Tighe began recalling more and more obscure bits of information about Ireland and nineteenth-century Irish life as the sessions proceeded. Eventually the whole life of "Bridey Murphy" was spelled out.

"Bridey (Bridget) Kathleen Murphy" explained through the entranced Mrs. Tighe that she was born as the daughter of Duncan Murphy, a Protestant barrister in Cork, and his wife, Kathleen, in 1798. She further claimed that she attended school supervised by a woman named "Mrs. Stayne," whose daughter eventually married "Bridey's" brother. "Bridey" also mentioned that she married the son of another Cork barrister when she was twenty years old. Brian Joseph McCarthy was a Catholic, but they were married in a Protestant ceremony. The couple, as the story went on, eventually moved to Belfast so that Brian could attend school; there he later taught law at Queen's University. A second (Catholic) ceremony was performed there by Father John Joseph Gorman at St. Theresa's church. The hypnotically elicited story ended with "Bridey" describing her death at the age of sixty-six and her burial (or being "ditched," as she said so colorfully) in Belfast in 1864.

When _The Search for Bridey Murphy_ was published in 1956 by one of New York's most respectable publishers, it became an instant best seller. It also became one of the most discussed books in the history of psychic research. The news that an everyday housewife in Colorado could recall a past-life incarnation was so stunning that soon a search for the _real_ Bridey Murphy was on . . . as newspaper reporters, skeptics, and believers alike searched through both Mrs. Tighe's background as well as Irish history to discover the truth behind her memories. It was all a mad romp that livened up the dull and conventional period of the sleepy Eisenhower years.

Historical research eventually verified some of Mrs. Tighe's memories but cast doubt on other aspects of her story. Most of the names that were communicated during the sessions were never verified. No records of Duncan Murphy, Bridget Kathleen Murphy, Brian Joseph McCarthy, or John Joseph

Gorman were ever located by anyone investigating the case. This in itself was not a damning indictment of the case, though, since vital statistics could not be found in Ireland dating back that far.

The real case for Bridey Murphy was uncovered by William J. Barker, a writer and reporter who was sent to Ireland by the Denver *Post,* which wanted the reporter to investigate, document, or expose the Bridey Murphy story. The plan was to underwrite an objective search in Europe, and the results of Barker's research appeared as a twelve-page supplement to the *Post* on 11 March 1956. Titled promisingly as "The Truth about Bridey Murphy," the report was both objective and scholarly, and it *partially* confirmed Mrs. Tighe's hypnotic claims. But as Barker was to write sometime later, "In summing up, I found neither for nor against Bridey."

What he was able to discover about the case was provocative nevertheless. During one of the later regressions, "Bridey" mentioned the names of two Belfast grocers from whom she bought food. The names were given as Farr's and John Carrigan. A search undertaken by Belfast's chief librarian at Barker's request documented that these two gentlemen were listed in the city directory for 1865-6. They were, in fact, the only two grocers in business at the time. What Barker found even more impressive was that several statements "Bridey" had made during the regressions turned out to be true, even though experts on Irish life were skeptical of them. The most famous of these was "Bridey's" claim that her husband was a barrister. This seemed unlikely, since Catholics were not emancipated in Ireland until the 1820s and therefore couldn't have practiced law during the early years of "Bridey's" marriage. Barker was able to learn in Ireland, however, that a Catholic Relief Act was passed in 1793, which ruled that Catholics could enter the legal profession. "Bridey" also asserted that she had lived in a house called "The Meadows." Barker was able to dig up a map of County Cork dating back to 1801, and while no house by that name could be traced, there was an area in Cork known by that bucolic designation. A house also called "The Meadows" could easily have once existed there.

Examples such as these could be cited on and on *ad infinitum,* but to go on with Barker's analysis would be to engage in a tedious history lesson about nineteenth-century Irish life. The few examples cited above certainly indicate that Mrs. Tighe's knowledge of nineteenth-century Ireland was prodigious. Some of her information was so detailed that it represented an *a priori* case for reincarnation despite the fact that no one was ever able to prove the literal existence of "Bridey Murphy" in Ireland.

Of course, there were charges and countercharges made about the case, especially by the press. Bernstein himself was even accused by one paper of promoting a hoax. More circumspect skeptics attempted to show that Mrs. Tighe had probably been exposed to all sorts of information about Ireland during her early youth. These attacks were more credible than the charge of fraud, since cryptomnesia and hypermnesia are two (allegedly) well-known byproducts of hypnotic regression. However, even most of these "investigative reports" into the Bridey Murphy case, which were often little more than debunking attempts, didn't hold up well when they, _too,_ were critically investigated.

The most apparently damning criticisms of the case were contained in a series of articles carried by the _Chicago American_ in May and June of 1956. They were later syndicated nationally by Hearst-controlled papers. The reports focused on the "discovery" that Virginia Tighe had lived for a time with an Irish aunt, Marie Burns, who often told her niece about her native country. The story sounded reasonable enough until Barker—still hot on the trail of the historical Bridey Murphy—discovered that the woman was really born in New York and had lived most of her life in Chicago. Although Marie Burns was genuinely of Scottish–Irish descent, she turned out to have very little interest in Ireland or its history. Many of the Hearst papers also carried stories that some of "Bridey's" memories were based on similar incidents from Virginia Tighe's own childhood. Barker discovered that many of these claims were simply the invention of the tabloid press. One of the few claims made by the press that did hold up concerned a neighbor of Mrs. Tighe's. It was reported that an Irish woman named Mrs. Anthony Bridie Murphy Corkell (the alleged model for Mrs. Tighe's "Bridey Murphy" of County Cork) had once lived across the street from Virginia Tighe's aunt and uncle. Barker looked into the matter and was able to locate the basis of the story. It was true that she once lived near Mrs. Tighe's relatives, but he could not document that her maiden name was Murphy. On the other hand, he did discover that Bridey Murphy was a rather common one in Chicago. The reporter also checked out Mrs. Corkell's background and found that she had lived in an area miles away from where "Bridey" and her husband purportedly lived. He, therefore, didn't believe that she could have been the source of Mrs. Tighe's memories and information.

And that is where the case rested for several years—unresolved and totally inexplicable.

Looking back at the Bridey Murphy affair after close to thirty years, the case still represents an enigma. The problem was that both the believers and the debunkers took an all-or-nothing approach to the mystery it presented. To the press and to the readers of _The Search for Bridey Murphy,_ the case either proved reincarnation or was the product of subconscious fantasy. Few partisans realized that perhaps the case represented a mixture of both elements—a tightly woven fantasy based on crytomnesia, role-playing, _and_ paranormally acquired information.

My own view is that some process along these lines may have been at the root of the case. There seems little doubt that Mrs. Tighe was able to tap into some source of information about nineteenth-century Ireland when she assumed the trance identity of "Bridey Murphy." Barker's search in old Erin certainly verified enough of "Bridey's" claims to prove that the case contained considerable merit. On the other hand, it can't be overlooked that some of Mrs. Tighe's information was based on just the sort of material that often emerges during the spinning of an hypnotic fantasy. Some strong evidence supporting this view comes to light when we make a detailed analysis of the names she communicated while hypnotized. Just such a revealing analysis was made in 1956 by Dr. George Devereux, an ethnopsychiatrist and former faculty member at Temple University in Philadelphia. His report appeared in a little-known and unappreciated article in the summer 1956 issue of *Tomorrow* magazine. Dr. Devereux devoted the crux of his report to revealing a curious anagram in the Bridey Murphy records. With typical psychoanalytical flair, he attempted to show a connection between the names of Morey Bernstein and Brian (or Brien) McCarthy. They seem to be anagrams of each other and all the left-over letters in Bernstein's name fit perfectly into McCarthy's second name, Joseph. Even if Dr. Devereux's fit was a bit procrustean, the two names come off suspiciously equivalent. The initials are the same, and the number of letters in both of their first and last names are identical.

"... The likelihood of these similarities being due to chance is probably much smaller than the likelihood that Ruth Simmons [Virginia Tighe] having once been Bridey Murphy," Dr. Devereux concluded.

This curious anagram wasn't the only psychologically suspicious aspect of the case, according to the psychiatrist. Dr. Devereux was also able to find several other psychodynamic connections between Virginia Tighe, Bridey Murphy, and Morey Bernstein. Since these connections can only be appreciated by understanding many of the precepts of Freudian psychoanalysis, their value tends to rest on how much stock the reader places in this form of analysis. (Many psychologists and psychiatrists are inclined to place very little in it.) But the close connections between the names of Virginia Tighe's hypnotist and her past-life lover is provocative and revealing. They suggest the possibility that Mrs. Tighe somehow gained (paranormal?) access to information about nineteenth-century Ireland, which she then wove into the fabric of her psychodynamically revealing reincarnation fantasy.

In conclusion, the case of Virginia Tighe and her past-life memories as "Bridey Murphy" can actually be explained by adopting any one of a wide variety of speculations:

1. That Virginia Tighe genuinely recalled a past-life incarnation as "Bridey Murphy" and that all other suggestions are convenient and post-hoc subterfuges.

2. That the Pueblo, Colorado, housewife genuinely recalled a life in nineteenth-century County Cork but wove this information within the context of a fantasy–involvement with her hypnotist.

3. That the entire past-life memory was a fantasy based on the subject's buried memories and which evolved into a Freudian fantasy.

4. That Virginia Tighe was spinning a fantasy that she somehow fortified by drawing on clairvoyantly derived information.

Of these four very different explanations, we can probably reject only the third. Some of her information was too detailed to be the result of coincidence and too obscure to be credited even to cryptomnesia. But it is manifestly impossible to choose between the first, second and fourth lines of speculation.

The Bridey Murphy affair actually presents us with the same problem we faced when we analyzed the phenomenon of extracerebral memory. There is no doubt that something very curious lies behind the ontogenesis of the case; but it is difficult to determine just what paranormal dynamics gave rise to it. So while it would certainly be expedient to say that the case points to reincarnation, alternate explanations can account for it equally as well. These alternative theories simply can't be ignored.

In fact, some of these counter-explanations were considered even more viable than the reincarnation theory when _similar_ cases of veridical hypnotic regression cases began emerging at the beginning of the present century.

The famous case of Virginia Tighe and her life as "Bridey Murphy" was not the first such case to emerge within either psychology or psychical research. A fascinating story told by the late Sir Cyril Burt, the eminent and controversial British psychologist, from his student days at Oxford represents a case in point.

During his undergraduate years, Burt studied psychology under Professor William McDougall, one of the greatest psychologists Great Britain ever produced. Aside from his public support for the infant science of parapsychology, McDougall was also fascinated by hypnosis. Many years after his mentor's death, Burt allowed the following story to be published. It concerned some private work he and the veteran researcher had conducted at Oxford into the mysteries of hypnosis.

His most remarkable "subject" was a brilliant student of philosophy who was completely blind. One evening, under hypnosis, and speaking with an unfamiliar voice, he announced that he was the Egyptian carpenter who carved certain tablets "in the hollow tomb of the King in his Den . . . an eagle and a hand and a zigzag . . . and the God on the steps with the bright white crown . . . King of the upper and the lower world." His vivid description of the interior of the tomb was quite awe-inspiring, but seemed to savor somewhat of the imaginative fiction of those days. We were astonished, some eight or nine months later, to read a very similar account first in the newspapers and then in the publications of the Egyptian Exploration Society. At about the time of the seance, it appeared, Sir Flinders Petrie had been excavating the cenotaph of a king of the First Dynasty called Semti (c. 3200 B.C.), whose "Horus name" was Den. (A hand is the hieroglyphic for D and a horizontal zigzag the hieroglyphic for N, as carved in his cartouche. The "eagle" or rather hawk over the cartouche is the symbol of Horus, the sky-god, from whom the kings were descended. Den Semti, a great fighter and a patron of the arts, was the first to assume the title of "King of Upper and Lower Egypt.") In the tomb was a tablet representing the king dancing before Osiris (the father of Horus)—who was often entitled "the God on the steps" and was so represented, wearing his emblematic white crown. There is in the British Museum a small but very lifelike ivory figure, representing the First Dynasty king wearing a white crown, which may quite possibly date from Semti's reign.

The student himself claimed to know nothing of ancient Egypt beyond what was in the Bible; and, owing to his blindness, his reading was extremely restricted.

What is so interesting was that neither McDougall, Burt, nor Sir Flinders Petrie—who was soon recruited to help solve the mystery—*ever entertained the idea that their subject was reliving a past-life.* They preferred to believe that they were dealing with a case of either spirit communication, telepathy, or clairvoyance. Burt noted that the archaeologist "wholly rejected the notion that *he* might have communicated the information by telepathy to an unknown recipient in Oxford." He preferred to believe that a normal explanation for the mystery would ultimately be found. Burt and McDougall first opted for some sort of telepathic explanation before they later became discouraged by some of the discrepancies in the subject's account.

This provocative and little-known story demonstrates how any case of past-life regression can be explained by a great number of different and mutually exclusive theories. Merely assuming that even veridical cases necessarily point to reincarnation would be naive. The case also demonstrates the fallacy behind the claim, echoed by Drs. Zusne and Jones, that only hypnotists who believe in reincarnation come across such material. Past-life revivications, whatever their source might be, sometimes emerge spontaneously during the process of hypnosis. The crucial issue is whether reincarnation can explain such cases better then any other explanation. This is a tricky area of study and there are actually two ways by which it can be approached. The first is rather obvious. Can any clues be found within the cases themselves that indisputably point to reincarnation? But there is also another way of pursuing the problem, concerning the nature of hypnotic regression itself, that has often been ignored by writers and students of the rebirth question. If it can be demonstrated that hypnotic age-regression is a genuine method of tracing the past, this would indicate that past-life memories could be genuine revivications and not simple confabulations.* If, on the other hand, the evidence suggests the age-regression is the result of hypnotic role-playing, cases of past-life regression would also probably be best explained as the result of fantasy. So at this point, let's turn our attention away from the reincarnation question and explore the nature of hypnosis.

The whole area of hypnosis is controversial even within conventional psychology, and there are many schools of thought about the nature of this curious state of consciousness. The most important thing to remember is that hypnosis is not an objectively discrete level of consciousness. Unlike normal waking and sleeping, no brain-wave pattern or other psychophysiological con-

---

*The term "age-regression" used in this context refers to taking a subject back to a time in his or her *present* life.

comitants habitually accompany the state. We can't hook up someone to a polygraph and unerringly determine whether he or she is genuinely "hypnotized." The experience of hypnosis is primarily subjective and unique to each individual who undergoes it. If you and your best friend were hypnotized by the same practitioner using the same induction technique, each of you would probably enter a different state of consciousness. Some people don't respond to hypnosis at all, while others simply become very relaxed as they follow the instructions suggested to them by the practitioner. A few subjects apparently become genuinely entranced. Every individual who undergoes the process reaches his optimal level of hypnosis, which is why trying to say anything concrete or universal about the state is virtually impossible. In short, the state of mind contacted during the process of hypnosis represents one of psychology's biggest mysteries.

Even the existence of a genuine hypnotic trance has become a matter of debate. Some researchers believe that good hypnotic subjects genuinely enter a subjectively discrete altered state of consciousness. This is a state in which the subject yields his or her normal experience of the world and becomes enmeshed into the innerworld suggested by the hypnotist. This approach to the interpretation of hypnosis has been hotly contested by other researchers, however. Some psychologists argue that hypnosis is only a convenient ploy some people can use to engage in vivid role-playing. They believe that good hypnotic subjects are simply people who can willfully engage in fantasy, and that no true hypnotic trance actually exists. My own feeling is that possibly both of these responses to the induction of hypnosis exist, depending on the individual subject or subjects.

Whether a hypnotist can actually regress a subject back to his or her childhood has also prompted a considerable amount of debate among the experts. Certain authorities believe that a good hypnotic subject can literally "relive" episodes from his or her own early life after being regressed. Other authorities adamantly deny this possibility. They choose to believe that the subjects are only play-acting on the basis of their conscious memories, perhaps abetted by some newly recollected information. A center line between these two extremes has been adopted by R. Reiff and M. Scherer in their authoritative _Memory and Hypnotic Age Regression: Developmental Aspects of Cognitive Functions Explored through Hypnosis._ Their view is that while the revivication of early childhood memories will sometimes be accurate, regressed subjects usually use these memories as a backdrop only. They do not actually relive the past. The two experts argue further that "the revival of earlier functions is often incomplete or contaminated with functions of age levels other than those to which the subject is regressed." Even Dr. Ernest Hilgard, a psychologist at Stanford University who firmly believes in the existence of the hypnotic trance, agrees with these assertions. He has written that "the notion that regression is a complete revivication of an earlier experience, and shows an 'ablation' of all subsequent memories, is too extreme to be supported by acceptable studies."

On the other hand, Dr. Hilgard admits that age-regression is something more than simple role-playing. Studies were once conducted at his laboratory during which students were asked to play-act as though they were children, and their performances were then compared to subjects who were genuinely responding to hypnotic regression. Dr. Hilgard's colleagues found that both groups behaved similarly, but that their subjective experiences were different. It seems that the role-playing subjects usually behaved like children but maintained the thought processes of an adult. They didn't *experience* themselves as children, which was exactly the response of the regressed subjects. This was not a hard and fast rule, though. Dr. Hilgard had to admit that "some subjects within the simulating group reported . . . that they became so involved in their acting that they lost awareness of their adult age and felt as though they were children." This led him to suggest that perhaps these subjects accidentally drifted into hypnosis, which begs the whole question of just what hypnosis represents in the first place.

Despite these cautious opinions, some experts on hypnosis believe that in some rare instances, a subject may actually relive his past during the process of regression. Dr. Hilgard discovered two subjects during the days of his Stanford University research who recalled languages they had spoken as young children. They couldn't recall the languages during their normal waking hours. Even back in 1945, one enterprising psychiatrist tried regressing a former epileptic back to his childhood. The subject was being monitored by a polygraph and his brainwaves began producing abnormal spikes typical of epilepsy when the relevant years were invoked. Other researchers have taken their subjects back to infancy and have been able to invoke the Babinski reflex—a dorsiflexion of the big toe and fanning of the others when the foot is stimulated. (This reflex is commonly seen in babies but disappears by the fourth month.) This was an astounding finding since this reflex cannot be simulated willfully. Because of these various findings, even the die-hard skeptics Leonard Zusne and Warren Jones admit that age-regression " . . . is an actual regression, even though it is not a stable or permanent phenomenon. There are fluctuations between regressed and nonregressed states of the subject."

Even though some subjects will behave as though they are reliving the past during the process of regression, it is another matter entirely whether they can actually *remember* anything concrete from earlier periods in their lives. Findings along these lines have been rather contradictory, and even Dr. Hilgard found that his two subjects who remembered their "lost" childhood languages recalled them imperfectly. One approach to the problem has been to take hypnotic subjects back to their past birthdays, and ask them to specify the days of the week on which they occurred. These experiments have sometimes proved very successful, but they have not always been replicated on demand. This probably does not mean that the age-regression effect is bogus. The sporadic results of this simple experiment are probably telling us something that should be obvious by now. Each individual tends to respond to hypnosis in his own way, and a group of subjects may all respond to a specific hypnotic task very differently. Obtaining a 100 percent consistent effect while working with large groups of subjects is probably impossible. Despite this simple fact, there is considerable anecdotal, informational, and physiological evidence that sometime hypnotic age-regression entails a literal trip to the past. For some subjects it is more than mere role-playing and becomes a genuine re-experiencing of their pasts. This conclusion has an obvious bearing on the nature of past-life regression; for if one can trace a subject's past through hypnosis, there seems no _a priori_ reason that regression could not be used to trace past lives as well.*

Over the past several years, a number of fascinating past-life recall cases have been placed in the literature by hypnotists interested in reincarnation. In light of the above discussion, these cases deserve to be studied in greater depth than most students of the psychic field have been willing to yield.

In the pages that follow, six cases of hypnotically evoked past-life recall will be presented. Three cases have been chosen because they represent some of the most challenging and evidential material I have been able to find. Four of them will be taken from the published literature on reincarnation, while the others will be drawn from my own files. (One of these was subsequently published as a magazine article in a short-lived "new-age" publication.)

Doris Williams and Her Past-Life Death Aboard the Titanic

This case is notable because of the amount of detailed information the subject communicated within the context of only two sessions. I first heard about the case when Zelda Suplee, the hypnotist who first began publicizing it, told a group of us about her findings at a meeting of the Southern California Society for Psychical Research. Mrs. Suplee is an amateur psychic investigator with a zeal for hypnosis research. She spent many diligent hours documenting the following case before she brought it to public attention.

The subject of the investigation was Doris Williams, an elderly but active woman who works as a registered nurse. Originally from Ohio, Mrs. Williams moved to California in 1955. Although the subject has been described as "feisty and perky," for most of her life she suffered from a major problem: a terrible fear of deep water, ocean voyages, and small boats. When she once tried to enjoy a Hawaiian cruise, she suffered such unbearable anxiety that she actually became ill. Mrs. Williams learned more about her problem in 1960

---

*There is some evidence that regressed subjects can correctly describe the delivery rooms in which they were born and even their own position at birth. For more information on this finding, see _The Secret Life of the Unborn Child_ by Thomas Verny and John Kelly. (New York: Simon and Schuster, 1981).

when she visited a psychic in Venice, a picturesque Los Angeles community located on the ocean near Santa Monica. The psychic conducted an initial hypnotic session with her, during which she found herself aboard the ill-fated *Titanic*. The date was sometime in April 1912. She offered her name as "Blackwell and later expanded this to "Stephen Weart Blackwell." Mrs. Williams didn't take the session too seriously and at first believed that the whole story was a subconscious fantasy suggested by the nature of her phobia. The psychic responded by suggesting that the puzzled woman check out the possible accuracy of the name. A visit to the public library resulted in the discovery that a Stephen Weart Blackwell was listed as a passenger aboard the *Titanic* by Walter Lord in his famous book *A Night to Remember*. Mrs. Williams was shocked by the discovery since she had never seriously entertained the idea of reincarnation before.

Several months passed before Mrs. Williams decided to explore her memories any further. Her interest was kindled when she became friendly with Ms. Suplee, who is a charter member of the Association for Past-Life Research and Therapy, headquartered in Riverside, California. A follow-up session was held at Ms. Suplee's Hollywood home. The regression began as Mrs. Williams recalled (as "Blackwell") working in an office with transport bills and shipping requests at the Brown Shipping Company, located at 167 West State Street in Trenton, New Jersey. Even though she was under hypnosis, Ms. Williams could talk freely and without much of the labor many subjects have to overcome.

"I am forty-three, married," she said as she assumed her past-life identity. "My father was a farmer who brought the family to the United States when I was very young, to New Jersey, near Trenton. I wanted to go to medical school, but my mother wanted me to marry and settle down. I made frequent trips to England, as business required it."

Later in the session, the subject began talking about "his" uneasiness aboard the *Titanic*. "Stephen Blackwell" recalled that his cabin was toward the front left side, and reliving the disaster that sank the ship didn't cause him much anxiety. "There was a lot of noise," he explained. "I joined the people fully dressed in dark clothes, a dark hat, a cape draped about me, holding gloves. I went on top deck facing the front of the ship, water to my left, center of ship to my right, almost halfway to the middle of the ship which was listing. I watched lifeboats being lowered. There was lot of crying, music—religious music." The regression was obviously not complete, since Mrs. Williams tended to speak about her memories more than actually reliving them.

Mrs. Williams emerged from the hypnosis claiming that her hands hurt, an apparent carry-over (?) from her drowning experience.

These revelations did not cure Mrs. Williams' mental problems, and she remained uneasy about sea travel for some time even after this second regression. However, she began to feel more comfortable about the possibility that she was the reincarnation of a *Titanic* victim. She even attended the "Fifth Annual *Titanic* Tonite" anniversary at the Los Angeles Biltmore Hotel, where she was programmed to speak about her possible past life. But she was too unnerved by the atmosphere of the occasion to go on with the talk, and she was sick afterward for three days. Despite her strong emotional response to her past-life memories, her fear of ships finally began to lift, and three years later, she was able to enjoy yachting for the first time.

In the meantime, Ms. Suplee was busy trying to track down any information that might shed added light on her subject's memories. She consulted first with the president of the Oceanic Navigation and Research Society, who dug out an old copy of the U.S. Senate's investigative report on the disaster. Stephen Weart Blackwell was mentioned among the victims, and the listing also gave his address and mentioned his employment with the Brown *Shipley* Company in Trenton. This turned out to be the British representative of his American company. This information, correctly given by Mrs. Williams, was not included in any book Ms. Suplee could find on the *Titanic*. She also learned that Blackwell had been returning on the ship after a business trip to Europe. He was forty-three at the time of his death.

Doris Williams today is a very active seventy-year-old and teaches reflexology (a form of foot massage) in Los Angeles. She has no desire to explore her past-life memories any further.

Jane Evans and the Massacre of the Jews in Twelfth-Century York

This case was originally placed in the literature by the late Arnall Bloxham, a talented British hypnotherapist and a recognized authority on past-life regression. He was a careful and critical researcher, whose original interest in hypnosis had been an outgrowth of his plans for a career in medicine. The outbreak of the First World War put a damper on his plans, but did not interfere with his interest in the challenge of psychosomatic problems and the way hypnosis could help in their treatment. He began conducting his experiments in past-life regression in 1940 and continued on with them until his death. He was well thought of by his colleagues, who elected him president of the British Society of Hypnotherapists in 1972. Bloxham conducted his practice from his home in Cardiff, South Wales, and worked fairly quietly until the BBC became interested in his work. Jeffrey Iverson, who ended up writing a book about Bloxham's research, was sent by the BBC to investigate his work. His independent research threw added light on many of the hypnotist's cases.

Bloxham's best subject was Jane Evans, an otherwise normal young housewife from Wales. She originally met Bloxham while searching for a hypnotists who could treat her rheumatism. She ended up being recruited for a series of regression experiments even though she was not predisposed to any belief in reincarnation. During the course of several sessions, she recalled a total of seven lives. Her most astounding was as a young Jewish mother in twelfth-century York. Her memories of this life were very detailed and surprising because she was able to describe the political situation that led to the horrible massacre of the Jews in York in 1190. Not only were her observations correct, but some of the specific information she recalled was also accurate. She especially recalled how, as a Jew, she had to wear a badge signifying her religion. This at first seemed an anachronism, because Church authorities in Rome decreed that Jews in Christian countries had to wear these insignias only in 1215. Subsequent research undertaken by Iverson revealed that the practice was widespread in England, however, before the proclamation. Jane Evans also recalled the religious practices of the twelfth-century British Jews and even discussed the money-lending trades common among the Jewish communities in York and nearby Lincoln. The culmination of the regression came when Jane relived the York massacre, which resulted when the Christian populace— fired by rumor, distrust, and anti-Semitism—rose up and killed every Jew they could find. Bands of marauders took advantage of the chaos, and Jane Evans decribed how they broke into Jewish homes to kill and loot. The terror was so ghastly that Ms. Evans even correctly recalled that some of the Jews killed their own children rather than allowing the gentiles to massacre them.

Jane recalled hiding in a church in York, where she and her children sought safety in a crypt. Her flight was useless, she explained, for she was discovered and killed along with her young family.

This scenario may sound a bit like a rather banal and two-dimensional rehash of a book or historical novel she may once have read. Unfortunately, the foregoing brief summary can't do justice to her recollections with all their conciseness, accuracy, and drama. Jeffrey Iverson was so impressed by them that he contacted Professor Barrie Dobson, an authority on Jewish history at York University, to see how he would respond to the tapes of the sessions. Dobson too, was markedly impressed. He pointed out that some of Jane Evans' memories of the massacre were technically inaccurate but consistent with what the Jews of the day believed about the incident. During her description of the massacre, for instance, Jane talked about the soldiers who carried out the murders. According to historical fact, the massacre was never sanctioned by the British government, but England's Jewish population believed at the time that the king was behind the plot. This point suggests that Jane Evans was not basing her memories on something she had read but was actually reliving her past-life death as a York Jew. Dobson was, however, even more impressed by the sheer accuracy of Ms. Evans' recollections, since he felt that some of her information would be known only to professional historians.

The only puzzling feature of the case was Ms. Evans' description of the crypt in which she and her children hid. The churches of that era were not designed with crypts, so this element of her story sounded like a dramatization right out of her subconscious mind. On the basis of her detailed account of the site, however, Dobson was able to identify the church as St. Mary's in

Castlegate. The church is standing today. Dobson and Iverson were still curious about the mysterious crypt when new information about its possible existence came to light. This new discovery came six months after Dobson had been brought in on the case. St. Mary's was being renovated at the time, and Dobson was following the project. He was able to inform Iverson that: "During the renovation of the church, a workman found something that seemed to have been a crypt—very rare in York. . . . It was blocked up immediately and before the York archaeologists could investigate it properly.'

On the basis of the description given by the workman, Dobson was able to determine that the architecture of the crypt was either Norman or Romanesque, which predated 1190.

Iverson became more interested in the Jane Evans case the more he dug into it. What he found so remarkable was that the best known historical aspects of the York massacre were bypassed in her recollections; her accounts tended to focus on more obscure points of information. For example, it was well known that the Jews in York were offered safe conduct before they were brutally killed, yet this episode was never remembered by Ms. Evans. On the other hand, her revivications focused on the rather obscure business connections between various Jewish communities in England at the time. Iverson therefore argues that her past-life story was "not a straightforward re-working of history book versions of the massacre." He adds that, "If we view her regression as a fantasy based on a reading of history books, it is perhaps strange that she should have omitted to fantasize about the best-known features of most textbook versions of the massacre."

Ann Dowling and her Past Life in the Slums of Liverpool

Another hypnotherapist who has studied the reincarnation question is Joe Keeton, a highly skilled practitioner who lives on the Wirral Peninsula of the British Isles. Keeton is an intriguing figure since he personally has no vested interest in reincarnation. He tends to believe that the results he has achieved with hypnotic regression are due in most cases to some sort of genetic memory. Nevertheless, the somewhat ominous looking and bearded hypnotist judges each case on its own merits. He believes that a few of his cases point to fantasy, others to some sort of rebirth, and yet others to telepathy. He points to the case of forty-seven-year-old Ann Dowling as the one that best suggests reincarnation.

Ann Dowling is today a working-class housewife from Huyton who has undergone more than sixty hours of regression at the hands of Keeton. Her past-life identity as "Sarah Williams," an orphan who lived in the slums of Liverpool in the early nineteenth century, emerged during their first session. Her regressions have been replete with considerable historical data, as well as information and insights about the grueling existence of the poor at that time. Peter Moss, a British broadcaster who collaborated with Keeton on a book concerning his work, once remarked that through "Sarah" and her memories, "we can really feel the bigotry, the folk-feeling of the gutter, and the animal-like acceptance of unbelievable conditions of hunger, cold, and misery of the poorest level of industrial revolution society."

Ms. Dowling first consulted Keeton because of two recurring nightmares that were plaguing her. The dreams usually followed a prescribed order. She would first find herself sitting alone in a empty room enveloped by terrifying anxiety; then the scene would shift to a sleazy basement where a stranger was brandishing a knife in front of her. Being subjected to these dreams caused Ms. Dowling to feel uneasy all the following day.

During her first regression session, Ms. Dowling translated these dreams into literal memories of a past-life. She found herself in the basement of a house in some undefined place called Chaucer Road. When the hypnotist moved her ahead five years in time, she recalled being beaten in the bare room of her other nightmare. After reliving these two traumatic episodes from her puported life, Ms. Dowling gradually filled in—under Keeton's gentle guidance—the chronology of her life.

She described being a five-year-old girl who lived in Liverpool with her father in the 1830s. She lived in a tiny house hidden within a labyrinth of streets near the harbor. Her father was a dock worker and was her only parent since her mother was dead. These revelations weren't extraordinary, but Keeton believed that somewhere buried in them was the clue to her nightmare about being assaulted. The session continued as Ms. Dowling recalled learning about her father's death and recreated the pathetic scene when her own neighbors robbed their house of its few possessions. Ms. Dowling then recounted how she was taken to an orphanage or "home" of some kind by her father's employer, from which she later escaped. Becoming a street urchin was her only alternative, and many of the subsequent regression sessions dealt with her life in the slums. Her only friends, she recalled, were a Mr. and Mrs. Roper who allowed her to sleep in their lobby and offered her spare food and clothing. Some years later when she was a teenager, "Sarah" found another protector in a Jewish slum-lord and opportunist named Eric Wiseman (or Weitzman). He allowed her to live in the basement in one of his buildings, which she cleaned in payment. She was given no other remuneration for her work. There she died miserably at the age of twenty when she was attacked in her makeshift home. Ms. Dowling was even able to recall the address where she lived and listed it as 57 Shaw Street.

Some of this material began making considerable historical sense when Keeton learned later that such an address actually existed in Liverpool, where a Swiss merchant had lived in 1843. The names didn't jibe, but the address was at least genuine.

Joe Keeton and Peter Moss believe that the importance of the Ann

Dowling case lies not only in the historical accuracy of her memories but their coherence and consistency. Street life in the nineteenth century with its degradations and dangers is not the type of material a modern housewife is likely to know anything about, except for a few plots drawn from Charles Dickens. Yet these are just the details Ann Dowling usually recalled during her regressions. It is also interesting that although the subject was raised as a Catholic, she turned against the Church and had a very Protestant perspective during her trances.

But the real key to the case rests on the accuracy of the many names Ms. Dowling was able to communicate. She was not familiar with Liverpool when the experiments were undertaken, although she knew the names of some of the city's main streets. She had never lived there and had never studied its history. This proved no obstacle to little "Sarah Williams," whose humorous gutter-talk about street life bore out upon investigation. Chaucer Street in the Liverpool of today is largely occupied by warehouses, but in the mid-nineteenth century it was a residential slum area. During one of her regressions, Ms. Dowling also described a druggist's shop called "Sampson's." Keeton and Moss were able to locate a street directory from nineteenth-century Liverpool that proved that a John and James Sampson ran such a business near Chaucer Street in 1848. "It seems almost impossible that Ann Dowling could possibly have unearthed the name of this long-vanished business," Keeton and Moss explain in their engrossing _Encounters with the Past_, "but it is typical of the obscure flashes that keep turning up throughout the regressions."

Another one of these juicy tidbits concerned "Sarah's" memory of the various foreign or celebrated visitors to Liverpool. She described one as "... supposed to be a prince .... but 'is dad's _not_ a king." This memory dated from the 1840s. Research undertaken by Keeton and Moss eventually revealed that in March 1846, the Prince d'Musignara—a nephew of the Emperor Napoleon—traveled through Liverpool on his way to France and Italy from the United States. Ms. Dowling also recalled a visit by Prince Albert and explained that he stayed with a judge. This was an obvious allusion to a trip the nobleman made in 1846 when he stayed in Liverpool at the lodgings of Judge William Wharton, who lived near the neighborhood whose streets "Sarah" roamed. Among her other memories were correct details concerning the introduction of gas lighting into the city.

An even more curious reference came during one session when Ann Dowling as "Sarah" was asked by the hypnotist to go back to any year and explain what was happening in Liverpool at the time. Her bizarre response was that, "They've taken our time away, they've stole some of our minutes." This was a rather incomprehensible response until Keeton and Moss discovered that it probably referred to a curious incident in the 1850s, when it was discovered that Liverpool was not correctly synchronized with Greenwich Mean Time. There was some speculation that the discrepancy might throw off ship schedules.

Certain people tended to crop up in Ms. Dowling's accounts as well. Because she lived on the streets, little "Sarah" was familiar with the local police. She specifically mentioned a fat bobby named Bobby Edwards, who seemed to tolerate her presence on the streets good-naturedly enough. "Sarah" especially mentioned that his partner, P. C. Brownlow, was less concerned about the plight of Liverpool's street urchins.

What is so strange about these names and memories is how their accuracy is compromised by curious but directly pertinent inaccuracies. Keeton and Moss were unable to find any records of a Bobby Edwards who worked at the Rosehill Police station, which had jurisdiction over the Chaucer Street slums. Their subsequent search, however, uncovered the pertinent fact that a John Edwards had been an inspector with that station and had lived on Brownlow *Terrace*. These coincidences certainly seem evidential. The fact that "Sarah" got Edward's name (apparently) wrong is not a serious problem, because her allusion to him as "Bobby" could have been a reference to his occupation. But why did she take the curious name "Brownlow" and change it from a street into a person?

This odd juxtaposition suggests that Ann Dowling may have been tapping into a source of information about nineteenth-century Liverpool, while not actually reliving her memories of the city. This is a possibility that we will be exploring in the next chapter.

Many of "Sarah Williams'" recollections about Wiseman, the slum lord who exploited her impoverished existence, also contained bits and pieces of accurate information. These invariably focused on the ways of the Liverpool Jews of the 1850s. Wiseman played a prominent role in little "Sarah's" memories, and she described his religious observances and idiosyncracies several times during her regressions. Much of this material was essentially unverifiable, but during one session Keeton specifically quizzed her about the man. She, in turn, described the synagogue in which he worshipped by remembering that it was located at a place called "Hope." Two of his friends were named "Isaacs" and "Epstein," she added, explaining that the former was a furniture maker.

All these scattered allusions began to jell when Keeton and Moss checked into Liverpool's history. They learned that a synagogue had been founded at Hope Place, a location relatively close to "Sarah's" purported neighborhood, in 1836. It was run by two Jews, and one of them, a cabinet maker or joiner, was named R. D. Meyer Isaacs.

It should be pointed out that these various details of nineteenth-century Liverpool life were not offered piecemeal by Ann Dowling. They emerged within the context of her vivid and detailed description of her previous life in the slums. The various names and locations discussed above cropped up within the account almost off-handedly: they constituted little more than casual references "Sarah Williams" made while talking about her wretched existence. It is, therefore, no wonder that Keeton and Moss argue that "there seems no physical way in which Ann could have collected the factual material which comprised her story." They also point out that this material should only be considered secondary to the grimly colorful and consistent view she communicated about an age, thankfully now passed, spanning more than twenty years of Liverpool history. They also note that the sessions vanquished Ms. Dowling's recurrent nightmares permanently.

Jane Doe and Her Life in Sixteenth-Century Spain

Our fourth case has only recently been placed in the literature, and in many respects it is the most impressive of the six currently under discussion. It was reported by Dr. Linda Tarazi. Dr. Tarazi, a clinical psychologist currently in private practice in Glenview, Illinois, took her B.S. and M.S. at Northwestern University before finishing her doctorate at the Illinois Institute of Technology. Because she long nurtured a considerable interest in hypnosis, her interest in past-life regression was easily primed—it was an area of study to which she was exposed through her readings in parapsychology. It is unfortunate, however, that we actually know more about Dr. Tarazi than we do about her "star" subject, whose anonymity has been preserved by the use of a pseudonym. The case was originally reported to _Fate_ magazine by Dr. Tarazi, who privately provided the editors with the true name of her subject. But this report was only a summary of the records and was obviously based on an enormous amount of field work into information spread over several regression sessions.

Jane Doe first met Dr. Tarazi in the 1970s, when she approached the psychologist with the idea of undergoing past-life regression. Dr. Tarazi has not explained just why the subject felt that such treatment was necessary. The subject had undergone hypnotic regression before, so the seeds of her past-life memories were already being sowed by the time she started working with the psychologist in Illinois.

The actual progression of Jane Doe's past-life story is a bit more complex than we saw in the previous examples, because the story emerged in bits and pieces over the course of several sessions. During these sessions she remembered snatches of several past lives. Despite the fact that her past-life memories kept wandering, the subject continually focused on sixteenth-century Spain, where she recalled living as Antonia Ruiz de Prado. At this point Dr. Tarazi began concentrating her own interest.

The story Jane Doe told about her past life in Spain was colorful, but at first the final version did not appear to be evidential. She claimed that she had been born as Antonia Micaela Ruiz de Prado on 15 November 1555 as the only child of a Spanish military officer and his German-born wife. Her place of birth was (allegedly) their plantation on Hispaniola, an island in the West Indies. With her father away for extended periods of time, "Antonia" eventually traveled to Germany with her mother, who died tragically soon after. Jane or

"Antonia," as the story proceeded, then went to live with her uncle, who was an academician who took the girl along with him as he took up teaching posts at universities in Germany, what is now Czechoslovakia, and England. It was during these travels that the young girl first found herself in the grip of severe religious conflicts that served as the focal point of the past-life: her spiritual kinship was with the Catholic church of her father, but she couldn't help but be influenced by her uncle's free-thinking Protestant sentiments. Her uncle also instilled in her a fierce appetite for learning, and she even disguised herself as a man to attend classes at the colleges where he taught. Jane Doe's story became even more melodramatic when she claimed that, while at Oxford, she involved herself in the Catholic cause—an unpopular issue there because by that time Catholicism had been outlawed by the state. Jane (always appeaking as "Antonia") yearned to return to Spain, but even this move was fraught with difficulties. Her uncle feared that she had been too exposed to Protestant ideas to safely return there and to the ever-present eyes of the Inquisition.

Jane explained to Dr. Tarazi that Antonia was finally able to return to Spain when her father retired from military duty. Her life, and the story, was not to end on such a happy note, however. The free-spirited woman returned to Cuenca, Spain, only to learn that her father had died ten days before. Her only legacy was a heavily mortgaged inn, and—as her uncle foretold—she was twice brought before the tribunal of the Inquisition to undergo grueling questioning.

This story is, in itself, not exceptional. Even Dr. Tarazi initially throught that it was "interesting and romantic but it was not unduly impressive." She also noted that much of the information proffered during the hypnotic sessions could be found "in a good history book or encyclopedia." Her initial diagnosis was, in fact, that the story was based on some historical material the subject had once read. But Dr. Tarazi decided to delve into the case a little further, anyway. Between the mid-1970s and 1983 she found herself devoting more and more time to what would eventually prove an exciting and befuddling case.

The psychologist's first discovery was that many of the names, dates, and places listed or named by her subject could not have been lifted from any source of information readily available to her. While some of the names given during the sessions designated well-known historical figures, others were more puzzling. During her Oxford years, for instance, "Antonia" talked about a Jesuit priest named Thomas Cottam. After an extensive search, Dr. Tarazi actually found him listed in the *Catholic Encyclopedia*. Dr. Tarazi was also amazed that her subject could recite Catholic prayers in Latin while hypnotized, even though she was not Catholic and had not studied language, history, or religion in high school or college. Even today's Catholics don't learn these prayers in Latin anymore, the psychologist noted. Evidence such as this led the researcher to extend her search for the historical Antonia de Prado, which would eventually take her from achives here in the United States across the ocean to Spain. The pieces of the puzzle all began fitting together like clockwork the more she searched, and the result was more than impressive.

The first step in Dr. Tarazi's search was to verify that a college was once founded in Cuenca. Her subject had often talked of the college, even though no contemporary source of the information she consulted mentioned any such institution. Dr. Tarazi was finally able to verify this information when she consulted a seven-volume study in Spanish, _Historia de la Compania de Jesus en la Asistencia de Espana,_ which makes two brief mentions of a college in Cuenca founded in the 1550s.

Even more impressive, however, was Dr. Tarazi's attempt to locate the Inquisition building that played such a prominent role in some of "Antonia's" memories. She traveled to Cuenca in the summer of 1983 and, with the assistance of a local tourist agency, was able to find the notorious structure. She photographed it and then brought the prints back to Illinois where she showed them to Jane. Dr. Tarazi was surprised when her subject firmly claimed that this building was not the one she recalled from her past-life. This all seemed puzzling until the psychologist did some further checking and found that the headquarters for the Inquisition in Cuenca had been changed in 1583. She only found out this information by consulting yet another Spanish source, _Memorias Historicas de Cuenca y sur Obispado._

Despite these impressive aspects of the case, the crucial feature of Jane Doe's past-life recollections concerned the people she knew and named from sixteenth-century Spain. These included those of the local bishop, the chief magistrate of Cuenca, and one of the inquisitors. These names could not be verified in any book to be found in the United States, but Dr. Tarazi eventually found them in the municipal and Diocesan archives in Cuenca. Further checks into some historical archives housed at Loyola University in Chicago even verified the names "Antonia" had given for some of her fellow prisoners of the Inquisition.

If all this weren't enough, some of the more unlikely elements of Jane Doe's past-life romance also turned out to be true. The subject's past-life revivications were detailed and complex, and even Dr. Tarazi admits in her _Fate_ article that several aspects of the whole story could not be told because of space limitations. But one subplot concerned "Antonia's" uncle, Juan Ruiz de Prado, who was allegedly sent to Peru in 1587 by Spanish authorities to check on the activities of the Inquisition there. This sidelight to the Antonia story sounded just like something out of an historical romance, in which all-too-typical forays into exotic locales and adventurous heroes so often abound. Only long after this story was told did Dr. Tarazi locate a book in the archives of Northwestern University published in 1887 that talked about Juan Ruiz de Prado and his mission to the New World. This work, _Historia de Tribunal del Santo Oficio de la Inquisicion de Lima,_ was literally falling apart when the psychologist found it. It had obviously not been consulted for years by anyone.

To date, this is where this fascinating case rests. Followers of the case hope Dr. Tarazi will eventually publish a more detailed account of her research, complete with transcripts of the regressions and further bibliographic references to the documents validating them. Despite the fact that this case has not been reported as thoroughly as we might hope, it is difficult to disagree with Dr. Tarazi's verdict that "something paranormal" was involved in it. The fact that the subject speaks no Spanish and has not traveled in Europe makes the case doubly impressive. It should also be noted that, were the case the result of an elaborate charade, it seems logical that Jane Doe would want to bask in the limelight. She has instead decided to hide in the shadows of anonymity.

Charles Roberts and His Past Life in Northampton and London

Sometimes the memories that emerge during a regression session are somewhat confused or entail curious inaccuracies. This next case is drawn from my own files and has not been published in the literature. The chief value of the report lies in the fact that the physician who unearthed the evidence gave me access to many of the original records detailing it. While the solution to this case is not as definitive as we find in the prior cases, it includes so many provocative features that it deserves to be summarized.

The case emerged from the files of Dr. Eugene Jussek, a general practitioner who works in the fashionable Los Angeles suburb of Sherman Oaks, California. Dr. Jussek is German-born and his medical education is conventional and impeccable. He is an attending physician at St. Joseph's Medical Center in Burbank and the flight surgeon for Lufthansa German Airlines. Despite his formidable credentials, Dr. Jussek turned away from traditional medicine some years ago when he became interested in holistic health. This interest in (then) avant-garde medicine led him to employ acupuncture and hypnosis in his practice.

Dr. Jussek first met Charles Roberts* in the fall of 1977, when their two wives bumped into each other while browsing in a Los Angeles bookstore. Mrs. Jussek was talking to some of the customers about hypnosis when one of them suggested that her husband might benefit from such treatment. His problem was not a physical but mental one, she went on to explain, because he was plagued by enigmatic episodes of aggressive behavior. Mrs. Jussek suggested that her husband might be able to help resolve the problem, and the physician agreed to see him. Charles Roberts turned out to be thirty-nine years old and the father of an eight-year-old girl. He grew up in Los Angeles and attended high school and junior college, where he studied to become an electronics engineer. He eventually gave up his plan and decided to study singing and music but later took a job with a brewery in Los Angeles. He traveled to Europe once in 1974 but did not visit England. This is a critical point because England was to be the setting for some of his past-life memories.

---

*This is a pseudonym adopted to protect the subject's privacy, though I have been privy to his real identity.

Dr. Jussek attempted to regress Roberts during their first visit together. The new client turned out to be such an exemplary subject that the doctor undertook several additional past-life regressions beginning in July 1977. These sessions resulted in the revivication of several of Charles Roberts' past lives—as a banker in nineteenth-century England, as an angry Irish rebel soldier in the eighteenth-century, as a teenage Mexican girl, as a medieval Chinese man, as a German father, as a Roman soldier, and a last (and rather dubious) one on the (no doubt fictional) "lost" continent of Atlantis.

It is impossible to determine how much fact, fiction, or fantasy went into the construction of these lives; but Charles Roberts' life as a banker in England is perhaps the most interesting and potentially veridical of the series.

Roberts' past-life memories in nineteenth-century England first surfaced during a regression session conducted on 29 November 1977. The following story evolved from the first session:

Charles Roberts recalled his past-life as "James Edward Stewart," a banker who lived at 17 Yorkshire Road in Northampton. He recalled that he was born in 1801 and that his parents were William E. and Mary Stewart. He also recalled that his mother's doctor was a Dr. Williamson. His father owned a bank. "James Stewart" recollected going to school at a place called Creighton and also to a "Draidon" school, which was located towards the outskirts of town. The story continued to unfold as "Stewart" explained about a trip he took to London, a three-day journey from his home, when he was seventeen. He stayed at the Wayside Inn while en route and at the All Man's Club in London, where his father was a member. There was a little confusion over the name of this club, and "Stewart" later referred to it as the London Club.

The trip to London contained its share of bawdy pleasures, and the next pertinent information was evoked when Dr. Jussek asked the subject about his father's business. The young "James Stewart" recalled that it was located on Canterby or Canterbury Street in Northampton, and he also admitted working there as an assistant teller. His dislike for banking eventually took its toll, and "Stewart" told of moving back to London to his father's displeasure. But to his dismay, he had to return home to take over the bank when his father died. "I have no use for that type of life. I have hired an employee to oversee the bank's workings," he added.

More details about the conventional life of "James Stewart" came later in the session when Dr. Jussek advanced him to the age of forty. "James Stewart" announced that he was still unmarried. Further probing elicited the information that "Stewart" died in 1861 from what seemed to be pneumonia. He was attended by a Dr. Levitt or Lavitt and was buried in St. James Church, Northampton.

The transcript of this single session was replete with an enormous amount of checkable information. Since Dr. Jussek has close ties in Germany, he decided to use his next trip to Europe to investigate his subject's claims. The results of the search constituted a curious mixture of success and failure. The physician was able to uncover enough information to prove that his subject was familiar with nineteenth-century Northampton; but he was not able to document the literal existence of "James Stewart" in England.

Northampton is a cattle and leather town, whose outlying areas revolve around an industrialized center. Dr. Jussek, his wife, and his daughter visited London first, where they learned through historical documents that at least there really *was* a St. James Church in Northampton. This information encouraged them to visit the town in the hope that further documentation would be available concerning "James Stewart's" life. The church was their first stop after they set up headquarters in town, but it turned out to be a relatively modern structure no more than one hundred years old. So the Jusseks next decided to check the records of the local mortuary. There they discovered that any one who died in the parish was actually buried at another church, St. Giles, since St. James didn't have a cemetery of its own.

The intrepid team of investigators immediately checked at the cemetery but found that many of the gravestones had been removed. The church was closed. "We set out to find York Road," Dr. Jussek writes, "and indeed discovered that it was just around the corner from St. Giles, just as Charles had told us his home had been. The houses on the street were very old, some of them old enough to have been Charles's. We felt that this had once been part of the well-to-do neighborhood of old Northampton. Although the area around Number 17 had been torn down and replaced by brick buildings, the surroundings houses were a type described during our hypnosis sessions."

The Jusseks believed that they were finally on the right track, but a disappointing visit to the Town Hall revealed that the town records didn't go back more than fifty years. This made it impossible for Dr. Jussek to check any possible mention of "James Stewart" there.

The only hope left was to consult with the vicar at St. Giles. It was at this point in the investigation that Dr. Jussek made a strategic faux pas, for when he spoke to the assistant vicar on the phone, he explained that he was investigating a reincarnation case. He might have just as well admitted that he was the devil's agent, and even a visit to the curate's home didn't help matters. The minister's wife was so horrified by his query that she shut the door in his face when he arrived. Since it was now becoming clear that he couldn't document "James Stewart's" life in Northampton, Dr. Jussek decided to turn his attention to the proper names and locations "Stewart" mentioned in the tapes of the regressions:

> At this point in our investigation, we had a list of potentially verifiable facts about the Northampton life of James Stewart with us, if such a man really existed. Each of these statements had to be meticulously researched, verified or rejected. We were looking for a banker whose possible date of death was 1861. He died of pneumonia at the age of 59, and was buried either in St. James (St. Jimes) or in the other church nearby which had not been named by Charles. Both churches were near his house. He was attended by a Dr.

Williamson, or Williams in his childhood, and at his death by a Dr. Levitt. His father's bank was two blocks from his home. As a child he was a student at Great Creighton School, an institution for boys, and previously he had attended Draidon School.

With the help of the kindly historians in the abbey we found two old directories, the Slater's *Commercial Directory* of 1862, and Mercer & Crocker's *General Topographical and Historical Directory* of 1871. Almost immediately I found a Great Creaton School listed under academies and schools! It had been located just outside of town in the village of Spratton, but is no longer in existence. This was a revelation to us. So it seems that Charles' memories were valid after all. We now knew we were on the right track. A second school nearby was also listed in the directories. Dryden School was located only a few blocks from York Road. The school was founded in 1710 and the building now houses the leathercraft museum which we had seen on our first day in Northamptom. This was a second hit.

We also found reference to the Savings Bank on St. Giles Square, close to York Road. It, too, no longer existed. So far it seemed that Charles' geography was accurate, if we allow that the York Road today had been the Yorkshire Road to which he had alluded. The second school and the bank were within the distance he described as well. Charles had stated that the bank was situated on Canterbury Street, but the local street names had all been changed over the past 150 years and we could find no complete record of the names as they existed in Charles' day. There is no Canterbury Street today, and we found no listing in the directories for a Stewart who had been a banker at that time. But our sources were so incomplete that we didn't consider this too much of a setback.

Dr. Jussek's next job was to discover the possible existence of "Dr. Williams" and "Dr. Levitt." The same directories that listed the schools also fortuitively listed the practices of a Dr. William Williams and a Dr. Flewitt. It is Dr. Jussek's belief that he may have misheard this name as "Levitt," since Charles Roberts usually spoke in a whisper while reminiscing about his past life.

The case was becoming more and more tantalizing as these bits of information began falling into place. The only remaining problem was trying to uncover the literal presence of a banker named "James Stewart," who died of pneumonia in 1861. Despite the fact that the assistant curate at St. Giles had not been too helpful, Dr. Jussek was finally able to consult the church's death registry. There is where he found the information for which he was so diligently searching. The death registry recorded (on p. 068G) that a *John* Stewart had died of pneumonia in the parish on June 14, 1861. His address was given as Number 29 St. Giles St. and was within a few yards of 17 York Road. It looked as though Dr. Jussek had finally found his man, at least at first glance.

It soon became evident that this John Stewart was not the banker Charles Roberts was apparently recalling. There seemed little doubt but that the subject's information contained too many historical and geographical accuracies pertinent to this Stewart to be rejected as coincidence. The close parallels between the name, residence, and year of death are self-evident. But John Stewart had been a journeyman wine-worker. So it appeared as if Charles Roberts had been tapping into the memories of two different individuals—the wine-worker in Northampton and a banker who shared a similar name. So the search had to be continued, and Dr. Jussek felt that a search through historical London might uncover more clues about the mystery unfolding before him.

When Dr. Jussek realized that he was headed for a stalemate in Northampton, he lost no time getting back to London. There he was again able to verify the stunning accuracy of his subject's past-life memories. Historical listings revealed the existence of a London Club as well as a tavern called the Old Man's Club . . . and the old records revealed that the latter had especially catered to bankers.

Unfortunately, the Jusseks ran out of time and had to return to the United States, both intrigued and mystified by what they had uncovered.

George Field and His Past Life in the Old South

For those readers becoming a little jaded with obscure points of English history, the following case will present a refreshing change of pace.

The hypnotist who discovered this truly extraordinary case was the late Loring G. Williams, a high school teacher from New Hampshire who was also an expert practitioner of hypnosis. Although he was not a trained hypnotherapist or psychologist, Williams was active in the field of past-life regression for several years. He uncovered a number of interesting cases during the course of his experiments, but by far, his most provocative discoveries came when he started working with fifteen-year-old George Field.

George lived in the hypnotist's own neighborhood in Hindale, New Hampshire. Williams had been conducting weekly hypnosis sessions with volunteers recruited from the area when he found that the teenager was an exceptionally good subject. So beginning in 1965, he began working with him in more depth. Each time he was regressed, George became a Civil War farmer from North Carolina named "Jonathan Powell" who was killed, he would so often say, by "those damn Yankees." "Powell" also maintained that he had lived in Jefferson, North Carolina, from 1832 to 1863, the son of Willard Powell, who was a local miner. During the course of the first regression, young Field described the geography of his home town and designated the name of the local river (South Fork), the names of some of his relatives, and the location of the local Quaker church. Subsequent regressions focused on different periods drawn from "Jonathan Powell's" life. These tended to concentrate on his mother's death, his father's death in a mining accident, the beginning of the Civil War, and his interactions with some of Jefferson's local businessmen. He remembered his own death with special bitterness, because he claimed that he was killed by Union soldiers (wearing *gray*) when he refused to sell them potatoes. George Field, in his past-life guise as "Jonathan Powell," also remembered the local area well. During one session he named the county in which Jefferson was located (Ashe County), the position of the main roads in the town, and the name of the neighboring city (Clifton), as well as a number of other features.

Loring Williams realized immediately that the case for reincarnation could stand or fall on the basis of George Field's past-life memories; so he didn't lose any time rushing off the the library to check out some of his subject's geography. He was very familiar with Jefferson, South Carolina, but he was heartened to learn that there also was a Jefferson in North Carolina. It was located in Ashe County.

Because the hypnotist realized the importance of the case he now had on his hands, he decided to forego any further research until he could regress George in the presence of independent witnesses. This session was held shortly after the first, and several local college professors and a clinical psychologist were present. Williams prepared for the session by looking up several bits of historical data about North Carolina so that he could quiz his subject during the hypnosis. Unfortunately, his plan—well thought-out though it was—failed. That night's session began inauspiciously when George began by describing two other past lives that apparently predated his "Jonathan Powell" incarnation. Williams finally had to direct the boy to the year 1845 before the teenager once again adopted the personality of the Civil War farmer. George was only able to relive a few commonplace episodes from his past life, so Williams was never able to explore "Powell's" memories in the detail he wished. The only important added detail that came to light was the name of "Jonathan Powell's" grandmother, Mary.

It was becoming clearer and clearer that the case couldn't be investigated properly from New Hampshire, so Williams decided to take George on a field trip to North Carolina. He hoped that the location would jar George's conscious recollections and would help him to recall more about his past life.

Jefferson turned out to be a picturesque little town in the northwest corner of North Carolina. Its population was 360, which was hardly more than the three hundred or so residents "Powell" said lived there in 1863. It needn't be emphasized that George had never visited the town before, but this didn't keep him from reporting strong déjà-vu sensations when he first arrived there by car. George's psychological reaction to seeing the Jefferson of today was encouraging, so Williams decided to hypnotize the teenager before driving him around any further. "Jonathan Powell" immediately emerged and was surprised by what he was seeing, because the city was so different from the town of his own day. His puzzlement caused him to become disoriented and Williams had to give up his idea that the hypnotic persona would be able to help him in his search for the historical Jonathan Powell. He quickly proceeded to the Ashe County Courthouse in Jefferson instead. There he checked out the history of any Powell families in the area. He was dismayed to find that the courthouse records only went back to 1912, but he was able to dig up a registry of deeds in the archives. These records proved that a Mary Powell once lived in Jefferson, where she had taken possession of some property in 1803. That would have made her the correct age if she had indeed been "Jonathan Powell's" grandmother. Williams also learned that Powell was a rare name in the area, which further sparked his hope that he was about to solve the mystery of "Jonathan Powell."

Unearthing information about old Jefferson was becoming a more difficult task than he originally expected, so the next strategy was to enlist the cooperation of the town's local historian. They met at her home later that day. Although the woman (who requested that her name be withheld) was skeptical of the whole affair, she agreed to listen to the tapes of George's prior regressions. Williams then regressed the boy in her presence so that she could talk directly to "Powell." They focused the session on 1860, and the little experiment proved most revealing.

The historian first asked the entranced teenager if he remembered Joshua Baker, the high sheriff of Ashe County.

"I think that it was about ten years ago that he was sheriff," responded the hypnotized subject. "I don't think I've met him or anything, but I think it was about ten years ago that he was there."

This response impressed the historian, since Baker was high sheriff in Ashe about 1850, which was ten years before the date to which George was being regressed.

Unfortunately, George couldn't identify some of the subsequent names offered by the historian until she asked simply, "Were you acquainted with the rich merchant Wall?" George immediately recalled that he remembered a *Samuel* Wall. This was an evidential response, because such a person had lived in the town at the time, although he wasn't the wealthy merchant that the historian was asking about. It finally looked as though "Jonathan Powell" was getting into the swing of things. When the historian mentioned another prominent local resident of 1860, George correctly explained where in town the man lived. But probably his most amusing response came when the historian asked him whether he knew a Jonathan Baker in Jefferson.

"Yeah," the subject replied. "He lived down in the center of the villie, too. I've met him quite a few times, and I've seen him down there. He's got quite a bit of money, I think! And he always talks about it, too. I think he's got a few slaves."

Even the skeptical historian had to chuckle at the accuracy of the information, and the folksy way "Jonathan Powell" talked about him.

The session proceeded as the historian threw out more and more names. "Jonathan Powell" couldn't identify some of them, but the mention of a few evoked a flood of detailed memories. He was able to discuss their occupations, where they lived, and their financial status.

The final hit came as the interview was coming to a close, when the historian asked whether he remembered a brick house built in Jefferson by a local military man in 1848. The historian only asked about the house without any mention of the date, and Field responded:

"Yeah, I think it was about ten or twelve years ago. It was in the late 1840s."

This session represented the climax of the case, especially since Williams was unable to find any records proving "Jonathan Powell's" historical existence. He was only able to additionally substantiate that much of the geography the teenager recalled under hypnosis while still in New Hampshire was correct. South Ford river runs by the town, and Clifton turned out to be the name of a neighboring community. The curious story of "Jonathan Powell's" death also gained considerable credibility the more Williams looked into the local history. The hypnotist was especially intrigued by the claim that "Powell" was murdered by Union soldiers wearing gray (not blue) uniforms when he refused to sell his potatoes to them. The Civil War records Williams consulted indicated that there were no Northern troops stationed in North Carolina in 1863 but the local historian advised him that marauding bands of Union soldiers from Kentucky often plundered the North Carolina area. She didn't consider it unthinkable that some of them could have disguised themselves as Confederate soldiers by donning gray uniforms.

The denouement of the case came after Loring Williams published an initial account of his findings in _Fate_ magazine in 1965. A subscriber wrote to him, claiming that she was a great-niece of Jonathan Powell. She explained that her father had mentioned him and was under the impression that he had been murdered by Union soldiers. She couldn't recall any further details, but she added that Willard was Jonathan's brother and not his father.

The six cases summarized above are strong enough, in my opinion, to constitute grounds for some sort of _a priori_ belief in reincarnation. They certainly counter the claims of Leonard Zusne and Warren H. Jones that all cases of hypnotically evoked past-life recall are, "beyond the shadow of a doubt," the result of fantasy. This idea, while generally held by most psychologists, can't come close to explaining any of the cases cited in this chapter. These reports point to something more complex. The skeptic's immediate response will be that these cases probably resulted from cryptomnesia. In other words, the subjects were probably responding to latent memories buried deep within their subconscious minds. This explanation is, in fact, just about the only tenable one the skeptic _could_ adopt.

Before we invoke the ever-present demon of cryptomnesia, however, we should examine this possible complicating factor in more depth. Since the problem of cryptomnesia is a vital one in the study of hypnotic past-life regression, it is important to determine whether such a phenomenon really exists. If it does, it would then be important to discover whether hypnosis catalyzes the emergence of this type of information and how it might interact within the dynamics of hypnotic fantasy. These are the issues to which we will turn in the next chapter.

Conclusions

Despite the fact that most psychologists are skeptical of hypnotically evoked past-life recall, the phenomenon bears up surprisingly well when critically examined. There are several cases reported in the literature that cannot be explained as the result of fantasy, in which obscure but accurate historical information was communicated by the subject. This material includes mention of proper names, dates, and geographical locations. These cases have been unfairly ignored by many students of the reincarnation question. The only possible explanation for them is that they derive from memories hidden in the subconscious minds of the subjects. This would be a conjectural line of argumentation but one that deserves further study.

6

New Light
on Past Lives?

Hundreds of people believe that they remember their past lives. Some may have had such memories from early childhood. Others recollect their previous existences when visiting new cities or locations and experiencing strong déjà-vu reactions to them.

But the majority believe in reincarnation as a result of hypnotic age regression. Not only are several new-age psychologists regressing their clients in hopes of finding the causes for their current life problems, but more and more reincarnation workshops are springing up across the country. Whole groups of people are being regressed and taken back to their previous lives.

Dr. Helen Wambaugh, a psychologist headquartered in northern California, has made a virtual career out of conducting group regression sessions and has published several analyses of her data. Meanwhile in southern California, Dick Sutphen and his associates at his Malibu-based corporation have commercialized the procedure into popular seminars that he conducts across the country. Both of these seminar leaders say that the client's contact with his own past life can be not only spiritually uplifting but also a technique for developing one's human potentials. Most of the enthusiastic individuals who sign up for these seminars have no difficulty making contact with memories of far-off ages and peoples.

But are such memories really valid?

The only way to document the validity of these past-life remembrances has been to check through historical records to find out if the individual's memories are accurate. Often times this is no easy matter. Because of the very general nature of the information usually elicited during hypnotic regression, most past-life recalls can be neither confirmed nor invalidated. Every once in a while, though, someone under hypnosis will recall in detail a life in an obscure city, and a subsequent check will document all of the information that was proffered. These cases are quite rare, and the six reports summarized in the previous chapter represent the high points in a large body of literature often hardly worth wading through. However, these cases make great copy for the popular press, and the tabloids often announce them with screaming headlines. Yet these very cases have also long served as a bone of contention between believers and skeptics. The believers will point to these reports as absolute proof of reincarnation. The skeptics will suggest instead that such remembrances are fantasies based on information the subjects were once exposed to, perhaps years ago, but that has been consciously forgotten.

This debate became stalemated long ago. Both the concepts of reincarnation and the idea of hidden memory (or cryptomnesia) are difficult to prove. So the believers just go on believing and the skeptics go on dismissing the whole thing.

The problem with this protracted debate is that both groups of partisans have approached it naively. I pointed out in the last chapter that several alternative explanations can be found for cases of even veridical past-life recall. So it would be naive to assume that these cases necessarily prove reincarnation. The skeptics and debunkers who challenge this body of case material also approach their task rather simple-mindedly. They quote all sorts of experts who believe in the mind's role-playing capabilities and propensity for fantasy. The concept of cryptomnesia and hypermnesia sprinkle about in their writings like ground pepper on a freshly tossed salad. But while the skeptics assume that the hypnotic state is linked to the realms of fantasy and the resources of hidden memory, few of them have ever taken the time to study what formal research has demonstrated about these processes. As a matter of fact, the combined results of research on hypnotic hypermnesia have been contradictory. Some reports from the University of Waterloo in Ontario, Canada, for instance, recently demonstrated that hypnotized subjects tend to recall previously learned information inaccurately. Nor have many skeptics and debunkers ever tried to show how hypnotic fantasy might specifically apply to reincarnation studies.

Those skeptics who wish to reject the evidence for reincarnation take three responsibilities upon themselves. They must first show that the phenomenon of cryptomensia actually exists. They must then provide that the stories reeled out by hypnotic subjects about their past lives reveal direct evidence of psychodynamic fantasy. And they must show that these fantasies are formulated in conjunction with cryptomnesia. These are the crucial issues confronting the study of hypnotically evoked past-life recall, and they are the topics with which this chapter will be concerned. Each will be examined in turn.

There is little debate within psychology about the bare existence of cryptomnesia. Many examples of this anomaly have been placed in the literature of psychology, psychiatry, and psychical research. During the early years of parapsychology, not a few researchers found that the "communications" they were receiving from the dead through trance mediums had their basis in obituaries or news stories. This information was probably being assimilated unconsciously by the psychic, whose subconscious mind then rehashed it and presented it in the form of a spirit message. A different kind of cryptomnesia was recorded by Helen Keller in her autobiography _The Story of My Life._ When she was a teenager, Helen wrote a short story that was good enough to be published. She was acutely embarrassed later when she discovered that several features of the plot were drawn from a story by Margaret T. Canby, which appeared in her book, _Birdie and His Fairy Friends._ According to Helen, "The two stories were so much alike in thought and language that it was evident that Miss Canby's story had been read by me, and that mine was—a plagiarism." Miss Keller still didn't understand how she could have assimilated the Canby story, since it had been published in 1874, before she was born. It was later determined that when she was eight years old, she lived for a while with a woman who owned a copy of the Canby book, from which she used to read to Helen.

I must admit to a similar indiscretion myself. When I was studying musical composition in college, our professor instructed us to write an original melody along with ten variations. That night I sat at the piano doodling away until the first phrase finally came to mind. The impasse was broken and soon the entire melody was written. I was quite proud of the tune until I realized later that I had unknowingly reconstructed the main line of a keyboard piece by J. S. Bach.

Very similar cases started appearing in the literature of psychical research after the turn of the century. Professor Charles Richet, who was one of France's leading physiologists as well as a pioneering psychic investigator, discovered the case of a trance psychic who wrote scripts in Greek while dissociated. He was able to show that many of the passages in the scripts were being cribbed unconsciously from a Greek/French dictionary. Probably the most intriguing case of cryptomnesia reported from this historical period was carried in the 11 May 1936 issue of the (London) _Morning Star._ It was contained in a letter from L. S. Lewis, who wanted to report an incident he had recently shared with his wife. During their travels through England, they once chanced upon a glen with a little pond. Both experienced strong déjà-vu reactions that were so marked that they began to think that perhaps they had lived there in some previous life. They only discovered the source of their memories when they returned to London and visited an art gallery they had frequented before their travels. There they found a painting of the same pond, which had apparently served as the (forgotten) basis for their unusual experience.

There seems little doubt about the existence of cryptomnesia, so let's go on to examine the whole area of hypnotic fantasy and how it bears on the reincarnation question.

As I suggested earlier, the skeptic could only effectively argue against the validity of hypnotically evoked past-life recall by drawing on one line of evidence. He or she would have to show that a subject's "past-life" scenario contained unmistakable psychodynamic connections to his or her present life. The problem with this approach is that it invites the skeptic to engage in a curious and questionable type of armchair psychoanalysis. Nonetheless, some scattered research into the manner by which subjects draw upon early life experiences while creating hypnotic fantasies has been reported. The most pertinent research along these lines was conducted by Dr. Edwin S. Zolik at Marquette University in the 1950s.

His interest, sparked by the controversy engendered by the Bridey Murphy affair, was to experimentally demonstrate the psychodynamic basis of "previous existence" fantasies. Dr. Zolik's plan was to hypnotize a subject and regress him to his past life, induce post-hypnotic amnesia, and then rehypnotize him. The catch came during the second critical session. Dr. Zolik's idea was to ask the subject to trace the source of the information that was serving as the basis for the original scenario. The subject eventually chosen for the experiment was a thirty-two-year-old married college student of Irish descent, whose past-life story revolved around his existence as Brian O'Malley, a British solider of the Irish Guard in County Cork. The subject became very upset when asked about his death but continued questioning revealed that he died in 1892 after being thrown from a horse. The subject wasn't rehypnotized until four days later, at which time he was asked to trace the source for his past-life identity. The subject hedged a bit but then explained that his grandfather had once spoken to him about an O'Malley. They had served in the army together, and apparently there was a great deal of animosity between them. The subject first heard about the man when he was only seven years old. He emphasized that his grandfather wanted him, too, to become a soldier and also indicated that his relationship with the elderly man was an ambivalent one bordering on open hostility.

Dr. Zolik's conclusion was that his subject's past-life story was a psychodynamic expression of his own desire to emulate his grandfather, while at the same time setting himself up as his adversary. There seems little reason to accept any other interpretation of the case.

Since at least some hypnotically evoked past-life scenarios are apparently psychologically derived fantasies, it has often been assumed that cryptomnesia is regularly employed during their construction. The case Zolik published has sometimes been cited as an example of cryptomnesia, but it is debatable whether his subject was consciously unaware of O'Malley's identity. This question was never probed during the course of the sessions. The possibility that cryptomnesia and fantasy can unite in an unholy hypnotic alliance was only experimentally explored years later. This breakthrough came during the 1960s when Reima Kampman, a psychiatrist at the University of Oulu in Finland, began following up several leads suggested by Zolik's work. He borrowed his progenitor's methodology but also expanded it by working with several subjects. He not only replicated Zolik's work but was able to explore the structure of past-life regression fantasies in more depth. He was also able to demonstrate that the ability to recall a past life while under hypnosis is a normal capability of the healthy mind.

From what I have just said, you may be getting the idea that Dr. Kampman is a skeptic of the psychic field. This would be an inaccurate impression, since the Finnish researcher is very much interested in scientific parapsychology and is currently supervising Finland's first doctoral student in the field.

Dr. Kampman began his research in the late 1960s and has continued on with it to the present time. His research into the dynamics of hypnotic regression was the result of his interest in whether past-life memories might actually represent the manifestation of a subsystem within the human personality. Such a phenomenon would be akin to the type of subsystem(s) that emerge(s) in multiple personality, but which is neither as radical nor aggressive as it appears in mental illness. To study this idea more fully, the innovative psychiatrist began hypnotizing his subjects in a search to locate this subsystem. He also wanted to find out just _where_ these subpersonalities might be picking up their sometimes all-too-accurate information about the past. To date he has published one monograph and a half-dozen technical reports on his research; research that has an important bearing for anyone interested in either hypnosis or reincarnation.

His first project was conducted with the aid of Finland's public school system. When Kampman announced his plan, close to two-hundred students, aged 12 to 22, volunteered for the study. By testing these individuals in small groups at his lab, he soon discovered that "past-life" recall is a relatively common hypnotic phenomenon. The subjects were simply asked to "go back to an age before your birth, you are somebody else, somewhere else." About seven percent of those tested accepted the suggestion and produced memories of a past life. So Dr. Kampman followed up with another study that employed the talents of seventy-five additional students who seemed to be exceptionally good hypnotic subjects. He found that thirty-two of them were able to produce past lives easily while the other forty-three failed. This finding puzzled the psychiatrist, as it might puzzle anyone who believes in reincarnation. Why shouldn't age-regression produce past-life memories in everyone? What factors determine a person's ability to recall a so-called past life?

These were the very questions that led Kampman to study the individual psychologies of his subjects. Psychological tests were administered to each participant, who also underwent a standard psychiatric interview. And as Kampman proceeded with his work, a fairly good picture of just who tends to remember a "past life" under hypnosis soon became clear. Kampman was able to determine that people who can conjure up reincarnation memories are indeed different from those who cannot. They are mentally healthier. He found that his two groups of subjects didn't differ at all when questioned about their home lives, attitudes toward religion, sexual views, or childhood rearing. However, those students who were capable of producing "past lives" were much less neurotic, handled stress better, and were better adjusted sexually than the others. They were also less repressive.

These factors led Dr. Kampman to reject any notion that his subjects were coming up with genuine memories of previous incarnations. He preferred to believe that such memories are fantasies a hypnotic subject can create at the whim of the therapist, if he or she has a healthy ego. Well-adjusted people can engage in these fantasies, he suggests, because they are so mentally well-adjusted that the ego is not threatened by these little adventures in make-believe. It doesn't create a potential conflict for them because they are so totally self-accepting. A more neurotic person might reject the suggestion, because the idea that he may be "someone else" may be very threatening to his concept of "self."

Now of course, any believer in reincarnation could easily dispute these views. Maybe mentally healthy people simply remember their past lives easier. The believer might also point out that a purely psychological interpretation of the past-life recall phenomenon cannot explain *how* hypnotized subjects so often come up with minute and accurate details about peoples and cultures they have never studied.

Dr. Kampman's results also seem to contradict the findings of many psychologists and psychiatrists who specialize in what is called "past-life" therapy. They regularly take their (often neurotically disturbed) patients back to their past lives through hypnosis to trace the basis of their problems.

These points are serious ones, but Dr. Kampman has gone on to study these issues in great depth. He has proven that the human mind does indeed tend to hoard little facts and pieces of data that it can draw upon in a normal way when called upon to create a "past-life" memory. He documented this phenomenon many times during the course of his research.

One of Dr. Kampman's subjects was a fifteen-year-old girl with artistic interests, with whom he first began working in 1968. While under hypnosis she was guided back to a previous life. She said that her name was "Malina Bostojevski" and that the year was 1780. She gave an accurate description of the historical era in which she lived before the hypnotist regressed her still further back. She eventually remembered five alleged previous lives. She recalled these same lives when she was rehypnotized a month later, yet when she was hypnotized again in 1975, she produced a totally different set of lives. "The place of residence, name, features of character, and life attitudes of the secondary personalities were very different," the psychiatrist reported, "as compared to the personalities induced seven years earlier." But just where did she come up with the information that seemed to give credence to her past lives? The answer to his puzzle came when Kampman began questioning his subject under deeper hypnosis.

The most interesting life produced by this subject was one she allegedly lived as a seven-year-old boy. His father was Aitmatov, the captain of a small boat. The hypnotized subject gave the name of the lake on which they worked and told how he drowned when he jumped overboard while imitating the fish he saw following the craft. It was a credible story overall, but Kampman wasn't willing to leave the tale so unresolved. He brought the girl out of hypnosis and made sure she had forgotten what she had just revealed. Then he rehypnotized her and asked her to go back in her present life to the moment when she first came across the information she used to create this particular past-life memory. The subject had no difficulty recalling that, many years before, she had read a novel whose plot matched that of her past life. The name of the lake was the same and the book's author had been recast into the name of her past-life father.

An even more remarkable case surfaced when Kampman began work with a nineteen-year-old student who was able to produce eight past lives; the most amazing as a thirteenth-century English country girl named Dorothy, the daughter of an innkeeper. The subject gave a detailed account of English life of that time and even sang an old English folksong for the startled psychiatrist. The song was sung in Middle English and seemed absolutely authentic. When questioned after the session was over, the subject had no idea where she normally could have come across the song. Another one of this subject's fascinating past lives was that of Karolina Prokojeff, who lived during the frightening years of the Russian revolution. She described the period accurately and gave several names of her family members. She also recalled a life as a girl in China who died after falling from a cliff.

If all this weren't enough, this same subject created a series of four new past lives when hypnotized several years later. The whole sequence of (now) eight past lives was mutually consistent. None of them overlapped and they represented a credible progression of incarnations from ancient China to the present. One of these new lives was of a seven-year-old child named "Kaarin Bergstrom" who died in 1939 during an air raid. She recalled the raid over her native Finland in detail and even offered her address, the names of her parents, and the exact date of the Nazi raid.

The real challenge to this case came, however, when Dr. Kampman began tracing just how his subject could have come up with such accurate information. His procedure was, once again, to rehypnotize her and ask her to trace the source of the information. It didn't come as any great surprise when the subject was able to explain where she had accumulated these bits of data.

"Probably the most astonishing detail," Kampman wrote when he reported the case to his psychiatric colleagues, "was the song that the subject sang several years earlier. . . . She went back to the age of 13, when she once by chance took a book in her hand in the library. She did not read it but only ran through the pages. In hypnosis she was able to tell the authors of the book, who were Benjamin Britten and [Imogene] Holst. Further, she could remember accurately where the song was in the book." Kampman didn't waste any time trying to verify his subject's revelations. He procured a copy of the book and there he found the precise song his subject had sung for him in her past life—even the language was the same.

The psychiatrist found a similar solution for the life of Karolina Prokojeff. The entire story had actually been pieced together from the girl's childhood memories. One of her mother's relatives has been named Prokojeff. Even more revealing was the "Kaarin Bergstrom" lifetime. Research undertaken by the psychiatrist into some old archives proved that no such person actually died during the particular air raid the subject had so vividly described, although a raid had indeed taken place on the day indicated. When pressed for the source of "Kaarin's" life when she was next hypnotized, the subject recalled thumbing through a patriotic book as a child, which included a picture of a seven-year-old girl who had been subsequently killed along with her mother during the air raid in question. The date of the raid was also given along with the address where the bombs had fallen. All this information matched the hypnotic past-life revelations of the subject. The girl had obviously adapted this information and incorporated it into a past-life fantasy.

Dr. Kampman also discovered that the subject's life as Ving Lei in China had a psychological basis to it. Her tragic death by falling might actually relate to a traumatic experience disinterred from the subject's current life. So he hypnotized her and specifically asked her to go back into her present life to the emotional source of this past-life memory. The subject immediately recalled how, as a small child, she had once fallen from a second-story loft.

In the light of these and several similar cases, Dr. Kampman is skeptical of all reincarnation claims. His overall conclusion is that any type of past-life memory is based on hidden information stored in the brain or on symbolized references to traumatic events experienced in one's current life.

These findings have an obvious bearing on the phenomenon being seen more and more often by those clinical psychologists and psychiatrists who use hypnosis to treat the phobias and other mental problems of their clients. Many clinicians have been promoting what they call past-life therapy, which entails instructing a hypnotized patient to trace the source of his or her problem. It isn't rare for these individuals to slip back into a previous life in which some horrible trauma occurred that has been imprinted on the present personality. A patient with a fear of water, for instance, may recall drowning in a past existence. These past-life recalls are usually produced at the direct suggestion of the therapist, though they can occur spontaneously—with or without hypnosis. However, far from serving as evidence for reincarnation, Dr. Kampman feels that these recollections are most likely fantasies built on a trauma suffered in the patient's present life that is still too threatening to confront.

The whole study of past-life therapy will be treated in depth in a later chapter, but it appears wise to introduce it now since Kampman's discoveries bear so significantly on the topic of hypnotic past-life regression.

Support for the view that past-life therapy prompts the emergence of events drawn from the patient's present life came when Dr. Kampman and two of his colleagues began treating a twenty-year-old hysteric at the University of Tampere (Finland). The woman had been referred to the university by psychiatrists in Sweden. She complained of bouts of momentary amnesia, headaches, and eye flickerings and had a terrible fear of sex. Since a physical work-up had revealed no organic cause for her somatic symptoms, the psychiatrists decided to treat her with psychotherapy. They soon learned that their patient was a very unhappy woman. Her father had remarried when she was quite young, she was poorly adjusted sexually, and she had experienced intense sibling rivalry. The psychiatrists diagnosed her as a hysteric and decided to use hypnosis as part of her treatment.

The cause of some of her problems came to light during the first hypnotic session, when she recalled that her stepbrother had attempted to rape her when she was only six. Two other siblings, aged two and three, looked on. This revelation of a long-forgotten incident resulted in the patient's immediate improvement. But this was only temporary, and the woman's symptoms reestablished themselves about a week later. Deeper psychological probing helped the patient recall other traumatic sexual (mis)adventures, and it was at this point in the therapy that Dr. Kampman decided to ask the patient to produce a past life in much the same way as pro-reincarnationist therapists are doing around the country today. The patient immediately recalled a life served in Egypt as a twenty-three-year-old woman named Isabel Abdul, the mother of two children aged two and three. She described a scene in which she was about to fill a basin with water and carry it home. She went on to describe her fiancé but could not remember his surname. Further suggestion prompted the emergence of a second past life as eighteen-year-old Briitta in Finland. The patient regressed to the year 1865 and this personality, too, explained how she was at a well drawing up water through the use of a lever system. The patient complained that the system was broken.

It didn't take much insight for Dr. Kampman to determine the symbolic nature of these past lives. He eventually interpreted them as fantasies drawn from incidents in his patient's present life and then transformed into past life fantasies. The fact that "Isabel" was twenty-three years old seemed to relate to the patient's own two children, who were two and three years old. The fantasy also seemed to relate to the two children of the same age who had watched the rape attempt to which she had been subjected as a child. The description of Isabel's fiancé also closely matched that of the stepbrother who had attacked her—perhpas the symbolic reason (psychological denial) she couldn't remember his surname. The consistent theme of raising water from a deep well might relate to a child's conception of the female sexual anatomy. The broken lever is also symbolic, according to Kampman, since it could well relate to the patient's conception of her own body as being "broken."

These interpretations might strike the reader as arbitrary and perhaps as a lot of psychoanalytic "mumbo-jumbo." But Dr. Kampman did not produce these explanations out of thin air nor in a last-ditch effort to deny the cogency of the reincarnation theory. Many of them were offered *by the patient when she was specifically questioned about their meanings during subsequent hypnotic sessions.*

The upshot of the case was a happy one. The hypnotherapy and counseling were effective and the patient was cured of her problems. A follow-up over a four-year period revealed no return of her symptoms.

All these cases, data, and explorations raise a million-dollar question. This is a crucial one in light of the data that was presented in the previous chapter. Do the research and findings of Dr. Kampman disprove reincarnation?

There is really no clear-cut answer to this question, but in the long run it appears to be no. The work of this enterprising Finnish psychiatrist has certainly done much to throw cold water on those believers and psychologists eager to find proof of reincarnation in the stories offered by their hypnotized subjects and patients. But this research cannot explain the many well-documented cases of children who remember their past lives from birth, instances of people who have spoken strange foreign languages during their regressions, or those rare instances in which hypnotized subjects have come up with specific names of obscure people who lived uneventful lives in other times and places. It should be also be borne in mind that Dr. Kampman only uncovered his few instances of genuine cryptomnesia after wading through dozens of cases. He had to cast his net in a sea of cut glass before pulling in a few gems, while other researchers have totally failed to replicate his work. Cryptomnesia may be a phenomenon just as rare as genuine past-life memory.

The real message in Dr. Kampman's research is that reincarnation is a treacherous area to investigate. He has also shown that the human mind is capable of registering all sorts of trivial information, filing it away, and drawing upon it in the most amazing ways during hypnotic regression. If nothing else, these studies have shown that much reincarnation research conducted in the past has been badly done. So while not discrediting the notion of reincarnation, Dr. Kampman's research teaches us that any future investigations into this mysterious subject should be conducted with caution.*

*The reader may be getting the incorrect impression from Dr. Kampman's research that cryptomnesic memory is simply a replay of information taken from a single source. Since his research was undertaken, our understanding of cryptomnesia has undergone a significant revision in this regard. During a joint conference undertaken at Cambridge University by the S.P.R. and the Parapsychological Association, Dr. James McHarg expanded our understanding of this strange phenomenon. He reported on a case from his clinical practice in which a brain-injured patient suddenly insisted that he was a Civil War officer. His knowledge of the American Civil War was impressive. Dr. McHarg was finally able to show that the patient had assembled his information unconsciously from two independent sources. The exposures to this information were made years apart. It would therefore seem that cryptomnesia can sometimes be a complex and creative phenomenon architected by the mind and brain.

In light of Dr. Kampman's findings, perhaps we should now go back over the six cases presented in the last chapter and see how well they stand up. Armed with the knowledge that past-life memories are often psychologically meaningful fantasies, and that the mind has the capacity for storing odd bits of information, we have to ask a potentially embarrassing question. Is belief in reincarnation still tenable on the basis of only a few selected cases? The following comments represent my own analysis:

The Doris Williams Case

This is probably the one case that can most easily be dismissed as the possible result of cryptomnesia. Very little information was communicated during the crucial session other than the subject's past-life name, address, age and cause of death. This is just the type of information that the subject might have come across during her years of casual reading. Certainly every literate adult is exposed to information about the _Titanic_ disaster at some time in his or her life. Ms. Suplee claims that she could find no generally available books on the tragedy that included all the information Ms. Williams communicated. When I first heard about the case, I conducted my own limited search and my findings support this view. So while the case contains several earmarks of genuine cryptomnesia, it is still hard to ascertain the source from which the subject derived her information. Probably the best way to explain this case would be by considering it either genuine or the product of a deliberate hoax. The fact that Ms. Williams is totally disinterested in following up on her revelations seems inconsistent with the latter view.

The Jane Evans Case

Here, too, there is a distinct possibility that the data Ms. Evans spun out while hypnotized was caused by cryptomnesia. While no specific source for this data has yet been found, the story of her past life tends to read very much like something drawn from an historical novel. The problem is confounded by the fact that Ms. Evans is prone to displays of cryptomnesia while hypnotized. Ian Wilson took a special interest in this case when it was first published. He had no difficulty showing in the American edition of his book that one of Jane Evan's _other_ hypnotically evoked past-life personas was based on a novel by Louis de Wohl. Wilson suggests that her twelfth-century life in York was probably derived from a similar source. He even writes that "there are indications suggesting the primary source of this latter [life] was an as yet untraced BBC radio play." Unfortunately, it is hard to take this claim very seriously because Wilson has not been more specific. It is difficult to understand how he can claim that the information about Ms. Evans' life in York was based on a play, when the very existence of this unnamed play is debatable. But the case is certainly contaminated by a curious form of guilt by association. Remember that there is no reason why a hypnotic subject could not recall a genuine past life during one regression session, yet spin a fantasy on another occasion.

The crux of the Jane Evans case rests on the discovery of the unknown crypt in which she claimed she was killed and which was actually discovered months after her revelations. The skeptic could rightfully object that this development was actually the result of a lucky coincidence. Most people tend to envision old churches and structures as complete with crypts and hidden passage ways. Perhaps Ms. Evans's description was a subconscious invention that was fortuitously borne out. The believer might reply that it is too coincidental that the subject (a) described a church with a crypt; (b) that matched the description of a church that actually existed in York in the twelfth century; and (c) where a crypt was later discovered, even though such a feature was rare for that period.

In the final run, the Jane Evans case is very provocative, but it falls short of representing proof of past-life recall. It remains only suggestive.

The Ann Dowling Case

This is the first of the six cases that cannot be glibly dismissed as the product of cryptomnesia. The investigators of the case scoured a great deal of archival material before tracing down the obscure people mentioned in the account. Perhaps we can dismiss the historical data the subject remembered, positing that this information was based on things she had read but forgotten. But this is as far as we can go. The whole issue of cryptomnesia versus genuine past-life recall revolves around a simple issue: Could the subject have come across the information he or she subsequently remembered during the process of regression? In the case of Ann Dowling's recollections, it seems very unlikely that she could ever have come by so many peculiar yet accurate names. These names designate people who never made any mark on history and who lived and died in general obscurity. The Ann Dowling case seems best explained by some form of reincarnation or paranormal cognition.

The Jane Doe Case

This is, of course, probably the most difficult case in the entire literature to ascribe to cryptomnesia. It ranks alongside the Ann Dowling case in that the historical accuracy of much of the pertinent information concerns people, places, and events, hitherto lost to history. While the story itself sounds like a fantasy or rehash of an historical novel, too many of the names of rather incredibly obscure people bear out. These verifications are distinguished by several convincing features. Some of the identifications were not made from source material available in the United States but were only uncovered in Spain. Since the subject of the regressions has never crossed the Atlantic, this certainly limits how far the "hidden memory" theory can be extended to account for it. The fact that even those archival records uncovered in the United States that bear crucially on the case were in Spanish is also impressive. To her credit, Dr. Tarazi actually taught herself Spanish to undertake her search into Jane Doe's incredible story. This alone testifies to the obscure nature of the information she was finally able to exhume and calls into question the idea that the story was an hypnotic confabulation.

There is another interesting point about the case that deserves noting. The action and _personae dramatis_ of Jane Doe's story focused on the city of Cuenca. This drab city is not known as a runaway tourist attraction, nor has it ever drawn much attention to itself. It would be the least likely setting for an unconsciously hoaxed story.

The Charles Roberts Case

Many of the same points of evidence presented in the Ann Dowling case apply to this report as well. There was, admittedly, a great deal of confusion about Roberts' memories, since his past-life scenario seems to be a composite drawn from the lives of two people. He was conceivably picking up information about some so far untraced banker as well as about a wine journeyman who lived and died in Northampton. Since Roberts has never been to England, it is difficult to explain how he was able to come up with and amalgamate so much scattered information about people and places drawn from the nineteenth century. We could feasibly reject his hypnotic knowledge about the streets and churches of Northampton. This information could have been derived from books, movies, or TV programs to which he was exposed during his early life. The names of the two doctors he offered were actually near-misses, so perhaps they, too, can be dismissed. But it would still be up to the skeptic to figure out how a brewer in Los Angeles correctly determined that a man named Stewart lived in a particular parish in England, and died there in 1861 from pneumonia. It may be objected that "Stewart" is a common name, but Dr. Jussek discovered that it actually wasn't in that part of England where "James or John Stewart" had once lived. So while a puzzling and largely unsolved case, some psychic factors probably lie at the root of it.

The George Field Case

This provocative account seems, at first glance, to represent the strongest case in the literature. We must remember, however, that the teenager could have been exposed to a great deal of information about Jefferson, North Carolina, when he visited the town with Loring Williams. They had, after all, been roving around the city for quite some time before George was hypnotized in the presence of the town historian. For the sake of analysis, we should actually break this case down into two parts—the information communicated *before* the trip to North Carolina and that which emerged *during* the visit.

Most of the information communicated by the subject when he was originally regressed in New Hampshire can probably be dismissed. This data could have been obtained from any atlas or map of the state. The only unusual information offered was the name of Mary Powell, which matched the name of a former resident of the town.

The most critical aspects of the case only emerged during the trip Williams and the teenager made to Jefferson. We know that Williams initially checked the records of the county courthouse, where he discovered a registry of deeds. What we don't know is what George was doing during the time. It is conceivable that he was helping Williams during their attempts to track down the historical "Jonathan Powell," thereby accumulating considerable information about the former residents. The skeptic couldn't be faulted for believing that the information George later communicated was based on data he came across at this time.* On the other hand, I find it difficult to believe that cryptomnesia can explain this case, even granting that the young man had some access to information about historical Jefferson. Williams makes it clear that the courthouse records only went back to 1912, so they couldn't have contributed to the teenager's knowledge of the nineteenth-century townsfolk. That leaves us with the registry of deeds, and it is indeed likely that Williams discussed what he found with his subject. This registry could have alerted him to the names of some of the landowners of the period in that area.

In rereading the transcripts of Field's interrogation by the town historian, however, I personally doubt that this registry could have been the source for all of the boy's information. George, as "Jonathan Powell," was obviously familiar with where in the city various residents lived, their financial status, specific dates pertinent to their lives, the marital status of at least one individual, and a host of other trivial bits of information. What is so remarkable about George's performance was the variety of information he revealed about so many long-deceased townsfolk. The information he recalled did not follow any sort of consistent pattern. If he was basing his responses on a single source of information, just such a consistency should have arisen, yet the material he recalled was incredibly diversified. The mention of different names elicited different types of recollections. The diversification of his information simply doesn't point to cryptomnesia.

---

*Loring Williams died a few years ago and can no longer shed any light on this problem. However, his son traveled with him on the trip and it would be interesting to discover whether this gentleman remembers how George Field was engaged while the county records were being consulted.

An added distinction in this case is that the literal existence of a "Jonathan Powell" was eventually corroborated. Unfortunately, we do not know the identity of the woman who wrote to Williams about her knowledge of "Jonathan Powell." So this aspect of the case can no longer be independently verified. But the letter seems to have been an honestly written document, since the writer actually corrected some of Field's information. A crank or someone seduced by false recollections probably would have confirmed everything the teenager reported.

Probably the single most impressive aspect of the collected information communicated in the above cases is its raw obscurity. As I pointed out above, to dismiss or substantiate a case as the product of cryptomnesia, a person must show that the subject somehow gained access to information about it. Such access can only be *inferred* if the pertinent data is traceable to a readily available source. Certainly the historical information offered by some regressed subjects cannot constitute strong evidence for reincarnation *per se*. This is just the type of data that anyone might pick up over the years but might consciously forget. But *some* cases of past-life recall contain points of information that are not currently matters of public knowledge or interest, nor ever were. This is why the recollections of Ann Dowling, Charles Roberts, and George Field point so strongly to some psychic process at work. It is hard to believe, even fully appreciating the role cryptomnesia can play in such cases, that these subjects were ever exposed to the veridical information they communicated about their past lives.

It is hard to comprehend just how difficult it has been even for reincarnation researchers to document some of their best cases. Since these researchers have encountered so much uphill work documenting obscure names and dates, it is illogical to assume that their subjects could have ever come across the information.

This was just the situation that plagued one of the most famous of all reincarnation cases. The case of Joanne MacIver was brought to public attention in 1968 by Jess Stearn, a journalist from the Los Angeles area. His book *The Search for the Girl with the Blue Eyes* has become a classic of popular reincarnation literature. Unfortunately, the case never made much of an impact on serious parapsychology, probably because its chief investigator was a journalist and not a scientist. The report stems from October 1962, when Joanne fell into a hypnotic trance while watching her father working with another subject. MacIver was a government auditor who lived with his daughter in a town outside Toronto. He was an eager believer in both reincarnation and the powers of hypnosis. When he realized that his own daughter was a successful deep-trance subject, he naturally recruited her for a series of experiments. During each subsequent session she readily became "Susan Ganier," who apparently lived during the middle of the nineteenth century in a town nearly 100 miles from Joanne's home in Orillia. "Susan Ganier" communicated a great deal of specific information about her life, including her marriage to a man named Thomas Marrow and her pathetic death in 1903 as a recluse. Her husband apparently died previously as the result of an injury he sustained when he was stabbed by a pitchfork. "Susan Ganier" also recalled the specific names of several landmarks near her home close to the community of St. Vincent, Ontario. Joanne was only fifteen years old when the regressions were undertaken and had never visited this area.

MacIver first set about documenting his daughter's claims by checking into old records and maps. He was able to authenticate the historical existence of many of the local landmarks mentioned by his daughter. He was impressed with her accuracy, since many of these landmarks no longer existed. He also interviewed an elderly man in the area who recalled "Susan Ganier" (as the widow Marrow). Jess Stearn reinvestigated the case, even though MacIver was still actively pursuing his own search, and he was able to independently substantiate Joanne's hypnotic claims. Although some of her memories were never traced, enough of them were so accurate that they made quite a stir when the case hit the press.

This brief summary of the case doesn't do justice to the painstaking legwork both MacIver and Stearn undertook while trying to document it. They confronted considerable difficulties while working in the locations where "Susan Ganier" apparently lived and died. It is therefore hard to believe that Joanne accidentally accumulated all her information consciously or unconsciously. She was living in a town nearly one hundred miles away and had spent little time away from it.

The climax to the case came when the researchers learned that a "Susan Ganier" actually once lived in Ontario. MacIver was only able to trace one gentleman who recalled the woman. Arthur Eagles still lived on a farm in the area and was found when other local residents suggested that he might be able to shed some light on the case. When MacIver first met him, Eagle was in his eighties and recalled the woman from his early youth. The fact that only one person could document the existence of "Susan Ganier" or "Susan Marrow" demonstrates just how obscure her life had been.

Because only one person in St. Vincent could identify the historical "Susan Marrow," some critics, in fact, remain skeptical of the case. They argue that MacIver probably suggested the name to Eagles in his zeal. This claim is specifically made by Benjamin Walker, a knowledgeable British author on the occult, in his skeptical book on reincarnation, *Masks of the Soul*. This claim is directly contradicted by the testimony Stearn quotes in his book about MacIver's meeting with the elderly man. A friend was traveling with him that day and witnessed the critical interview with Eagles. This was in October 1963. Paul Uhlig was a local shopkeeper who willingly shared his memories when Stearn sought him out. He specifically told the journalist that "I didn't want MacIver handing him a lot of leading questions and I made him agree that we would not mention the Marrow name first; it would have to come from Eagles." MacIver kept his word. As Uhlig also told his visitor, "Eagles spoke about people he had known sixty years ago and more. . . and then voluntarily brought up the widow Marrow. That's how he referred to her, throughout."

The informant also told Stearn that Eagles recalled her husband, Tommy, and knew about his being injured in an accident. He and his father felt sorry for the reclusive widow and sometimes chauffeured her about town.

With only a few cases of this quality in the literature, it would be rash to wholly reject past-life regression as valid evidence for reincarnation. To assume that cryptomnesia can account for all hypnotic past-life revivication is incredibly uncircumspect. It would be encouraging if more fully documented cases existed in the literature, but the serious student of the field simply cannot ignore the few sensational ones that do exist. While cryptomnesia and hypermnesia are ever present possibilities and dangers, they do not represent inescapable problems for the researcher interested in past-life regression. Brilliant as the researches of Dr. Edwin Zolik and Dr. Reima Kampman have been, they do not disprove the notion that a case will occasionally go beyond anything conventional psychiatry is prepared to handle.

Because some cases of past-life regression point away from cryptomnesia, this does not mean that they necessarily suggest reincarnation. I pointed out in the last chapter that a number of theories could be proposed to account for them. Reincarnation is only one alternative we should be considering. To invoke reincarnation as the probable explanation for some cases of hypnotic past-life recall, the believer would have to show that the rebirth doctrine explains these cases _better_ than any competing theory. What impresses me most about the six cases we have been examining is how certain of their elements point in a different direction than simple rebirth. Recall how, for instance, Ann Dowling (speaking as "Sarah Williams") transformed the name _Brownlow_ from an address into a policeman. Charles Roberts' memories were apparently a composite drawn from the lives of two people who lived in nineteenth-century England. These peccadillos and juxtapositions are not consistent with typical slips of memory. The believer could well argue that Ms. Dowling's slip _was_ a normal error of memory to which anyone might be prone, but this suggestion isn't too reasonable. "Sarah" apparently knew Bobby (or John) Edwards very well. It is inconceivable that she would have slipped up so badly about the name of his alleged partner. The confusing identity of the real "James Stewart" is also hard to explain as a simple error of memory. It is also curious how this case resembles the past-life memories of Imad Elawar (chronicled in Chapter 3), who also remembered a past life apparently derived from two sources. The problem we find in the Ann Dowling and Charles Roberts cases suggest that both subjects were tapping into a source of information about the nineteenth century but not that they were recalling personal memories of their own past lives.

If the cases of Ann Dowling and Charles Roberts were truly unique, perhaps we would be justified in ignoring their implications. But they are not. A case very similar to the Charles Roberts report cropped up in Joe Keeton's practice. It represents his most challenging case. The subject of the regression was a twenty-seven-year-old former nurse named Pat Roberts, whose past-life identity emerged as "Frances Jones." This persona claimed her birth in Bootle (England) as "Frances Mary Rodrigues" in 1840. "Frances" further explained that she married a "Frederick Jones," whom she was in the habit of calling "John." They lived in the fashionable Canning Street section of Liverpool, where she died in 1913. She also recalled a second marriage to an "Alfred Johnson," who owned a sailing vessel called the *Franconia*.

The phenomenal accuracy of these various names came to light when Keeton and Peter Moss checked old records in Bootle and Liverpool, where they discoverd the historical existence of "Frederick Jones," "Frances Johnson," and a "Frances Jones" . . . who indeed died in 1913. They even documented the existence of the *Franconia*. The problem came when the investigators tried to trace the true life stories of these people. It turned out that while all of Mrs. Roberts' names represented real people, not all of her information about their interrelationships was consistent. The clue to the whole mess only came when Keeton and Moss discovered that a real Frances Jones once lived on Canning Street in Liverpool in the 1870s. The coincidences mounted when they learned that a "John Jones" had also lived in the same street, and that *another* Frances Jones and *another* John Jones lived there during the next decade. As they further inspected the information communicated during the regression sessions, it began to appear that Mrs. Roberts had been drawing information from the lives of *all* of these people. This hardly looks like reincarnation. It seems more as though some sort of psychic process was taking place whereby Mrs. Roberts was tuning in on the lives of several different people—people who shared similar names and who lived close by one another over a twenty-year period.

If we decide to follow the lead suggested by Sir Cyril Burt so many years ago, perhaps we could suggest that Mrs. Roberts simply became very psychic while hypnotized. Perhaps the process of hypnosis allowed her to clairvoyantly tap into the information about the two Frances Joneses and the two John Joneses. There is a considerable body of experimental evidence that certain levels of hypnosis represent "psi-conducive" states of consciousness.*

This theory is superficially viable but unsatisfactory in the long run. The strength of Mrs. Roberts' revivications rests in the astonishing number of dates, names, and places she recollected. This is the very type of information that psychics are not prone to communicate. In general they find it difficult to communicate specific names and dates. When proper names *are* successfully elicited, it is often the result of several fumbling attempts. They don't gush out

*For a popular review of this evidence, see my previous book *Our Psychic Potentials* (Englewood Cliffs, N.J.: Prentice-Hall, 1984). A critical review of the experimental evidence was published in the *Journal* of the American Society for Psychical Research 63 (1969) 214–52.

facilely, which was typical of the way Mrs. Roberts communicated while regressed. Neither can the idea that she was drawing on simple clairvoyance while creating her past-life scenario explain the perverse lawfulness of her information. . . information drawn from the lives of several people who shared common names but who probably never knew one another.

In reading over the literature on reincarnation and hypnotic regression, I have actually been able to find only a single case where it appears as though telepathy played some sort of a role. In 1975 a psychologist/hypnotist in Kansas City, Missouri, announced that she had discovered the reincarnation of John Wilkes Booth. The subject was a college student who first approached the hypnotist innocently enough because he wanted to learn self-hypnosis. Dr. Dell Leonardi was teaching regression techniques as part of her class when she discovered that her new recruit was a gifted subject. He soon became "John Wilkes Booth" when regressed and spun out an elaborate story about the actor's life and his escape from justice. The plot of his flight after the assassination of Abraham Lincoln wasn't very credible, but the subject was, nonetheless, able to communicate a great deal of factual information about Booth. These facts kept Dr. Leonardi continually on her toes as she tried to stay one step ahead of her prize subject. A few indications exist in Dr. Leonardi's report that the subject was coming up with bits of obscure information about Booth shortly after she herself had stumbled across them. This certainly indicates that the psychologist was "leaking" information to the subject telepathically.

Certainly the cases of Charles Roberts, Pat Roberts, and Ann Dowling point to a much more complicated psychic process. It seems to me as though they were psychically assimilating a great deal of information from a certain area and time period but were somewhat unable to sort it all out properly. The past-life memories that sprung from their minds therefore took the form of confused compilations. The subjects tended to be catching hold of memory constellations—random bits of information linked together tenuously by time, place, and name associations—rather than genuine personal memories.

To understand the point I am trying to make, think back to what happens when you dab a drop of ink on a piece of fabric. The ink spreads in all directions by following along several of the threads. Something figuratively akin to this may have occurred when Charles Roberts, Ann Dowling, and Pat Roberts made their psychic contacts with the past. Their psychic senses latched onto a source of information in one time framework but then spread to associated networks of information. The results were past-life memories drawn from various constellations of information that are improperly amalgamated into confused and contradictory scenarios.

Just as with the extracerebral memory syndrome, there is considerable evidence that some cases of hypnotically evoked past-life memory represent a genuine form of psychic phenomenon. But what at first glance appears to be evidence for reincarnation looks, at a deeper level, like something quite different.

Conclusions

Despite the fact that some cases of past-life recall result from cryptomnesia and fantasy, those based on psychodynamic principles cannot explain all cases of hypnotic past-life recall. The best cases continue to hold up well no matter what objections are raised. The material communicated in some of these reports is so obscure that it is unlikely the subjects ever had the opportunity to gain normal access to it. On the other hand, these cases are not clear cut. They often include curious distortions. These anomalies cannot be explained on the theory that the subjects were virtually recalling their past lives. It appears instead as though they were psychically tapping sources of information but were not responding to memories derived from their own previous existences.

7

Xenoglossy I: Psychic Links with Ancient Egypt?

Attempting to track down and validate the memories of people who recall their past lives is excruciatingly difficult. Many people who remember such lives recall living several centuries ago, usually as obscure people in obscure places. Even verifying the simple historical existence of these people, or checking the historical accuracy of what is reported is nearly impossible in most instances. Nor is it an easy matter to prove that hypnotic subjects who come up with such stories did not already have the information stored somewhere in their unconscious minds. We pick up so much information about foreign people and places through our exposure to television and other media that our minds (both conscious and unconscious) have become cluttered repositories of a nearly infinite amount of data. Under the right conditions (such as hypnosis), such material is bound to surface. Given the fact that most people who are interested in past-life recall already believe in reincarnation, it shouldn't seem odd that these recollections surface in the guise of "reincarnation" stories.

So how can you authoritatively verify the validity of past-life recall? There seems no foolproof way, but one line of evidence has always struck those interested in this subject as probably *the* most crucial aspect of the extant literature on reincarnation. If a person were to suddenly develop a skill that related to a previous life, such a phenomenon would be strong evidence favoring reincarnation. For instance, if an auto mechanic remembered a previous life as a violinist and also remembered how to *play* the violin—and really could do it— that would be true evidence of reincarnation. A skill is a learned attribute. We learn it by practice, and one cannot master a technical skill without this practice. Now, one skill we all learn during the course of our lives is language. We learn to speak by a process of cognition, imitation, rehearsal, and practice. If a person could recall and correctly use a language he allegedly spoke during a past life, this could be considered valid evidence of reincarnation. However, as more than one skeptic has pointed out, people who remember their past lives—either spontaneously or through hypnotic regression—rarely can demonstrate this skill.

But skeptics are often a hasty lot of people. The fact remains that a few reincarnation researchers *have* found their subjects talking in foreign languages. This phenomenon represents one of the precious few lines of evidence that reincarnation (or at least something akin to it) really occurs. It is, though, still a controversial area of exploration, as the following classic case illustrates.

Dr. F. H. Wood was an obscure British musicologist and organist who lived in Blackpool, England. Born in 1880, he would have lived an uneventful life had his brother not been tragically killed in a car accident in 1912. Since Wood held a long-lived interest in the paranormal, he immediately set about making post-mortem contact with him. England was full of mediums during this heydey of post-Victorian spiritualism, but it wasn't until 1927 that Wood embarked on what would become one of the most complex cases in the annals of psychical research.

It was in that year that a friend of his, an amateur musician and singer, began experiencing spontaneous trances and bouts of automatic writing. Miss Ivy Carter Beaumont (called simply "Rosemary" in all the published reports on her mediumship) was a school teacher some thirteen years his junior. She knew of his interest in the paranormal and immediately told him about the strange experiences that were disrupting her life. Wood, ever hoping to find evidence proving the survival of the soul, took an immense interest in the case. His search to make psychic contact with his brother was soon abandoned, though, when an abrupt turnabout occurred in the case and Rosemary began bringing through messages from ancient Egypt. Not only did she begin speaking in the alleged language of those ancient times, but she gradually began recalling her own previous life along the Nile in some detail. By 1940 Wood had written three books on his investigation into the Rosemary affair, had collected some 5,000 phrases of ancient Egyptian, and had presented psychical research with a case so complex and controversial that even today it remains the focus of considerable interest.

Dr. Wood tells the story of Rosemary's mediumship in his first book, *After Thirty Centuries,* which appeared in 1935. When he first met her, the young school teacher's automatic writing had fully developed and she was receiving messages from a deceased Quaker woman. Messages were also being received from England's late prime minister.* This phase of the Rosemary

---

*Some of these communications were veridical; that is, they revealed information the psychic could not have come by normally. Since this aspect of the case does not bear directly on the case for reincarnation, it will not be discussed here.

mediumship abated about a year later when a new entity appeared as a control. "Lady Nona" initially revealed only that she had lived in ancient Egypt, that her name had been Telika, and that she had been sent to Egypt from her native Babylon to wed the Pharaoh. Her nexus with the medium, she explained, came from their association in that past age in which Rosemary had led a previous life as a Syrian captive. Wood was naturally fascinated by the story and pressed the entity to explain how she could communicate so well in English. The entity responded by explaining that she could communicate by directly influencing the psychic's brain.

The appearance of Lady Nona also heralded a curious development in Rosemary's mediumship. The psychic now began receiving clairaudient messages from the Egyptian communicator that gradually augmented and superseded the automatic writing. Soon Lady Nona was deluging Wood with information about her Egyptian life. These communications also caused Rosemary to recall her own incarnation in Egypt by way of vivid mental pictures. Some of Lady Nona's revivications contained historically accurate information about ancient Egypt as well, primarily about the reign of Amenhotep IV (Iknahten), which impressed the investigator.

The truly unique aspect of the Rosemary mediumship was, however, Lady Nona's claim that she and the medium had lived at the same time in those ancient days. This created a special bond between them and added a surprising element to the case because talk of reincarnation was not at all popular among mediums, psychics, or spiritualists of the time. This bond allegedly gave Lady Nona the power to deliver, through her reincarnated friend, messages purportedly in the ancient language they had spoken together. These language tests, and the controversy they ignited, soon became the critical focus upon which the validity of the case ultimately hinged.

The story of how these language tests came about is itself a fascinating one. Wood had by 1931 written several articles about the Rosemary mediumship for the popular psychic press. Eventually he received a letter from an Egyptologist in Brighton seeking more information about the case. Alfred J. Howard Hulme was basically an amateur Egyptologist but was skilled enough to have compiled an Egyptian dictionary. His interest in Egyptian linguistics naturally prompted him to ask Wood whether Lady Nona could deliver any message in the ancient tongue. Such an accomplishment, he explained, would have a dual value. Not only would it help validate the Rosemary mediumship in general, but a number of such communications could well shed light on the ancient Egyptian language itself. Hulme explained that Egyptian writings are constructed solely on consonants and scholars have no idea how the language actually sounded, since the unrecorded use of vowels is unknown to us. We can _read_ Eqyptian, but no one today knows how to speak it.

It wasn't until three months after Hulme first contacted Wood that Lady Nona complied with Hulme's request. It came toward the end of a seance, when Rosemary clairaudiently mumbled a phrase she had heard Lady Nona speak. "Ah-yít-ah-zhúla," she intoned. Wood was curious and sent the phonetically recorded phrase to Hulme in Brighton, who was able to reconstruct and translate the phrase as "Saluted art thou, at the end." A collaboration soon resulted between Hulme and Wood, who began doggedly recording hundreds upon hundreds of Egyptian phrases dictated by Nona through the medium. It was Hulme's eventual opinion that the language delivered through Rosemary was internally consistent, accorded well with ancient Egyptian vocabulary and grammar, and shed new light on the hitherto mysterious use of the vowels. Hulme even identified the language as that used in the Middle Kingdom of Egypt, which dated between 2400 and 1356 B.C.

Not only did Hulme translate Rosemary's utterances, but he also constructed "test questions" he delivered to Wood, who, in turn, enunciated them to Lady Nona. It was hoped that she could reply intelligently. These tests were invariably successful and constitute the most intriguing linguistic aspects of the case.

On one occasion, for instance, Wood delivered an Eqyptian phrase through Rosemary meaning "Hail to Thee, Princess Nona." Nona's reply was "Ah-neésh-u-en. Pah-ah-sée-man." Hulme later translated this as meaning "Protected ones are we. This is indeed established."

Wood was immensely impressed by this message. "Now the significance of this prompt answer is more subtle than might even appear at first sight," he wrote in *After Thirty Centuries*. It seems that a word Hulme had used in his original phrase had two possible meanings, depending on the usage. He had not told this to Wood. Nevertheless, the communicator had taken the word as used by Hulme and inserted it into her response by using the word's *other* denotation. "Such an answer," Wood explained, "finally disposes of the theory that these language tests might be received by telepathy from Mr. Howard Hulme, 200 miles away."

Incidents such as these led Wood and Hulme to deliberately test Lady Nona with several dozen language tests between 1931 and 1936. They were structured along four different lines. Sometimes a question was given to Lady Nona through Rosemary in English with the request that a meaningful reply be given in Egyptian. A variant of this procedure was to give the communicator a request in Egyptian and ask for a pertinent response in the same language. Sometimes, to test the communicator's understanding, they would request an English reply to a question posed in the ancient language. A fourth type of test was more impromptu, in which Lady Nona would deliver an Egyptian phrase while Rosemary offered a rough translation that could later be checked.

This last type of test especially intrigued Wood, who devoted an entire chapter to it in his subsequent *This Egyptian Miracle*. During one session, for instance, Rosemary heard Lady Nona say "Zee ésti donk. Pa ńeeta, Kheem sáb." Rosemary herself added that the phrase concerned "something to do with your having a lot to find out." Wood indeed found later that the phrase translated as "To write the report gives work—this editing, when ignorant or without the knowledge of a master-scribe."

The upshot of these tests came in 1937 when Wood and Hulme published a book primarily directed toward analyzing the linguistic aspects of the case. _Ancient Egypt Speaks_ included a detailed analysis of the language delivered through Rosemary, as well as a discussion of some of the language tests. Hulme's main contribution to the collaboration was to show that Rosemary's language was based on correct vocabulary and Egyptian grammar. He even went so far as to write that "in cases where the Egyptians habitually made exceptions to certain grammatical rules, Nona never fails to observe these breaks from rule." Unfortunately, though, Rosemary never transcribed any hieroglyphics, which could have further documented her mediumship. This is actually quite understandable, since Lady Nona claimed to be Babylonian and may well have been more familiar with spoken Egyptian than its complex written counterpart. But in 1936 the medium did visit the offices of the London-based International Institute for Psychical Research, which was then under the direction of Dr. Nandor Fodor. A grammaphone record was made of Rosemary speaking from Lady Nona's dictation, and more than fifty phrases were recorded for posterity.

The revivication of the ancient Egyptian language corresponded with greater and greater recall on Rosemary's part about her own past incarnation. These, in turn, corresponded with Lady Nona's own willingness to reveal more and more about her own terrestrial existence. Both women came out with fascinating material and often historically accurate insights. A tablet unearthed in 1887, for instance, fully confirmed that a Babylonian princess had indeed been sent to Egypt during the time Lady Nona claimed to have lived. Rosemary's memories were, however, less detailed and more impressionistic. She described court life, the rule of the priests, the Pharaoh's palace, herself and her dress, and the great cities she had seen. She also described religious rituals and even sung snatches of Egyptian hymns, which Wood, as a musician, transcribed with relish. The exciting point about these communciations was that Rosemary herself had little interest in Egyptology, so Wood could not believe she had picked them up through casual reading. They also represented an independent source of possible verification of the mediumship.

Dr. Wood tried to validate Rosemary's memories with the same zeal and determination he had used to evaluate her linguistic material. His ultimate opinion was that some of Rosemary's descriptions uncannily matched photographs of Thebes and Karnac that he was able to procure in England. He also published what he felt was her unmistakable prediction of World War II.

Wood published little after the outbreak of the war. He eventually learned the fundamentals of Egyptian grammar itself and during the later phases of the case relied less and less on Hulme's expertise. Wood died in 1963, several years after his collaborator and two years after Miss Beaumont, who had remained a spinster schoolmistress. The Rosemary case still remains a classic and is often cited by reserachers and scholars interested in the evidence for life after death and reincarnation.

But even though the case is a classic, it is not without its share of controversy. Although the case was originally reported more than fifty years ago, a hot debate is still being waged between those who feel it to be one of the most important in the annals of psychical research and those who feel it is total nonsense. There has also been some debate over whether the case should be evaluated as evidence for reincarnation or simply for trance mediumship. It can stand, it has been argued, purely as an example of spirit communication without any reincarnation-linked overshadowings clouding the issue. The crucial aspect of the controversy, however, is that the communicator (Lady Nona) herself emphasized that the retrieval of the ancient Egyptian language was contingent on Miss Beaumont's ability to gain psychic access to buried memories that had carried over from her previous life. This claim obviously ties in with the psychic's own personal recollection of an Egyptian incarnation that emerged as her mediumship developed. In light of these facts, it seems that the entire Rosemary case simultaneously serves as potentially excellent evidence for both reincarnation *and* post-mortem communication. The validity of either aspect of the case automatically contributes to the validity of the other.

So did the Rosemary mediumship, as Hulme claimed, "completely restore the spoken language of Ancient Egupt?" This is a question that today is as perplexing as it was forty-five years ago. Even many psychical researchers don't quite know how to evaluate the case. The late Professor C. J. Ducasse, a philosopher at Brown University and a keen student of the survival issue, dealt squarely with the case in his 1961 classic *A Critical Examination of the Belief in a Life after Death*. His view was that if all aspects of the case can eventually be validated, then the case is "explicable at all only on the assumption that Nona is the surviving spirit of an Egyptian or an ancient person who now uses Rosemary as medium for expression, or that Rosemary is the reincarnation of the spirit of such a person or both." Ducasse is quick to emphasize, however, that *if* is an awfully big word. Dr. Ian Stevenson of the University of Virginia, who is today's leading authority on the evidence for reincarnation, has also acknowledged the importance of the case. But he bemoans the fact that no true expert on ancient Egypt and its language, who could have shed extra and objective light on it, took a personal interest in the case when it was active.

Stevenson's view, that the case is "impressive" but unresolved, is perhaps the most logical way to assess the case. Looking over the case today and all that was written about it, it is clear that it was hardly as clear cut as Wood and Hulme made it out to be.

One problem is that Hulme was probably not as expert in Egyptology and the Egyptian language as he claimed to be. It is unfortunate that he never engaged other Egyptologists to examine the case and work with him on it. He was attacked on these very grounds as far back as 1937 when Professor Battiscombe Gunn, an Egyptologist at Oxford University, reviewed the coauthored *Ancient Egypt Speaks* for the *Journal of Egyptian Archaeology*. In it he argued that Hulme probably read into Lady Nona's utterances meanings that just weren't there. He also argued that Hulme, in his zeal, compounded his error by freely "correcting" the phonetic material Wood was sending him to better fit it in and find correspondences between the phrases and genuine Egyptian vocabulary. Since the vowel sounds of the language were totally unknown, it was Gunn's belief that Hulme merely took what were actually random vocalizations and then twisted them around until some meaning could be matched between them and Egyptian.

Gunn's assessment might seem damning but for the fact that not everyone schooled in Egyptology agreed with him. On the heels of Gunn's comments came the opinions of England's great Egyptologist, the famous Sir Wallis Budge, who was quite impressed by the case.

A more modern appraisal of the Rosemary records has recently been offered by Ian Wilson, a British writer and a firm skeptic when it comes to reincarnation. He offers a totally negative but fascinating judgment on the case in his recent book _All in the Mind?_, devoted primarily to the case against reincarnation. Wilson made several inquiries into Hulme's background while preparing his book and cites strong evidence that the Brighton scholar's educational background as an Egyptologist was indeed questionable. So to throw fresh light on the case, Wilson took the Rosemary records to John Ray, a reader in Egyptology at Cambridge, and asked him to go over the material and then offer a fresh evaluation. Ray's eventual conclusion firmly supported Wilson's suspicions, in that Hulme's understanding of the Egyptian language was certainly flawed. He found that the Brighton researcher had made inexcusable errors in grammar while trying to make sense of the Rosemary utterances and had even freely confused Middle Egyptian with the related but linguistically distinct language of later Egypt. He also found that Rosemary's visions included some amusing anachronisms, such as seeing camels used for domestic work in an era before they were actually employed for such purposes.

I might add at this point that several years ago I raised the question of the Rosemary mediumship with an Egyptologist who is also a keen student of the psychic field. His view was that Rosemary's memories of ancient Egypt were totally consistent with the information taught to most school children during their studies of ancient history—which was part and parcel of a formal Victorian education.

So just what is one to believe about this provocative case?

My own evaluation of the case remains pretty much neutral, although I can't say I find the criticism of Wilson, Ray, and Gunn all that destructive. It seems hard for me to believe, for instance, that Hulme and (later) Wood could have so consistently misinterpreted the material they were receiving. The consistent success of the various language tests is also hard to explain as mere misinterpretations. Nor can Gunn or Wilson's arguments explain how Rosemary could reply to Egyptian questions with meaningful replies in English. Either she (or Lady Nona) actually understood what was being asked, or the psychic could read the investigators' minds. Either way we have to admit that some element of genuineness was contained within the mediumship. The fact that Hulme sometimes had to revise Wood's phonetic descriptions of Rosemary's speech doesn't bother me very much either. Anyone who has tried to transcribe a foreign language with which he is not familiar will know how inexact such transcriptions invariably turn out. Cognitive psychologists have also been long aware just how subjective our sensory perceptions really are. Certainly one must take into account, as Hulme did but which Wilson does *not,* that a certain margin of error must have existed as Lady Nona spoke her utterances to Rosemary, who repeated them to Wood, who had to phonetically transcribe them. Just recall for a minute all the furor over the Watergate tapes. Several people worked on the tapes and had a hard time transcribing them and agreeing on what was sometimes said . . . and they all spoke perfect English.

In his zeal to dismiss the Rosemary case, Wilson also makes some dubious points about the vowels Hulme incorporated into the records. Remember that Rosemary enunciated words that included their vowel sounds. Hulme had to match these utterances against vowelless words in the Egyptian vocabulary. So a certain amount of guesswork had to be part and parcel of his job. Wilson feels that this was a crucial source of error to which Hulme became addicted. A word such as b-nd, to make an English language analogy, could be, for instance, matched against bond, bind, bend, or band. The same would be true of anything Rosemary said. If she had said something like (to use an English analogue) "bend," Hulme could try to match it with bond, band, or bind for the word to become meaningful in itself, or within the phrase he was translating. "On this basis," Wilson writes, "Hulme could conjure up an Ancient Egyptian meaning for any set of sounds produced by Rosemary."

This is, of course, nonsense. It just wouldn't work in actual practice. If Rosemary were speaking gibberish, she could have invariably come up with many words that, no matter how the vowels were interchanged or juxtaposed, would not turn out meaningful. Just take any three random consonants of our own alphabet and try to see how many meaningful words can be made by inserting vowels between them. Not many. And since Hulme was working with word groups that had to have an overall meaning, the dubious nature of the utterances would soon have become clear to Hulme and Wood as they made their translations.

But what of Ray's opinion that Rosemary's language—or at least Hulme's translation of it—was ungrammatical and confused different dialects? There is no need to argue this point. Although at the present time Ray has not published a report showing how widespread these peccadillos appear in the Rosemary records, his criticisms would not be too devastating even if such errors were rather widespread. When I read Wilson's evaluation of the Rosemary records, which included Ray's evaluation, I thought back to a cartoon I once saw while working as a professional musician. It had been tagged on a harp case and depicted a monkey holding a violin; his organgrinder owner stood next to him. The monkey had its hat held out to a passerby, who was standing there with a rather cynical expression on his face. He was saying, "Well, I don't know; after all, I've heard 'The Flight of the Bumble Bee' played a lot better." The point is obvious. The miracle of the Rosemary case is not that the language was perfect, but that the medium came out with anything resembling Egyptian at all.

Hopefully, though, the last chapter in the now fifty-year-old mystery of the Rosemary mediumship will soon be written. It may well be that within a few years the whole enigma of Rosemary and her Egyptian language will finally be resolved.

Dr. William Kautz is a staff scientist at SRI International in Menlo Park, California, where he has founded the Research Center for Applied Intuition. Being a computer expert by training, Dr. Kautz has long been interested in how the computer might shed new light on the Rosemary case. Thanks to a private grant, he has now procured Dr. Wood's original notebooks on the case (which include some 5,000 phrases) and hopes to apply modern technology to their evaluation. Dr. Kautz's main plan is to carry out a type of analysis unthinkable before the modern age of the computer. This entails running a series of complex analyses of the Rosemary material. As he recently explained to an audience attending a conference held by the Psychical Research Foundation in Chapel Hill, North Carolina:

> In order to establish the validity of the purported Egyptian language text of the Rosemary records, it will be necessary to establish a close and linguistically reasonable correspondence between them and the known Egyptian language of the late 18th Dynasty. The comparison may take two forms. Rosemary's vocalized Egyptian can be compared (1) directly with the vowelless and somewhat formal written language, or (2) with a _reconstitution_ of the vocal language. Reconstitution is a procedure sometimes involved in linguistic studies to re-create one member of a langauge family from other closely associated members, taking into account geographic and cultural affinities and based upon established principles of phonic and morphemic trends in langauge evolution. A full reconstitution of vocal Egyptian has never been attempted. Several studies have attempted to reconstruct some of the vowel sounds from later versions of written Egyptian (19th and 20th Dynasty forms, and also Coptic, which contains vowels but was spoken very much later) and words and communications shared with other contemporary written languages that contained vowel representations.

Dr. Kautz has not been blind to the problem this undertaking will entail:

> Rosemary was simply not able to reproduce the full range of 'gutterals' and other sounds we believe were employed in Egypt at the time. The source personality apologized several times for her inability to communicate some of the sounds through Rosemary's "alien throat."
>
> In spite of these expected differences between Rosemary's spoken Egyptian and the classical, written version of the language, there should be no funda-

mental difficulty in testing for a close correspondence between the two. Most important, however, there is no point in striving to prove the two to be identical (as Dr. Wood attempted to do).

The SRI scientist also hopes to find objective evidence that the Rosemary language is self-consistent, a claim first made by Hulme so many years ago.

This exciting project is, to date, only in its initial stages. All of the original Egyptian utterances have been procured and computerized and a library on Egyptology—including writings on the language used in its long history—has been assembled. An authority on Egyptology has also been hired to begin an independent reconstruction of the language most likely used in Rosemary's era. During the next four years Kautz will be busy computerizing a small dictionary of written Egyptian so that a meaningful comparison with the Rosemary records can be made by the computer. Several different types of linguistic analyses are planned.

If all Dr. Kautz's work pays off, what will be the result? It will be a major breakthrough for parapsychology and especially for those primarily interested in the survival controversy, including the case for reincarnation.

Conclusions

The Rosemary case represents a rather backdoor approach to the reincarnation mystery, since the evidence provided by the case is more inferential than direct. The fact remains, though, that it holds up well even after several decades. While the case is not without its difficulties, what seems so impressive is how critics have been unsuccessful at disposing of it. While the xenoglossy spoken by the psychic is complicated by the fact that the ancient Egyptian language remains somewhat of a puzzle to us, there is every indication that Rosemary had access to some sort of information about the structure of the language. It is highly unlikely that she came by this information normally.

Xenoglossy II: Speaking of Past Lives

Unfortunately, there are very few cases of past-life recall that include complete language revivications. The Rosemary case is fairly unique in the literature, though at least one recent case—to be discussed in full later in this chapter—certainly rivals it. It would undoubtedly be evidential if some child, of the sort Dr. Stevenson has been studying, could suddenly start speaking a foreign language both responsively and linguistically correctly as his past-life memories emerged. Such a case would add immensely to the case for reincarnation, because the possibility that such a young child, still acquiring mastery of his *own* native language skills, could have accidentally picked up a foreign language unconsciously seems unlikely. But such cases just do not exist.

There do exist, however, a few cases in which children have recalled past lives and have spontaneously employed small bits and snatches of the foreign languages they purportedly spoke. Ian Stevenson has run into this phenomenon no less than four times during his personal investigations of children in Asia, Alaska, and the Middle East who have recalled their past lives. That's not a great average, since he has investigated hundreds of cases. But this phenomenon, technically called *xenoglossy*, cannot simply be dismissed just because it is rare. The following case, which Stevenson includes in his monumental study *Twenty Cases Suggestive of Reincarnation,* is typical:

Swarnlata Mishra was a little girl who lived in a central Indian province where the native tongue is Hindu; yet at a remarkably young age she would sometimes start dancing while singing in Bengali. It was later discovered that these songs were based on poems by Rabindranath Tagore, a famous

147

Indian poet. It was alleged that the girl had never been introduced to this language, even though the songs were available on commercial recordings. Swarnlata claimed that she learned the songs and dances while living in the Bengalese city of Sylhet (now in Bangladesh) during a previous life. The case of Swarnlata Mishra is not a strong one, though, because she was only heard to *recite* a foreign tongue, not actually use it in an intelligent fashion. Nor can it be ruled out that the girl had, at sometime unbeknown to her parents, learned the songs from records.

A more impressive case uncovered by Stevenson is that of Wijanama Ariyawansa, a Sinhalese boy born in 1959 and living in Sri Lanka.

Wijanama, while still a child, began talking about a previous life as a Muslim. This was a surprise to his parents, who were Buddhists. (Buddhism is the primary religion of Sri Lanka). Unfortunately, the boy could not seem to remember specific details about his past life that could be checked out and verified. However, during the period of his life when he was under the influence of his past-life memories, the boy would often become somnambulistic and had the habit of sitting up in bed while asleep, crossing his legs and uttering phrases in a strange language. These episodes lasted for several years and only came to an end in 1970.

Because of the lack of potentially veridical information in the case, it is weaker than most of the reports Stevenson has published. The only strong interesting aspect of the case *was*, in fact, the xenoglossy. Wijanama would sometimes spontaneously use strange and foreign sounding words in his day-to-day conversation. The proper identification of these words is crucial to the case, and it is the one aspect that Stevenson has been able to follow up in depth. As he reports of this analysis:

> In November, 1970 I was able to obtain a tape recording of Wijanama's nocturnal utterances. Mr. T. S. Miskin, a member of the Muslim community of Kandy, listened to the tape recording and identified two of the words as "umma" and "vappa." These are corrupted Tamil words used by Kandyan Muslims for "mother" and "father." On the tape recording one can also hear Wijanama saying "Allaha," the Arabic word for "God." A fourth word "thungs" (to give its best representation with the English alphabet) has not been identified. Wijanama repeated the words several times during the mutterings, which apparently consisted of a kind of call to his (previous) parents and God. Mr. Miskin was particularly impressed by Wijanama's pronunciation of the words which he recognized and he stated that only a Muslim child could have pronounced them so well.

The youthful Wijanama sometimes also spoke another unfamiliar word on occasion. While taking his meals, the boy's parents sometimes asked him if he had eaten enough or whether he wanted more. If the boy were satiated, he would reply by saying *"podang"*. This is a Tamil word used by the Kandyan Muslims and translates as "enough." The Kandyan Muslims specifically use the word just as Wijanama was in the habit of employing it, to signify that they have had enough to eat. The corresponding Sinhalese word is quite different.

Dr. Stevenson is not the only researcher who has stumbled across this strange phenomenon. A similar case has been reported from Brazil by Hernani Andrade, one of that country's leading parapsychologists. Just as Dr. Stevenson has done in Asia and the Middle East, Dr. Andrade has made several studies of Brazilian children who have spontaneously recalled their past lives.

The subject of his investigation was Viviane Silvino, a Brazilian girl living in São Paulo, who at a young age began talking about a previous life she had lived in Rome. Although the girl was able to outline various facts about her previous life, Andrade was never able to trace any family in Rome that matched her description. Since the girl did not recall her previous family's name or address, this failure was perhaps inevitable. Nonetheless, on occasion the girl seemed able to use isolated Italian words and phrases. It should be noted, though, that her mother had a passing familiarity with Italian, which the girl might have picked up accidentally.

It should be fairly obvious that none of these cases are, in themselves, very impressive, because the xenoglossic languages spoken by the children were ones they could easily have heard during the course of their daily lives. Nor were they obscure dialects or so-called "dead" languages, which would be hard to "pick up" accidentally. It is not rare to hear Italian spoken in Brazil, just as it is not odd to hear Greek spoken in New York or Russian in San Francisco. All of us, even if we don't realize it, have ample opportunity to learn bits and phrases of several foreign languages. A chance watching of a foreign and subtitled film, following an opera libretto, overhearing two foreigners talking a mixture of their own language and English—these are experiences we all have had and might well imprint themselves onto our minds to be recalled later (and innocently) during the emergence of a past-life recall. There is even some evidence that a language picked up unconsciously can be used correctly and most creatively.

The case for this phenomenon is slim and controversial, though. The only documented case on record, in fact, is contained within the records of one of the most complicated cases of multiple personality ever placed in the literature. Multiple personality is a syndrome in which an individual "possesses" several different personalities who alternately control the body. Many of them will be totally oblivious to the existence of the others, while a few may be familiar with the other personalities and will consider them rivals. The case of Billy Milligan was (and is) a textbook example of this mental disorder. While still a young man living in Columbus, Ohio, he came to public attention in 1977 when he was arrested for rape. During the trial it came out that he was a victim of multiple personality and that it was one of his alter egos who was responsible for the attacks. He was eventually sent to a mental institution. One of the strangest aspects of the case was that one of Billy's numerous personalities (there were a total of twenty-three in all) could speak Croatian. It was later learned that, as a teenager, Billy had associated himself with some Gypsies in Florida and had "picked up" the language from them, although he was never actually taught it.* This case must be considered an anomaly since no other case resembling it has appeared in the literature on this disorder. But it does indicate that one should evaluate cases of xenoglossy with some caution.

There does exist one case, however, that relies on both xenoglossy *and* the fact that the subject was able to "remember" veridical information about a past life. The value of the case lies in the fact that a number of investigators have looked into it and were able to do so while it was still in its most active stages. It is also notable that these investigators have been uniformly impressed with the case.

The first publication of the case in the United States came in 1979 when it appeared rather innocuously as "A case of secondary personality with xenoglossy" in the *American Journal of Psychiatry*. The authors were Dr. Ian Stevenson and Dr. Satwant Pasricha, an Indian psychologist interested in reincarnation and parapsychology. The report concerned a young woman in Nagpur, Maharashta (India), who since 1974 has periodically fallen into strange trances. During these episodes she is taken over by the personality of a Bengali woman who apparently died more than a hundred years before. If all this weren't bizarre enough, the woman speaks only Bengali during these trances even though she has never formally studied the language in any depth. She also seems familiar with people who actually lived in Bengal during the early part of the nineteenth century and seems totally conversant in the customs of the period.

Drs. Stevenson and Pasricha are not the only researchers who have looked into the case at first hand. Several Indian parapsychologists have also been delving into it; chief among these has been Professor V. V. Akolkar of Poona, who has been following the case for several years now, although his privately circulated report on it has not yet been published.**

The main character in this eerie drama, Uttara Huddar, was born in 1941 in Nagpur, a city located in west India and hundreds of miles from Bengal. Her native tongue is Marathi, although she speaks fluent English and some Hindi. Her parents speak Marathi almost exclusively. Her childhood and schooling were relatively uneventful. She came from a family of five children and lived her early life with her parents in Nagpur, where she had little contact with any Bengal residents. She never visited that part of her native India and most of her formative years were devoted to learning. She was apparently an unexceptional student but took a special liking to dancing, dramatics, and San-

---

*This information was not included by author Daniel Keyes in his engaging book, *The Minds of Billy Milligan* (New York, Random House, 1981). The information came to light only after the book had been finished and was made public in a review of the book that appeared in the February 1983 issue of *Reincarnation Report* magazine.

**I would like to thank Dr. Akolkar for advising me of the existence of his report and providing me with a copy of it.

skrit. Science was her first choice in college and she eventually took a degree in biology. During her graduate study she concentrated on English and public administration, and after these studies were concluded, she began work as a lecturer at Nagpur University in the latter field.

This was hardly an auspicious beginning for what was soon to become a _cause célèbre_ for scientists interested in reincarnation.

The awakening of Uttara's past-life memories came in 1973. She had previously maintained a long-lived interest in religion and the spiritual path. Her father had introduced her to the practice of yoga and meditation when she was a youngster, and since 1965 she had been practicing meditation regularly. A turning point came in 1972 when she experienced an intense mystical experience while meditating at a local ashram. Several more of these experiences followed in subsequent months, some apparently reminiscent of the legendary "raising of the Kundalini." These experiences unfortunately had an ill effect on her mind, and in December 1973 she was hospitalized because of her recurrent headaches and blackouts. Even though the blackouts continued while she was hospitalized, her doctors were totally puzzled by them and never diagnosed the problem.

It was also during her hospital stay that "Sharada" first emerged. Sometimes when Uttara would go to bed she would awake as an entirely new personality who claimed to be a Bengali woman still living in the nineteenth century. She could only speak in Bengali and had a difficult time communicating to the people in the hospital who were generally unfamiliar with the language. These spells lasted only a few moments at first but they continued after Uttara was released and gradually became stronger and stronger. Between February 1974 and April 1977, for instance, there were some twenty-three instances when Sharada took total control of Uttara's body. These periods manifested in a variety of ways. Sometimes there were premonitory signs when Sharada wanted to "come out," and Uttara would feel odd crawling sensations over her head before passing out. But it was more often the case that Uttara would simply wake up in the morning _as_ Sharada, who seemed in control of both Uttara's mind _and_ body. She seemed totally unaware of who Uttara was and could speak only Bengali, much to the dismay of the Huddar family, who speak only Marathi. Nor did she even recognize the Huddar family at first. She insisted that her name was Sharada and seemed to think that she was still living in the Bengal of years ago. She was also apparently unfamiliar with modern tools, customs, and other elements of modern Indian life. What was even more distressing to the Huddar family, not to mention Uttara herself, was that the Sharada personality eventually was able to take longer and longer control of the body. By 1977 it was not unusual for Sharada to be in control for a week or so. Possessions of up to forty days were also noted.

But just who is Sharada?

By her own testimony and account, she is a Bengali woman living in the nineteenth century as the daughter of Brajanath Chattopadhaya and Renukha Devi. (It appears that she lived around 1810 to 1830). She has told

Uttara's family, as well as many investigators who have visited her in Nagpur, that she was raised by her maternal aunt, was married at seven, had two miscarriages, and traveled to several Bengal cities with her husband. She seems unaware that she is "dead." Her last memory is that she fell unconscious (and presumably died) from a snakebite she suffered while gardening. During these conversations with the Huddar family, investigators, and other visitors, she has mentioned the proper names of scores of her relatives and has revealed a wealth of geographical and historical facts about Bengal. She has, in fact, made a total of eighty-five specific statements about her life capable of being documented and verified.

This is essentially a summary of the case as it now stands. The Sharada personality still periodically controls Uttara to this day, although there is some evidence that she is slowly merging with Uttara's normal personality. The case seems to tread that infinite though obscure boundary between possession and reincarnation, though several attempts to document Sharada's life tend to indicate that reincarnation might be the more viable explanation.

The most detailed examination of the *historical* validity of the Sharada personality has been made by Drs. Stevenson and Pasricha, who traveled to Nagpur in June 1974 especially to study the case at first hand. There they were able to collaborate with two Indian investigators, P. Pal and R. K. Sinha, who helped to formally document and investigate certain aspects of the case. Dr. Stevenson and his colleagues were able to interview Uttara, take a detailed case history of her trances from the Huddar family, and chronologize the names and places mentioned by Sharada that related to her Bengali life. Dr. Pasricha was able to follow up the case by traveling to Bengal to further delve into the historical aspects of the investigation. What they have discovered is astounding. With the help of his Indian colleagues Dr. Stevenson was able to construct a detailed genealogy of Sharada's Bengal family, the Chattopadhayas, based on names volunteered by the personality. They were even able to locate the current head of this family in Bengal and were delighted to learn that he possessed a genealogy of the family that covered the early nineteenth century. He was able to verify that a Brajanath Chattopadhaya had actually lived during the time indicated by Sharada.

The existence of this independent (and probably accurate) genealogy also gave the investigators their chance to test Sharada's memory when she next controlled Uttara. They didn't have long to wait, because Uttara underwent another trance/possession soon after the genealogy was discovered.

In his official report on the case to the *Journal* of the American Society for Psychical Research, Dr. Stevenson explains how Sinha and Pal specifically questioned Sharada about her relatives after studying the genealogy but without mentioning anything to her about the information it contained. He and Dr. Pasricha reported in 1980:

> Sharada was asked whether she could give the relationships she had with members of her family other than her father. She mentioned 10 other male

relatives and gave her relationship to six of them. On the assumption that Sharada was the daughter of Brajanath Chattopadhaya (as she said she was), she gave the correct relationship she would have had to five of the male relatives of Brajanath Chattopadhaya whose names appear around his on the genealogy. For example, she gave her grandfather's name as Ramnath, and in the genealogy Ramnath is recorded as the father of Brajanath, who was, according to Sharada, her father. (The names of the five other persons Sharada mentioned do not appear in the genealogy.) The genealogy is exclusively a male one. Since no women's names appear in it, we cannot say that we have proved that a person corresponding to Sharada's statements existed. But the correspondence between the genealogy and her statements about the relationships of the male members of the family seems beyond coincidence.

Dr. Stevenson also noted that, while one name given by Sharada did not appear in the independent genealogy, subsequent research successfully documents this individual as yet another son of Brajanath Chattopadhaya. (They found his name signed to a nineteenth-century land document.) So it would appear that Sharada's memories are even more complete than the current Chattopadhaya family's own records. The only problem with this test is that part of the genealogy was published in a local Bengali magazine in 1907. But as Dr. Stevenson no doubt correctly notes, "We believe it virtually impossible for Uttara to have seen a copy of this magazine. It is not likely that any copy of it had ever gone out of Bengal, and she had never visited that state. Accordingly, we are confident that she had never seen the genealogy."

An even more critical aspect of the case is, of course, the language Sharada speaks during her periods of possession. It certainly appears that she can speak fluent Bengali. Her command of the language has been independently documented by Pal, among others, who spoke with the Sharada personality during the 1975 Stevenson investigation at great length. He was especially impressed by an odd idiosyncracy of her vocabulary and reported to Stevenson that Sharada had used no English "loan words" during their conversations. This impressed the scholar since modern Bengali was deeply infiltrated by the English language at the turn of the current century. Today, the Bengali language employs about 20 percent of these loan words. The Bengali of Sharada's era made no use of English and this is exactly how the personality used it. She instead used a great number of Sanskrit words, which is also historically accurate.

But could Uttara have learned this language in any normal way? This is an issue upon which investigators who have delved into the case disagree. Dr. Stevenson holds a negative opinion on the issue. While in India he traced back through all of Uttara's educational records. There he learned that she had taken a few lessons in Bengali script when she was studying Sanskrit but was only exposed to a passing acquaintanceship with it. He points out that Uttara learned only enough to read a few words but little more and could not even read full sentences. Nor was she taught to speak Bengali but only to *read* the script. He also learned that even her teacher couldn't really speak the language. It is his conclusion, then, that the Sharada case is a genuine example of paranormal xenoglossy—the psychic ability to speak a language never previously learned.

This same issue has also been studied by Akolkar, who personally investigated the Sharada case on behalf of the Parapsychological Research Institute in Poona. He conducted his investigation at about the same time that Stevenson was actively involved in the case but has come to a different conclusion. Akolkar also tried to trace any exposure Sharada might have had to Bengali during her schooling. As a result of several inquiries, he maintains that Uttara may possess a better command of the language than usually attributed to her. The major stumbling block came when the Indian investigator was able to locate a former classmate of Uttara's who claimed that they studied Bengali together. He further maintained that the two of them had learned enough to read an elementary primer in Bengali, but nothing more. He emphasized, though, that they had no detailed study of the language; but these revelations indicate that Dr. Stevenson has overstated the evidence the Sharada case presents for genuine xenoglossy. It is Akolkar's view that, however unfeasible, we must take into account the possibility that Uttara might unconsciously be more familiar with Bengali than may appear on the surface.

This does not mean that Akolkar believes that the case should be dismissed, however. In fact, he believes the exact opposite. He specifically notes in his unpublished report that Uttara's academic study of Bengali can only explain her familiarity with the *written* language and not how it is actually spoken. He also notes that her passing familiarity with the language cannot explain the fact that she speaks Bengali with a specific local dialect and accent, sometimes uses colloquial expressions, and can distinguish between the dialects and accents of her Bengali visitors. Nor can her academic learning explain her detailed knowledge of sometimes antiquated Bengali customs. "One had only to observe and listen to Sharada to feel convinced that it was not a case of a non-Bengali girl putting on an act," he concluded after making his investigation of the case and meeting the Sharada personality.

So just how can the case of Sharada and her strange appearance in twentieth century India be best explained?

Drs. Stevenson and Pasricha believe that either reincarnation or possession can account for the case. "The somewhat rapid onset and cessation of the Sharada phases as well as the marked differences of personality that occurred when the phases change," they report, "strongly resemble behavior observed in cases of the possession syndrome. Similarly, the amnesia each personality appears to have had for events occurring to the other, even though it was not total, suggests the possession syndrome more than a case of the reincarnation type. The feature of responsive xenoglossy, however, indicates that this is no ordinary case of the possession syndrome, but might instead be one of true 'possession.' This implies that Sharada is a discarnate personality—that is, that she consists of surviving aspects of a real person who lived and died in the early years of the nineteenth century, and who, almost one-hundred-fifty years later, came to dominate and control Uttara's body."

But the investigators do note certain problems with this explanation. They point out in particular that since 1976 the two personalities seem to be slowly fusing. This would indicate that a common memory base links Sharada to Uttara's normal personality. They also note that a few cases have been reported in the literature on the reincarnation memories of children who were similarly "taken over" momentarily when their past-life recollection began emerging. These were only passing phases of these cases, but Stevenson and Pasircha feel that the Sharada case may be generically related to these other reports.

Drs. Stevenson and Pasricha also bring up the possibility that perhaps Uttara Huddar is a distant offspring of Sharada and somehow "inherited" her memory. But since Sharada claims to have died before ever having a child, they reject this explanation.

"We are therefore entitled to conjecture," they conclude in their ASPR report, ". . . that Sharada was a previous incarnation of the person now identified as Uttara."

But can a clear line really be drawn between possession and reincarnation based on phenomenological criteria? This is a vexing question but one that must be raised. Can it be resolved authoritatively?

Perhaps not. But there is one aspect of the Sharada case that seems to weigh the balance in favor of reincarnation. It concerns a peculiar story that comes not from Uttara but from her mother, who has shared this strange ordeal with her daughter. While delving into Uttara's childhood, Dr. Stevenson learned that she suffered a snake phobia as a youngster. Now this may be linked to the fact that Sharada's last recorded memory was of falling unconscious after being bitted by a snake. Could it be merely coincidence that, while she was pregnant, Uttara's mother _had recurrent dreams of being bitten on the foot by a snake?_ Perhaps in some strange way, Uttara Huddar's mother was already being told just "who" her daughter _really_ was even before her birth— and years before Sharada was able to make her existence known to the astonished family.

But what about research on hypnotic regression, one might ask? What about people who are carefully _guided_ back to past lives? Shouldn't these subjects be able to recall the languages they spoke during their past incarnation relatively easily and _consistently?_ Several researchers are presently engaged in this type of study, including Helen Wambaugh in the United States, Thorwald Dethlefsen in Germany, and (until his recent death) Arnall Bloxham in England. But most of these researchers (with the exception of Dethlefsen) have tended to veer away from the problem of language recall. A typical case in point is Dr. Edith Fiore, a Saratoga, California, psychologist, who uses hypnotically induced past-life recall as part of her clinical practice and who has written, ". . . I have not had anyone speak in a foreign language. Lately, though, just to be on the safe side, before regressing subjects I suggest that they respond to me in English."

This typical unwillingness to explore a potentially important avenue of evidence has long marred the hypnotic investigation of reincarnation memories.

Of course, the whole issue of language recall, especially under hypnotic regression, may well be a phony one to start with. Keep in mind that we are dealing here with *memory,* and memory is a function of mental imagery and not necessarily langauge. In fact, cognitive psychologists have discovered that people tend to code incoming information for later memory retrieval in terms of an imagery code and a language code. We all rely upon both of these processes when we think and try to remember, although many of us will use one code more often and consistently than the other. Hypnotic regression obviously relies more on image processing than on verbal associations, which is why hypnotically elicited past-life memories would probably not include much language recall. For instance, try the following experiment. Close your eyes and think back to something that happened when you were five years old, as you might under the direction of a hypnotist regressing you. Then verbally describe what you see as though you were actually reliving it. Although your vocal inflections might change a bit, note that you are still speaking with the vocabulary and nuances of an adult. This is very similar to what happens during formal past-life hypnotic regression. It might therefore be inappropriate for us to expect a regressed subject to actually speak in a foreign language. However, by careful questioning, it might be possible for a regressed subject to recall bits of a language he spoke in a previous life—while he is reliving some past event—or perhaps any odd words or phrases that might have been spoken *to* him during the episode in question.

Just such a case did, in fact, come to light in the mid-1970s when Dr. Joel Whitton, a Canadian psychiatrist associated with the Toronto-based New Horizons Foundation, reported that one of his hypnotized subjects had apparently come out with words and phrases in two obscure languages while undergoing past-life regression. Both languages were "dead"—that is, no longer commonly spoken—so, Whitton claimed, the subject couldn't have picked them up by accident.

Whitton discovered his prize subject, an unnamed thirty-year-old psychologist, during a project he was undertaking into the phenomenon of past-life regression. Whitton certainly didn't begin his project as a believer. Before discovering this star subject he had written, "Perhaps the Bridey Murphy case served to popularize the subject of hypnosis and reincarnation memories more than any other single instance. . . . Yet at no time previously or in the subsequent two decades has the use of hypnosis in studying the reincarnation theory been analyzed. The validity, reliability, advantages, and disadvantages of hypnosis as an appropriate research tool in investigating reincarnation have not been examined." On even a more pessimistic note, Whitton had written,

"There is no reason as yet to suspect that hypnosis will successfully carry the burden of proof of reincarnation."

It was with these considerations well in mind that Whitton began his own experiments in hypnotic regression in 1973. Only subjects who could achieve a very deep state of hypnosis were used. The investigator also included as part of his study an analysis of his subjects' subsequent dreams, to see how and if elements of their alleged past lives were inserting themselves into their unconscious minds.

Whitton's subject may have done quite a bit to overcome the psychiatrist's initial skepticism toward hypnotically evoked past-life memories. Whitton only describes him in his report as a single man, "educated in the field of psychology and [holding] a responsible position in the assessment and treatment of children with learning and behavioral disorders." Since Whitton is employed as a psychiatrist for the Toronto educational system, we may assume that his subject is probably a colleague and someone who has been known to him for some time. By checking into his background, Whitton has discovered that, besides English, his subject has some familiarity with French, Hebrew, Rashi, Yiddish, Greek, Latin, and Italian. He has been additionally exposed, at one time or another, to several other languages from Hindustani to Norwegian and from Arabic to Ojibway. While under hypnosis, however, this psychologist has spontaneously remembered two previous lives, one as a Viking living about 1000 A.D. and another as an ancient Iranian. While remembering his Viking life, the subject has often heard his previous incarnation, named Thor, talking to him. This has enabled him to recite several words and short phrases of Norsk, an old language and a precursor of modern Icelandic. These words, given phonetically by the subject, have been recorded by Whitton himself. A few of the words seem polluted by Russian and Serbian derivatives. What is most impressive is that most of these words, which the psychologist cannot himself understand, deal with the sea—just the sort of words a reincarnated Viking might be most prone to remember and just the words Whitton encouraged his subject to come up with.

Only portions of the phonetically transcribed phrases and words have been successfully translated by independent "raters" familiar with the language. This may tend to make the case appear less impressive than it really is. However, phonetic transcription of phrases and word groups are extremely hard to correctly render and interpret. As Whitton points out:

> A subject who is naive to a certain language can experience considerable difficulty in phonetically writing that language. For example, another subject was slowly reading the following Icelandic sentence: _Enn bar staka jaka af og til ad lani vid Hornbjargsvita_, which means, _At Hornbjargsvita single ice floes were occasionally still drifting ashore._ As the subject was reading word by word the Icelandic sentence by one of the raters (whose native tongue is Icelandic) the subject wrote the following phonetics: NYR STARKA VAKA RFOTV

ARLADI BIF HORVSRWEDA. It can be appreciated that only three or four of the phonetic groups would be recognized in their translation.

Whitton's subject has also recalled a life as a young man living in Mesopotamia in 625 A.D. and has been able to write out a few scripts in the language he allegedly spoke. Sassanid Pahlavi was the language used in that area from the third to the seventh century. It has not been used since that time and has no relationship to modern Iranian. Yet the subject's scripts have been recognized as correctly written Sassanid Pahlavi by Dr. Indrahim Pourdradi, an expert on the language at the Near Eastern section of the Library of Congress. Some of these writings resulted when Whitton asked his hypnotized subject for *specific* equivalents of commonly used English words. This indicates that the subject can make intelligent use of the language and is not merely repeating chance words he has picked up (unlikely though that is) or perhaps even fraudulently memorized.

If Whitton's subject was unique, the case would be suspect. However, other hypnotists experimenting with age regression have, on rare occasions, come across similar cases. Thorwald Dethlefsen, the director of the Munich-based Institute of Extraordinary Psychology, is one of the few researchers investigating the reincarnation issue who has made an attempt to explore the phenomenon of language recall. He reports in his recent book *Voices from Other Lives* that he was able to regress one of his subjects to a life in ancient Israel. During the regression the subject said at least two words in correctly spoken Aramaic. While this is the only example of xenoglossy reported in the book, Dethlefsen claims that this phenomenon is quite common. He specifically notes that, while a regression session is conducted in German, "I can command the subject to give certain answers in the 'original langauge.' The command is usually obeyed, although at first the foreign language is not spoken fluently or with ease." Unfortunately, Dethlefsen gives no examples of this phenomenon in his book other than the one case cited above.

No doubt the most exhaustive study of such a case has (once again) been contributed by Dr. Ian Stevenson. The complete history of the case came to light in 1974, when he published a detailed monograph on it. The report itself dates back to 1955, the year that a Mrs. T. E. (whose identity has remained a secret at the request of the subject) underwent several hypnotic regression sessions at the hands of her husband, a qualified physician who sometimes used hypnosis in his practice.

Mrs. T. E. was a thirty-seven-year-old housewife living in Philadelphia. She came from Russian-Jewish lineage and to this day still lives in the city of her birth. Her husband died in 1970. The emergence of her past-life memories came duirng a two-month period when her husband was attempting hypnotic regression with her. At first the sessions only left Mrs. T. E. with a painful headache; this seemed linked to a dim recollection of being hit on the head. The dramatic climax to the case came about a week later when, during yet another hypnotic session, Mrs. T. E. took on the personality of a character who called himself "Jensen Jacoby," and who claimed to be Swedish. He communicated by speaking a mixture of a strange language (presumably Swedish) and broken English. This personality subsequently appeared and spoke Swedish during eight sessions held in 1955 and 1956. To document the language the entity so often spoke, several of the sessions were tape recorded by Mrs. T. E.'s husband. Swedish-speaking acquaintances of the couple were also invited to the sessions and were amazed to discover that Jensen could not only speak Swedish but could also reply in Swedish to questions asked in English. Responsive conversations conducted solely in Swedish were also undertaken during some of the sessions.

The personality of Jensen Jacoby (a common name about as unique as "Bob Smith" would be in the United States) gradually developed his own singular identity. He claimed to be a simple peasant, and although he described his life and trade in some detail, he did not reveal any detailed knowledge of Sweden. He did, however, describe the incident that apparently terminated his life and that obviously related to the headaches Mrs. T. E. suffered during the first abortive regression sessions. He told how he and his fellow countrymen had engaged in a battle with some enemies. During the conflict he was killed by a blow to the head he suffered while wading in a pool of water. This memory may have related to the Swedish-Russian wars of the sixteenth and seventeenth centuries. Several additional clues given during the sessions led the first investigators to conclude that Jensen, if he were indeed a genuine personality, probably lived in a small village on the west coast of Sweden in the seventeenth century. Such a geographic location also helped explain why the Jensen personality spoke Swedish with some Norwegian influence.

From a purely veridical and historical standpoint, the case presented little material of any interest. Aside from the xenoglossy Mrs. T. E. was able to display, the only impressive element that arose from the early phases of the case was a unique test some of the first investigators designed. They borrowed some artifacts from the American Swedish Historical Museum in Philadelphia, and presented them to Jensen during one of Mrs. T. E.'s hypnotic trances. He was able to name them spontaneously, often in proper Swedish. It is doubtful that Mrs. T. E. could have studied up in advance to perpetrate a hoax either, since some of the artifacts were rather unusual, such as a Scandinavian wooden container used for measuring grain, which Jensen identified correctly.

But the truly evidential aspect of the case is, as mentioned above, the uncanny versatility Mrs. T. E. displayed when using the Swedish language during the hypnotic sessions. Not only did she speak the language while entranced, but she also used it correctly and perfectly in keeping with a personality that lived in the seventeenth century. This important fact was documented by many visitors to the original sessions and by several experts brought in later to evaluate the tape recordings. For example, Dr. Nils Sahlin, a Philadelphia resident who once taught Swedish, took part in some of the 1955–6 sessions and was able to carefully observe the Jensen personality. Some years later he told Stevenson:

> There were innumerable indications that Jensen was totally unacquainted with modern articles, tools, and exotic fruit. On the other hand, he showed immediate familiarity with articles and things dating back to and before the seventeenth century, many of which had existed in like form for centuries before that. While Jensen apparently understood modern Swedish and Norwegian without difficulty, he had no modern vocabulary, no words for things of exclusively modern date. His usage had a clearly Norwegian flavor, which in my opinion lies closer to the language of the Middle Ages than does Swedish.

Dr. Sahlin also reported that Jensen spoke the language without even a trace of an accent.

> Most remarkable to me was the medium's pronunciation of the words she used, whether ours or her own. She did not speak her Scandinavian as an American would. She had absolutely no difficulty with the umlaut sounds or other peculiarly Scandinavian sounds and accents. By and large she used the correct articles (attached to the noun in Scandinavian) and correct inflectional endings. Having taught Swedish, I know how difficult it is for an American even to repeat after the teacher the correct endings.

Nor did Jensen merely make use of words that had first been spoken by the Swedish speaking interrogators. Sometimes novel yet cogent words were introduced into the conversations. As part of his investigation, Dr. Stevenson also checked with Mrs. T. E.'s relatives and investigated her childhood to see if she had ever had the opportunity to learn Swedish normally. The search came up nil. The only possible contamination to an otherwise clean slate was that Mrs. T. E. had once seen a series of television plays dealing with the life of Swedish immigrants in the United States. Some Swedish had been spoken during the course of the plays.

In short, the collective verdict of the several researchers and Swedish speaking parties who took part in the experiments was that Jensen Jacoby really could speak intelligent Swedish and could carry on impromptu communications in the language. A complete transcript of these conversations runs to more than one-hundred fifty pages and was contained in Stevenson's detailed monograph.

The case, though, is not as impressive as Stevenson—who believes it to be genuine case of xenoglossy—makes it appear. This is especially obvious if we take the time to make a detailed study of the transcripts taken from the original tapes of the sessions. The first thing that is rather noticeable is that Jensen hardly ever uses verbs. This certainly seems suspicious. Verbs and their correct conjugation are the hardest element of a language to learn and master. If a hoaxer wanted to fake a case of xenoglossy, his best bet would be to memorize nouns and short phrases, while avoiding the use of verbs. And this is just what Jensen seems to do during his little conversations. Sometimes verbs are quite obviously and awkwardly avoided. The case is also polluted by the fact that fraud played a role in the subsequent phases of the case. Mrs. T. E. eventually began entering an involuntary mediumistic trance during which she would deliver messages on scientific topics. Even Dr. Stevenson admits in his report that on at least one occasion the topic of one such oration matched some notes found scribbled on a piece of paper in the woman's handbag. Mrs. T. E. claimed not to know how this material got into her possession, a claim that Stevenson apparently takes at face value. The more skeptical reader may well come to a more felicitous and pessimistic conclusion about the woman's integrity.

On the other hand, Mrs. T. E. has passed a lie-detector examination and genuinely seems to be speaking in a dialect of Swedish common to the fourteenth and fifteenth centuries. These positive aspects of the case cannot be ignored either.

Whether or not hypnotically regressed subjects really can recall languages they have never studied is still an unresolved issue. Some evidence exists, but this evidence is not unequivocal. It is obvious that much more research needs to be done on the question. Whitton has made a good start in this direction, and a professor of psychology and expert in psycholinguistics at the University of Southern California is currently planning a similar project. Only time will tell how valid the remembrances of foreign words and languages during hypnotic regression really are.

Conclusions

Xenoglossy, which is potentially one of _the_ most important lines of evidence for the reincarnation doctrine, is also an area of research that has yielded impressive evidence. While many cases of xenoglossic speech can be explained as resulting from cryptomnesia or unconscious learning, a few detailed cases have come to light that cannot be easily dismissed. The fact that, in a few of these cases, so-called "dead languages" have been spoken in an intelligent fashion is especially evidential. Much of this evidence is admittedly still clouded in controversy and the number of cases that withstand critical scrutiny is small. So while cases of xenoglossy cannot serve as independent and definitive proof of reincarnation, they must nonetheless be considered one of the strongest lines of corroboration currently pointing to the rebirth doctrine.

9

Past-Life Therapy

Ma Tin Aung Myo's parents couldn't understand the problem. Since they lived in the rural village of Na-Thul in Upper Burma, their daughter had been shielded from most of the horrors wrought by modern technology. But every time an airplane passed overhead, the girl would be driven into a panic. Ma Tin Aung Myo's peculiar phobia was inexplicable enough, but things really got out of hand when she started talking about her previous life as a Japanese soldier.

The bizarre phobia of little Ma Tin Aung Myo opens a curious chapter in the history of reincarnation research, for it suggests that some mental problems that develop in our present lives may actually be "carry-overs" from our (purported) previous existences.

Ma Tin Aung Myo was born in December 1953. She was the fourth child of U Aye Maung (her father) and Daw Aye Tin (her mother), who died when she was ten. Daw Aye Tin later told investigators that, even when she was pregnant with the girl, she had a peculiar series of dreams that may have related to her daughter's curious claims. She dreamt that a stocky Japanese soldier appeared to her and claimed that he was coming to stay with her family. He appeared to her stripped to the waist. She had this disturbing dream three times, and it is certainly understandable why the woman was distressed by it. The Japanese had made few friends when they commenced their wartime occupation of Upper Burma in 1942. Daw Aye Tin could still remember how allied bombers had frequently straffed the area to protect the crucial railway lines that bordered her town. The bombers were known to gun down anyone on the ground, so the Burmese often evacuated the area during the day. The village of

Na-Thul was the center of these raids when the American and English armies finally managed to drive the Japanese from Burma in 1945.

Ma Tin Aung Myo apparently began talking about her previous life when she was only about two or three years old, and Dr. Ian Stevenson first learned of it some years later and traveled to Burma to meet with the girl and her family in 1972. Ma Tin Aung Myo's mother explained to Dr. Stevenson that her daughter often began to cry and speak cryptically about wanting "to go home" every time a plane flew overhead. When her father asked her why she was afraid, the little girl would invariably answer that she was afraid that she would be shot . . . a curious statement since she was much too young to know very much about the horrors of the war years. Ma Tin Aung Myo retained her phobia for several years, even though her family assured her over and over that the planes couldn't hurt her. The girl's mother also told investigators that Ma Tin Aung Myo was terrified even when a harmless helicopter once landed in the town. She ran indoors to escape from it even though the craft was quite a novelty in the town. Most of the local folk, she added, deliberately scurried outside to see it. Ma Tin Aung Myo continued to talk about going back home all during these formative years.

The girl's behavior became even more perplexing as the years went on. She began complaining about the local climate, couldn't stomach spicy Burmese foods, preferred half-raw fish, and would sporadically throw crying fits about going home to Japan. Eventually the actual memories of her past life became clearer to her, and she explained to her astonished family that she had been born in Japan in her past life, in which she had been a man, had married, and had fathered children. She recalled becoming a soldier during the war and had lost "his" life while stationed in Burma. She further recalled just how she had died. She (or "he") had been outdoors cooking a meal over an open fire very close to where her present family now lived. She had just taken off her shirt and was wearing short pants and a belt when she spotted a plane zeroing in on her. She tried to run, but a spray of bullets ended her life. One struck her in the groin and killed her.

The strange case of Ma Tin Aung Myo is bizarre enough. So could this be a genuine case of past-life recall? It is hard to say.

The description Ma Tin Aung Myo gave of her previous life obviously tied in with Daw Aye Tin's dream of the Japanese soldier, though it is impossible to determine whether Ma Tin Aung Myo had known about the dreams before she first began speaking about her past life. Since she was so young when she first began speaking about her previous existence and first developed her plane phobia, it is unlikely that her parents had specifically told her about the dreams. But she may well have overheard them talking about them. So her description of her past life could have somehow been suggested to her by her parents. This idea supposes, of course, that the girl was cognizant enough at two years old to incorporate these influences into her own self-concept. But this issue is only one of the many uncertainties that surround this strange case. Even Dr. Stevenson, who made an intensive study of it between 1972 and 1977, admits in his report that he failed to track down any events that might shed light on Ma Tin Aung Myo's story. A chief stumbling block was that her parents could remember no incident in which a Japanese soldier was gunned down near their home. Nor were their daughter's statements about her past life in Japan specific enough to trace.

This, in fact, is probably the most embarrassing aspect of the case. It's rather inexplicable that the girl could remember the basic outline of her past life, but couldn't recall her previous name or place of birth. So the skeptic might rightfully argue that Ma Tin Aung Myo had probably internalized information she had picked up from her parents at a very young age and had later used this information as a basis for a fantasy. This fantasy may have eventually become a psychological reality for her. On the other hand, the believer in reincarnation could justifiably point out that Ma Tin Aung Myo's memories were fleeting, vague, and certainly not very complete. Perhaps only a dim outline of her past had been available to her, while more specific details had been wiped from her future memory during the rebirth process.

So from the strict standpoint of evidence, the case of Ma Tin Aung Myo remains a stalemate. But what *is* so impressive about this report is how her rebirth memories have permanently influenced Ma Tin Aung Myo's behavior.

As she grew older she eventually lost her fear of airplanes. This in no way compromises the legitimacy of her original phobia, since many children outgrow their irrational fears. But her memories of her Japanese life have, to the present day, severely affected Ma Tin Aung Myo's sexual identity and orientation. Although many of the specific memories of her Japanese life have faded, she still perceives herself as a man.

Ma Tin Aung Myo refused to wear women's clothing even as a young child and insisted on dressing like a boy. She wore the typical Burmese ankle-length skirt but tied it with a knot in the middle and wore a checked design typical of masculine attire. She was pronouncedly tomboyish as a child and her favorite game was, naturally, playing soldier. This may all sound simply like typical adolescence, but her masculine identity became even more pronounced after she reached puberty. She insisted that her friends address her by masculine honorifics, and she even dropped out of school when the local authorities refused to allow her to attend classes dressed as a boy. Ma Tin Aung Myo continued dressing in this manner over the objections of her family, who were no doubt embarrassed by the entire affair. She never longed for a boyfriend and by the late 1970s was actively courting other village girls in or near her home town.

This overwhelming cross-gender identification made quite an impression on Dr. Stevenson when he finally met Ma Tin Aung Myo. "When I met Ma Tin Aung Myo first in 1972," he reported to the *Journal of Nervous and Mental Diseases* in 1977, "she was overtly masculine in her sexual orientation. She said that if conventions would permit she would associate with boys. She had no wish to marry a husband and expressed instead a desire to have a girl as a wife." Yet despite what may appear to be an overt pathological adaptation to the girl's life situation, Dr. Stevenson does not believe that it resembles anything that comes within the purview of conventional psychiatry. "Since she has not asked for transforming surgery we should not call her a transsexual, but I am quite sure she has never heard of such surgical operations," he notes. "Nor can we call her a transvestite if we restrict this term to persons who obtain sexual pleasure from cross-dressing. So far as I know, Ma Tin Aung Myo dresses as a male because she thinks she is a male and she dresses thus habitually."*

Dr. Stevenson does not present the strange case of Ma Tin Aung Myo in support of the reincarnation theory. But he does suggest that the specific dynamics of the case can best be explained by taking it at face value rather than by interpreting it within the framework of orthodox Western psychiatry.

The case is also pregnant with several implications that should be of interest to parapsychologists, psychiatrists, and theologians alike. For with the strange case of Ma Tin Aung Myo we have a report in which two forms of anomalous behavior—an extreme fear of planes and a paradoxical sexual identity—seem linked neither to a genetic nor a learned causation. These traits appear to be directly linked to memories of a past life. The case thereby suggests that many of the mental problems we face in our present lives may really be carryovers inherited from our unacknowledged past lives.

Certainly this implication has not been lost to Dr. Stevenson, despite his formidable training in conventional psychiatry. Shortly after finishing his research on the Ma Tin Aung Myo case, he addressed this very issue in a paper on "The explanatory value of the idea of reincarnation," which also appeared in the _Journal of Nervous and Mental Diseases_. The psychiatrist sets up the theme of the paper by pointing out that much of what psychiatry believes about child development and personality theory is essentially theoretical. It is not truly empirical in nature. He further argues that "most psychiatrists and psychologists today believe that infancy and childhood are more important periods in the formation of personality than any later periods; but this idea is only an assumption, as I mentioned some years ago. Cases of the reincarnation type challenge it and suggest that although personality is indeed being formed in childhood, its development actually begins much earlier in other terrestrial lives anterior to the child's present life." Dr. Stevenson goes on to take the even more radical stance that "if we allow ourselves to think of the formation of human personality as extending further back in time than conception or

---

*Dr. Stevenson's views are a bit debatable since transsexualism is marked by the psychological belief that one is essentially (emotionally) a member of the opposite sex. This could well fit the dynamics of the present case. Some transvestites cross-dress because they over-identify with the opposite sex, even though they might retain their own gender identity. This, too, might explain some of the dynamics of the present report.

birth, we may be able to explain better than we now can a number of anomalies in child development and human personality . . . "

It is important to note here that Dr. Stevenson is not adapting the reincarnation doctrine as a comprehensive framework by which to explain psychological development but only as a complicating factor that may exert a confounding influence on personality formation.

Dr. Stevenson proceeds to cite a number of cases that he has investigated in which disturbances in childhood purportedly reflected traumas experienced in previous lives. He points out, for instance, that some children who drowned in their previous incarnations have been inexplicably frightened by water and motor accident victims have been afraid of automobiles; one child was even repelled by a food by which he was previously poisoned. Stevenson also believes that the reincarnation doctrine can explain the strong interests children develop in the most unlikely areas of inquiry; peculiar affinities toward skills that can only be mastered through practice; disturbances in parent–child relationships; gender identity conflicts; internal diseases; and the sometimes overt psychological differences seen in identical and Siamese twins. These differences are especially noteworthy because these twins share common genetic information and prenatal environmental conditions.

Even when these primarily psychological disturbances are not accompanied by specific memories of a past life, reincarnation may still be a viable explanation for them. Dr. Stevenson suggests that it is the behavior itself in such cases that presents a strong case for reincarnation. He notes toward the end of his paper that he has investigated a number of such cases. "In one case," he explains, "an apparently ordinary white American boy was unusually partial to American Indians. He liked to wear their dress and regularly took their side in any view of the history of relations between Indians and white persons or in any current controversy between them and white persons." No one else in the family shared his preoccupation. Oddly, the child did not appear to have any specific memories of a previous Indian life but merely behaved as if he had. Stevenson also investigated a case in which a young boy developed an absorbing fascination in ships and the sea, even though he lived in the central part of the United States. No one else in the family shared his interests or feasibly contributed to it. Stevenson, of course, realizes that these cases cannot serve as proof of reincarnation, although they are consistent with the possibility.

The lesson we can learn from these possibilities is that reincarnation *may* be an unrecognized factor in personality development. But there are even more pertinent issues at stake. *If* certain negatively toned or inhibiting factors brought over from our past lives can disrupt the smooth running of our present lives, can these problems be treated? Could the various psychotherapeutic procedures normally used in psychology and psychiatry uncover past and "forgotten" information to help cure these difficulties? In fact, might not these strategies be more successful in some cases than orthodox treatment when geared toward uncovering traumas experienced in our past lives?

Dozens of psychologists and psychiatrists are actively involved in this sort of past-life therapy in the United States today. The basic procedures they use are fairly standardized. Past-life therapy usually entails taking the patient back to a trauma he experienced in a purported past life, usually through hypnosis, and making him relive and acknowledge it. This process allegedly helps the client to understand the dynamics of his present behavior and thereby helps him to overcome it. There can be litte doubt that many mental health workers who are employing these techniques are qualified professionals who are very dedicated to their work. The data they uncover also represent a considerable body of evidence that could feasibly support the reincarnation doctrine. So the rest of this chapter will be concerned with several key issues raised by past-life therapy. These will include whether psychotherapeutic techniques are valid for uncovering genuine memories of past lives; if past-life therapy actually works; and, if so, if reincarnation is the best explanation for these clinical successes.

Because the practice of psychotherapy is an individualized one, it is hard to generalize about the specific dynamics of past-life therapy. Every professional currently working from this perspective has evolved his or her own private techniques to a limited degree. In general, though, the many forms of past-life therapy currently practiced in the United States can be broken down into three main categories: (1) formal past-life therapy implemented through hypnotherapy and hypnotic regression; (2) cases in which the past-life recollections have therapeutically emerged spontaneously during conventional therapy; and (3) treatment monitored through memory-association procedures.

Let's take a look at each of these approaches and/or phenomena and see just what they contribute to the case for reincarnation.

Hypnotic Regression and the Case for Past-Life Therapy

Hypnosis as a psychotherapeutic tool has had a controversial history during psychiatry's curious and often-troubled history. Before the development of Freudian psychoanalysis, it was a popularly used form of treatment for a number of disorders, including hysteria. It was considered one of the few roads to the unconscious until Freud discovered that the secret environs of the mind could be explored by less cumbersome means. His tools included dream interpretation, free-association, and slips of the tongue. Hypnosis was soon banished as a standard form of therapeutic treatment and only returned to conventional psychiatry many years later when its effects were rediscovered by more eclectic psychiatrists.

One of the hypnosis's most powerful processes is regression, during which the clinician guides his patient back to a previous episode in his early life. The fact that hypnosis can also be (allgedly) used to trace previous lives soon led some metaphysically oriented therapists to explore an obvious possibility. Perhaps regression could also be used to trace the causes of disturbing behavior to past lives as well.

Probably the first psychiatrist to implement this procedure was Dr. Denys Kelsey, a British psychiatrist who was fortunate enough to be the husband of Joan Grant, a psychic who has written extensively about reincarnation and her own far memories. Dr. Kelsey could be considered the spiritual father of past-life therapy, a possibility he began exploring in the 1950s—well before interest in the rebirth doctrine became popular in the West. Dr. Kelsey was a conventionally trained therapist, a member of the Royal College of Physicians, and a clear-headed thinker when it came to the subject of reincarnation.

Dr. Kelsey's approach served as a prototype from which many other contemporary past-life therapists have derived their own procedures—acknowledged or not. It is important to note, however, that the London-based psychiatrist only felt that reincarnation should be explored as an explanation for a behavioral problem when more conventional approaches had already failed. (He would therefore probably eschew the facile way in which the reincarnation doctrine is bandied about by many pop "new age" psychologists today.) Dr. Kelsey's experiments were novel in another respect as well. He relied not only on hypnotic regression to trace the memories of his clients but also used his wife's clairvoyant faculties. He always invited Joan to attend the sessions so she could use her psychic sense to help validate the information a patient was coming up with. This procedure allowed him to cross-check information arising from the session, because he felt his wife could easily spot the difference between a memory and a fantasy.

Dr. Kelsey conducted his first clinical past-life exploration soon after he moved (date not given) to London. He was approached at his office one day by a patient who was suffering from a curious obsession. The patient was a young man who harbored the neurotic belief that he was responsible for his father's arthritis. This delusion apparently related to an incident that had occurred when the young man was only seven years old. He explained to Dr. Kelsey how he had run a damp cloth over the mattress of his parents' bed during a time when he had deep resentment towards his father. When his father actually developed arthritis thirteen years later, the patient could not shake the irrational delusion that he had somehow caused it. Dr. Kelsey's first therapeutic approach to the problem was eminently reasonable. He assumed that the patient still felt guilty about the repressed hostility he was harboring toward his father—hostility that he had never been able to resolve. Dr. Kelsey assumed that, at a deeply unconscious level, the young man really wanted to injure his father and was now paying the penalty for his wish. Even though this was a natural assumption from which to work, Dr. Kelsey simply couldn't make any headway with the patient. He found himself at a clinical dead end after eighty sessions. The best he could do was to help the young man deal with his irrational delusion. But a crisis in the case was to erupt two years later.

The young man had learned to live with his preoccupation. It wasn't a problem that seriously affected his ability to function normally in everyday life, and its importance in his life had gone by the wayside. But when his father suddenly died from a stroke, the patient once again found himself overcome by the delusion that he was the cause of his father's misfortune. This led him to resume treatment with Dr. Kelsey.

Since conventional therapy had not worked, Dr. Kelsey and his wife decided to try reincarnation-oriented hypnotic regression. They soon discovered that the patient was an exemplary hypnotic subject. He entered a hypnotic trance easily and immediately reported seeing a young woman dressed in Edwardian attire waiting by a mansion. He eventually came forth with an elaborate story about the woman. She had been orphaned, he explained, while still a teenager. Her parents had been the victims of a cholera epidemic that had swept India, and she had been sent home to England to live with a maternal aunt, who lived in a large house out in the country in East Anglia. The patient couldn't remember the name of the town but felt that the young woman was, at this time in her life, financially dependent on her aunt and thought she would always be. She only learned otherwise when she reached twenty-one and found that a trust had been left for her. The money was still controlled by the aunt but was destined to pass to her when she married. The catch was that the marriage could only take place with the aunt's approval. The patient became more emotional now as he described how he, in his past life as the young woman, eventually fell in love with a local curate. This was a match his aunt disapproved of. It eventually transpired that the girl had tried flicking water on the aunt's bed in the hope that the elderly woman would take ill and die. The plot had been uncovered by the aunt, who went into such a paroxysm of rage that she had a stroke. She was bedridden for the rest of her life and the young woman found herself even more trapped, for now she had to care for her aunt. She had become her own victim.

The above account is, of course, only a summary of a lengthy case report. Joan Grant was present at the session and shared in the recollections by "tuning in" on them psychically. She helped guide the session by handing her husband notes about the patient's memory that helped to elucidate key elements in the story and guide it in the most effective direction.

Dr. Kelsey was surprised by the upshot of the session. "When I brought the patient slowly back to the present day and out of hypnosis," he recalls in his book _Many Lifetimes_, "he had a clear memory of all he had been telling us and felt no doubt at all that it was a part of his own long history. He was completely satisfied that at last he had discovered the true source of his guilt—guilt that became transferred to his father." Dr. Kelsey implies that a dim memory of the act the patient allegedly performed in his previous life had come back to haunt him when he carried out a similar transgression as a child. What was even more amazing was that the patient found himself cured of his obsession from that day onward.

Dr. Kelsey followed the patient's progress for several years. The young man never suffered a recurrence of his *idée fixe*. So in this case reincarnation therapy obviously worked where conventional therapy had failed.

Dr. Kelsey didn't have to wait very long before replicating his little psychotherapeutic experiment. Soon after he had completed his first reincarnation-linked therapeutic success, a patient the psychiatrist describes as "a tall, wiry, athletic young man" showed up at his office. This unfortunate patient suffered from the delusion that there was something effeminate and shameful about the shape of his hips. He went on to express the sense of shame and inferiority he felt because of his irrational delusion. His obsession had even caused him to drop out of his career training. He bemoaned the fact that he was just too uncomfortable around both men and women to function very well socially, although he fully realized that his self-image was irrational. Dr. Kelsey approached the case by using conventional hypnosis and supportive psychotherapy. He was able to help the patient deal and live with his delusion and discharged him when it was clear that his life was at least on the right road again. No permanent cure of his problem had been effected, though.

Because the young man had responded to the initial treatment, Dr. Kelsey was surprised when he heard from the patient more than a year later. His symptoms and insecurities had returned—this time with a vengeance.

Dr. Kelsey decided to implement past-life therapy during their first subsequent session. This was a course of action the young man found intriguing, so the psychiatrist hypnotized him and suggested only that he allow his mind to wander back in search of the source of his current feelings. He also suggested that the patient feel no inhibitions about revealing any pertinent information that came to mind. The patient responded fairly rapidly and described how he saw a young woman involved in a panoramic series of situations—at the theatre, on the deck of a yacht, and in a pasture. He also saw a handsome escort at her side at each location. Joan Grant was attending the session, and her immediate impression was that the patient was perceiving this woman as she idealized herself and not as she really was. Dr. Kelsey responded to his wife's comments (passed to him in writing) by suggesting to his patient that he see the woman more concisely. This suggestion had a powerful impact on the young man. He began identifying more closely and emotionally with the woman and explained that she was the daughter of a local tradesman and had fallen in love with a student. She expected to marry him and eventually enter high society. The relationship was doomed, though, by her possible pregnancy. The young man deserted her, and in desperation the young woman had tried inducing a miscarriage. Failing in her constant attempts, she underwent an abortion by an unskilled midwife who butchered her badly. She died during the operation when she lost too much blood.

Dr. Kelsey believed that the scene reflected the patient's own past life, and that the horrible conditions under which she had died had caused an element of the girl's personality to split off and wander through space. It had now been reborn and revitalized by the patient's mind. Although the young man had never consciously recalled this past life before, Dr. Kelsey suggests that the trauma of the death was now manifesting in the form of his peculiar delusion that there was something feminine and shameful about his hips.

This revelation had the predicted effect. "His symptoms . . . were cured in a single session," Dr. Kelsey explains. "I think the word 'cure' is justified, for he had had no recurrence of symptoms during eight years, and he is very happily married."

Dr. Kelsey takes a theoretical as well as empirical approach to the whole issue of reincarnation therapy. He believes, for instance, that the evidence he has amassed in support of the reincarnation doctrine is a result of more than just his clinical successes. He has also been interested in using hypnosis to explore the prenatal (interuterine) lives of his patients. This has led him to evidence suggesting that the newly conscious embryo is capable of reacting to its environment suspiciously similarly to the way he or she will react to life stresses as an adult. This was, of course, a radical suggestion to make back in the 1960s even though many psychologists interested in prenatal psychology have now reached a similar conclusion. But the British psychiatrist has taken these fascinating findings one step further. He argues that because some elements of our personality are already "set" at birth, these aspects must be carry-overs from past lives.

Despite this essentially metaphysical view of life, Dr. Kelsey does not believe that hypnotic regression is a cure-all for every problem the mental health professional will face during the course of his or her practice. He candidly admitted that he has often been wrong about ascribing a patient's problems to a past life and that many subjects will not recall a previous life despite extensive hypnotic promptings to come up with one. This has led him to warn his colleagues that "I cannot emphasize too often or too strongly [how] recognition that the current life is but the most recent of many is by no means a panacea. In the majority of cases the root of a neurosis lies in the present, can be found in the present, and can be resolved in the present."

It is only unfortunate that Dr. Kelsey, who is such a cautious and insightful psychiatrist, has not explored the possibility that the memories his patients sometimes dredge up may be only therapeutically effective fantasies. His only response to this view is that most of his clients have _not_ come up with past-life revivications even when asked to produce them, thus indicating that those who _do_ recall their past lives are indeed responding to genuine information. This is a debatable point and will be discussed later.

Another interesting point Dr. Kelsey raises is that reincarnation memories will sometimes surface spontaneously during hypnosis even when no specific suggestions have been given to produce them. He cites only one example of this curious phenomenon in his book, but it is a most impressive one.

The patient was a staunch Anglican professional man who had been a practicing homosexual for more than twenty-five years. He apparently was uncomfortable with his sexual orientation because of his history of failed relationships with other men. He entered treatment with Dr. Kelsey hoping to overcome his life problems and panicked during the course of the therapy when he suddenly found himself attracted to a young man who lived in his apartment building. Dr. Kelsey responded by recommending that the subject undergo hypnosis. During the trance the patient was given the suggestion simply to see "who" was causing him to harbor such feelings. No mention of reincarnation was made and the psychiatrist insists that the topic had not been approached during the earlier phases of treatment.

This fact didn't keep the subject from slipping into a past life, though. The patient responded by describing his past life as the Hittite wife of a tribal ruler. A long and colorful story emerged in which he saw himself traveling with her husband through wild and dangerous territory, often entailing a horrendous amount of self-sacrifice on her part. The climax of the story involved her husband's betrayal when he deserted her to form a liaison with a young boy. Her rage was so great, the subject said, that she had plotted to put a curse on her husband. Her rage ultimately turned on herself and she was eventually murdered.

Dr. Kelsey was surprised that a proper Anglican would come up with such an amazing story, so he questioned him carefully after he had emerged from the hypnosis. The patient immediately explained that he had indeed been the Hittite in his past life, even though he had never evinced any interest in reincarnation. She had been a power-mad and scheming woman whose only interest had been to control her husband, he added. He now realized that his current homosexual predilections were a karmic debt he was paying for the sin he engenderd by way of his past-life rage.

Although he now recognized the source of his unhappiness, the patient still didn't know how to deal with it. Dr. Kelsey merely suggested that, because he was a devout Anglican, perhaps it would help to pray for absolution from his past-life sins. The patient and Dr. Kelsey prayed together, and the result was exactly what the psychiatrist hoped for. The patient totally reversed his sexual orientation from that day onward, found himself attracted to women, and was eventually able to commit himself fully to heterosexual relationships.

This case is especially interesting for two reasons. The first concerns the nature of the reversal itself. The behavioral trait Dr. Kelsey was treating is notoriously difficult to handle even with patients who—usually for social reasons—wish to change. Such cases are so recalcitrant that most therapists today believe that homosexuality probably isn't a behavioral disorder at all and nothing that really can or should be treated. Yet Dr. Kelsey reports that this gentleman's long-lasting sexual preference was apparently reversed in a single session. This is an outcome that no psychotherapist would dare predict or expect. The suddenness as well as the nature of this cure is therefore astonishing. It is also interesting that no direct suggestions were given for the subject to trace his problems to a past life. The emergence of the past-life memories apparently came as a surprise to both the therapist and the patient. Now the skeptic will undoubtedly argue that the patient may have previously known about Dr. Kelsey's interest, but this is a weak point since the gentleman's strong Anglican background would have probably led him to reject the idea. This is why Dr. Kelsey never even brought up the subject in the first place.

Is the spontaneous emergence of past-life information during the course of hypnotherapy a genuine phenomenon? Such a finding would certainly countermand one of the chief objections skeptics have raised against the conceptual validity of reincarnation therapy—that these therapists come up with reincarnation evidence simply because they overtly or covertly brainwashed their clients into producing it. So let's now explore this issue in some depth.*

The Spontaneous Emergence of Past-Life Recollections During the Course of Conventional Hypnotherapy

The criticism that past-life memories revive during hypnotic regression only when the patient is specifically instructed to do so is simply false. There is, in fact, ample evidence that even hypnotherapists who do not believe in reincarnation sometimes come across these cases in their practice. Sometimes the amazed psychiatrists will find their patients inexplicably cured or helped by the emergence of such memories.

Probably the most fascinating case of this type has been recently placed on record by Dr. M. Gerald Edelstein, who is a staff psychiatrist at Herrick Memorial Hospital in Berkeley, California. He was formerly the head of the emergency service and the department of psychiatry there. Although an expert in the application of hypnotherapy, Dr. Edelstein doesn't practice past-life therapy and rejects the idea of rebirth. But this hasn't kept him from confronting the revivication of past-life memories as a result of his own hypnotic explorations. These memories, explains Dr. Edelstein in his newly published text _Trauma, Trance and Transformation,_ sometimes surface spontaneously when the therapist employs a technique called the "affect bridge." The hypnotherapist has many tools he can use when trying to treat a behavioral problem, and the "affect bridge" is one of the most popular. It is roughly derived from psychoanalytical theory that states most behavioral problems are rooted in the dimly recollected past. This procedure is particularly used when

---

*By leaving the topic of formal hypnotic past-life therapy at this point I do not mean to slight other psychologists engaged in work similar to Dr. Kelsey's. These primarily include Dr. Edith Fiore in California, as outlined in her _You Have Been Here Before_ (New York: Coward, McCann and Geohegan, 1978), and Thorwald Dethlefsen in Germany, who chronicles his work in his _Voices from Other Lives_ (New York: Evans, 1977). Their work is subject to the same strengths and weaknesses as Dr. Kelsey's.

the clinician wishes to trace the root of a phobia or current conflict by uncovering the previous trauma that produced it. The subject is hypnotized, told to experience the current emotional response to the conflict (such as anxiety), and instructed to go back in his life to the first time this emotion was felt. The hypnotized patient will often spontaneously recall a traumatic experience early in life that had long been repressed from memory. The therapist then helps the patient deal with the memory and resolve it. Improvement usually follows.

It is during the regression stage of this technique that spontaneous reincarnation memories sometimes surface, even if the therapist has made no mention of such a possibility to the client. "This sounds so bizarre to most people that I would be hesitant to mention it," Dr. Edelstein explains in his text, "except for the fact [that] therapists working with the affect bridge will occasionally uncover this response and should be prepared to handle it."

Although Edelstein will openly tell his clients that he doesn't believe in reincarnation, this has not dispelled the clinical benefits that arise from these memories. "These experiences, for reasons I cannot explain, almost always lead to rapid improvements in the patients' lives," he admits candidly.

The case that particularly intrigued Dr. Edelstein was that of Shirley, a legal secretary in her late thirties who was having sexual difficulties with her husband. She didn't enjoy the activity very much and only found it passingly enjoyable by engaging in violent rape fantasies. Edelstein's initial feelings were that his patient didn't want to take responsibility for her sexuality or was somehow responding to the emotional loss and anger she had felt when her mother entered a tuberculosis sanitarium when the patient was two years old. (After her release, the mother was never very affectionate to the child.)

To trace the basis of his patient's fantasy, Edelstein initiated a course of hypnotherapy using the affect bridge. Shirley responded during her first hypnotic session by going back to the time when she first learned to associate sex with violence. She described a scene when she was a newborn infant, watching her mother bleed to death as a result of her birth. This response puzzled the psychiatrist because it was at variance with her real infancy. He then asked her what year it was, and to his surprise, Shirley said that it was 1793. She went on to describe the log cabin in which her family lived, her father's occupation as a trapper, and how a neighbor had acted as midwife for her birth.

Both patient and therapist were nonplussed by these very unexpected revelations. They certainly went far astray from what they both expected to discover under hypnosis. Things got even more complicated during the subsequent week, when Shirley reported that her difficulties with her husband were definitely improving. This was an unexpected result, because she had not responded at all to any prior form of therapy. But there was a negative side effect to the improvement. Two new problems arose. Shirley now found herself frightened that she would hurt someone or that she herself would be hurt as a result of her improvement.

Dr. Edelstein hypnotized Shirley at their next session to discover the source of her first fear. The affect bridge was used once again. Shirley soon slipped into yet another past life in nineteenth-century France. She was attending a ball while her husband remained ill at home. There she met a would-be suitor and a brief liaison resulted. She explained that her husband learned of the affair and died from his illness shortly thereafter. Rightly or wrongly, the patient was left to blame herself for his death.

Once again these memories made little sense to the psychiatrist, but they obviously had great significance for his patient. Shirley was able to report at their next meeting that her fear of hurting someone as a result of lovemaking had vanished. This now left her with only the morbid fear that she _herself_ would be hurt. A susequent hypnotic session now revealed that the patient had been raped by her father as a child in fifteenth century Spain. Uncovering this memory had the predictable result of curing Shirley's last remaining anxieties. In fact, Dr. Edelstein was able to discharge her as cured of all her problems after only seven hypnotic sessions. This was in stunning contrast to the totally ineffective two-year course of traditional "insight" therapy to which she had been previously subjected.

Dr. Edelstein was loathe to admit the possibility that his patient's problems stemmed from another life or lives. This skepticism led him to explore Shirley's life in great detail in hopes of finding a normal explanation or source for her memories, but what resulted was a series of psychological dead ends.

His first thought was that Shirley's reincarnation recollections were screen memories—false memories produced by the unconscious mind to guard the conscious mind against remembering an event or events still too traumatic to handle or confront. Perhaps the Spanish rape experience was only a symbolized scenario drawn from an early childhood fantasy or possibly a real experience, he thought. He even hypnotized Shirley to explore her childhood in search of such a clue, but the session yielded no evidence supporting his theory. Nor should the elicitation of such screen memories, Dr. Edelstein believes, have resulted in such a rapid cure.

Dr. Edelstein next toyed with the idea that perhaps such past-life memories may be based on traumatic childhood dreams. All of us have dreams now and then that are deeply disturbing to us, and Dr. Edelstein suggests that children may experience similar dreams which are actually reflections of traumatic events drawn from their own immature lives. These dreams, like the traumas themselves, may be repressed from memory. Hypnotic regression may revitalize the _contents_ of such a dream, he suggests, but not the fact that the information was encapsulated in one. A past-life "fantasy" may result from such a process.

As for the case of Shirley, Dr. Edelstein could nonetheless find no direct evidence for any natural explanation for her memories and her cure. "I do not accept reincarnation for this case," he writes, but does admit that conventional psychological theory cannot explain it either. "It is entirely conceivable to me that . . . some theory, as yet announced, may lead to a better understanding."

Another and more important conclusion could also be reached on the basis of this case—that past-life "therapy" really does work, and it doesn't matter whether the therapist believes in it.

Some related observations have been recently made by Dr. Lewis Wolberg, who is one of this country's leading authorities on hypnosis and hypnotherapy and a practicing therapist in New York. Wolberg has also run into this phenomenon during the course of his own practice. But he does not share his colleague's view that these cases are necessarily inexplicable.

Dr. Wolberg illustrates this phenomenon in his book *Hypnosis—Is It for You?* by drawing on a case he encountered while treating a young woman who suffered from a chronic neck condition. His patient's trouble had lasted for two years and had been unsuccessfully treated by internists, neurologists, and psychiatrists. Dr. Wolberg decided to treat her with hypnosis. While she was entranced he asked her if she had any notion about the cause of her symptoms. The young woman excitedly described a previous existence as a member of a royal family. She described how she had been hanged in a public square by a revolutionary mob. Her performance was extremely impressive, and she fell into a deep sleep after narrating the events.

Dr. Wolberg believes that such cases are symbolized fantasies that are constructed in the same way that dreams are formulated. He writes that "I have listened to dramatic outpourings of previous lives in many of my patients, and in each instance I was able to trace the tales to forgotten impressions of early childhood, which had been experienced by or told to the subjects." This accords with the views and evidence of Dr. Reima Kampman, whose research was discussed in an earlier chapter. Dr. Wolberg has no difficulty disposing of the above case by pointing out the psychodynamic meaning of her false memories. It seems that as a child the patient had to endure the cruelty of an older sister, who often beat her around the neck. Now as an adult the patient was still repressing and turning away her own anger by somatizing her conflicts and converting them into neck pain. Her reincarnation fantasies seemed to be highlighting her desire to express the way she felt exploited by her own family. She perceived herself martyred by them.

This does not mean that Dr. Wolberg eschews the potential value of these fantasies or the therapeutic benefits that might arise from them. He even writes that "the very fact that [the patient] has an opportunity to spill out his fantasies without restraint and to conjecture on the source of his difficulty in the presence of a kindly, nonpunitive authority may suffice to alleviate his symptoms."

So there you have it. You can either follow Dr. Wolberg, who argues that all such cases of spontaneous past-life recall can be explained psychologically, or you can follow Dr. Edelstein, who says that sometimes the roots of these memories cannot be traced. This conflict of professional opinion gives you an idea of the difficulties inherent in coming to any conclusions about this admittedly strange phenomenon.

Past-Life Therapy Through Memory-Association

The contradictory views expressed above indicate how touchy hypnotic regression can be when used as a tool in reincarnation therapy. The patient is placed in a highly suggestionable state, he is eager to please the therapist, and is functioning in an altered state of consciousness in which fantasy and reality often mix. This is why a few therapists have attempted to devise forms of past-life therapy that do not rely on formal hypnosis. If the memories of our previous lives do in fact exist deep within our minds, there should be alternate ways of gaining systematic access to them. Perhaps some past-life therapists have learned from Freud in this regard, since he, too, gave up the use of hypnosis when he discovered alternate methods of exploring the unconscious.

A curious form of free-association procedure, which has been designed as one alternative to formal hypnosis, has been successfully used by Dr. Morris Netherton, a Los Angeles psychologist primarily engaged in past-life therapy. Dr. Netherton's technique may sound absurdly simple, but it is apparently just as successful as hypnosis. The key to the system rests in the clinician's ability to pick up verbal cues from his patient. During his initial meeting with a potential client, Dr. Netherton will focus on a key phrase the patient has used and that seems to sum up his problem. These cues, he feels, invariably relate to a past-life trauma. He will then ask the client to relax, sit back, focus on the phrase and its meaning, and then wait for mental pictures to form. This imagery procedure, argues the Los Angeles psychologist, often catapults the patient to a previous life and usually the source of his current problems.

Dr. Netherton believes the key verbal phrases we habitually use in our lives reflect response patterns we learned during our prior existences. He also believes that his innovative techniques help the patient stay in control of the regression, which in turn helps him more efficiently use the information that emerges from the sessions. "It must always be the patient, and not the therapist, who does the work," he explains. "To do so, he must be fully aware of what he is playing back, and how it affects him. My object, therefore, is to reach the unconscious without destroying the presence of the conscious."

Dr. Netherton structures his procedure more systematically than do most past-life therapists, because he believes that successful therapy involves four discrete experiential stages. The patient must first make contact with his or her past-life memories while the conscious mind remains active; he or she must then reconstruct the pain and emotional trauma experienced during that life; and the patient must next explore his or her own death and reexperience it. The goal of the strategy is to help the patient become detached from the influence of the past life by consciously reliving it. The final stage of the system entails helping the patient explore his or her prenatal experience, birth, and early childhood years. This step helps the therapist discover what present life problems triggered the emergence of the past-life influence. The Los Angeles psychologist does not expect to see instant cures from his procedures. An average session lasts for more than two hours and the therapy itself often takes up to three months. Dr. Netherton also believes that his procedure can be used to treat a wide variety of problems, including sexual inadequacies, phobias, and even recurrent medical problems.

To give a better idea of just what Dr. Netherton's system entails, the following cases will illustrate how his procedures can be used in dealing with two very different problems:

Alcohol addiction is an extremely difficult disorder to treat, because contemporary psychiatry and medicine are far from sure about its cause. It is apparently the result of both physiological and psychological factors. But everyone who has ever dealt with the disorder realizes how totally debilitating it can be. In his book *Past Lives Therapy* (which he co-authored with Nancy Shiffrin), Dr. Netherton discusses his treatment of a patient he calls Ben Plummer. The patient had been a successful manager of a Los Angeles-based wholesale business before his descent into alcoholism. He saved the business from decline and had turned around its profits but began running into conflict with his boss. She was a very dominant woman who resented the threat he posed to her, and she began pressuring him out of the business. This had led the patient to such severe drinking that he had entered an alcohol treatment hospital, where he lapsed into a deep depression. Dr. Netherton first met the subject just after he had been released, although he was still nearly psychotically depressed.

The patient made constant reference during his first consultation to the feeling that his mind was active but that his body was dead. He seemed to equate the destruction of his work with the physical deteriorization of his own body. These are, of course, just the type of key existential statements upon which Dr. Netherton likes to seize. So he asked his patient to lie down, close his eyes, and focus on these phrases. It didn't take long before the subject began reporting some pertinent mental imagery. He saw himself as a naked body incarcerated in a large and empty concrete room. The sound of dripping water was heard in the background. The patient realized that he had been incarcerated there by his mother, who claimed that he had killed his brother . . . a charge he adamantly denied. He found himself so profoundly depressed by the situation that he recalled killing himself by beating his head against the wall.

There is an obvious tie-in, of course, between this revivication and his present problem. Note how in both cases a powerful woman is the (direct or indirect) cause of his incarceration and depression. This led Dr. Netherton to theorize that his patient was responding, in his present life, to a history of betrayal by a significant woman in his past life.

Dr. Netherton expected the patient to follow up on this suggestion when it was pointed out to him but was somewhat surprised when he didn't.

The observation merely prompted the patient to report a series of unrelated images apparently emerging from yet another past life. This time he found himself in Japan or China, and once again he perceived himself as a prisoner. He saw himself incarcerated and tied up while a man approached him with a bowl of fermented cereal. He was instructed to eat the cereal to cleanse himself of his sins. The patient's next memories concerned tasting the awful gruel and then being led to another room and killed.

Re-experiencing his own death in this past life prompted the patient's mind to wander from life to life, where alcohol had invariably played an important role. He subsequently described several instances where the wonders of alcohol were praised by his friends and/or co-workers. He also recalled an incident from his present childhood in which he became drunk at a picnic, much to the amusement of the adults present, who encouraged him with the promise that alcohol had the power to smooth out the problems of daily life. This incident triggered yet another past-life recollection as a carousel operator in Germany or Bavaria, where he would often drink at night to combat the boredom he felt with life.

The psychologist conducted several past-life sessions with this patient, but a crisis in the treatment came during the second meeting. During this session the patient relived a life in which his wife caught him drinking and had him sent to a hospital. Her action was not motivated by her concern for him, but as an expedient method of getting him out of the way. He was apparently having an affair, and his wife knew about it. Having him incarcerated was her way of revenging herself. But even in the hospital he was able to gain access to his beloved alcohol and simply drank himself to death.

These past-life memories also seemed to be exacerbating the fact that the patient had been an unwanted child, a fact Dr. Netherton discovered through even more probing.

He was not able to totally cure this patient's serious problem. "He had done severe damage to his liver," he explains in his book, "even in the relatively brief period of intense drinking. His heart and arteries were also adversely affected. No amount of understanding could reverse this situation, so I cannot honestly say that he came through therapy restored to his former state of health. The physiological addiction remained." The best the psychologist could do was to warn him from ever touching alcohol again. "I could only hope that his new understanding would make it possible for him to abstain," he concludes.

It is clear from his case reports that Dr. Netherton takes this case at face value. His interpretation is that the patient's current problem resulted from a long history in which he learned to deal with scheming women by drinking. His current conflicts with his boss had merely instigated a replay of this neurotic and self-defeating pattern. The Los Angeles psychologist also implies that, because the patient brought forth this information while remaining conscious, they were most likely true memories and neither fantasies nor confabulations.

At this point the skeptic could easily disagree with Dr. Netherton's assumptions. It seems clear (at least to me) that these revivications were not true memories but—on a deeply symbolic level—simple restatements of his problem masked in various revealing guises. His first fantasy, for instance, seems to be a restatement of how he perceives himself and his present life situation—as a small and innocent (naked) victim thrown into prison (both literal and figurative) by a dominant woman. There really doesn't seem to be any reason to conclude that this series of images was reflecting a past life. It reads very much like a dream the patient might have had during this difficult time in his life. The second fantasy, in which he found himself a prisoner in Japan, probably symbolized his need to drink when placed in "binding" and hopeless situations. Note once again how the scenario represents a rather transparent statement about the nature of his addiction. It doesn't take much psychiatric training to appreciate the meaning of the patient's German past life, either. Here he is apparently making a very significant statement about how drinking helps him to escape the endless merry-go-round of life.

It is my feeling that Dr. Netherton could have made more headway in the case had he used these past-life "memories" to explore the psychological dynamics of his patient's alcoholism. His drinking seemed to be a response to his feelings of personal inadequacy coupled with a severe inability to deal with his repressed anger towards women. The patient was merely turning his anger inward through his self-destructive behavior. There is little reason to invoke reincarnation to explain the case and the subject's fantasies.

Some practitioners of past-life therapy believe that their techniques can be used to treat some medical as well as psychological problems. Dr. Netherton shares this view and has treated problems ranging from migraine to hyperactivity to cancer. The discovery that some medical problems might also have roots in the distant past would be an important factor for physicians to consider. This idea is a logical extension of past-life therapy, especially because more and more doctors are realizing that many purely physical disorders are often complicated by psychological factors. One medical condition that is often the result of both psychological and physiological factors is migraine, a disabling recurrent headache that constitutes a living hell for anyone suffering from it. Dr. Netherton explains in his book how he successfully cured a case of migraine when he accepted a patient he calls Harrison Lask for treatment.

Lask came in for treatment shortly after he had left his wife, infant son, and his optometry business. He felt he could no longer cope with life. He also felt that he had been vying with his son for his wife's attention, but his real reason for seeking treatment was to eliminate his blinding headaches. They were recurring daily, and the only thing the patient could do to relieve them was to ingest caffeine. Since the headaches were the patient's most pressing problem, Dr. Netherton decided to focus on it immediately. So he had his new client lie down and concentrate on the moment right before he usually got up and when the headaches were at their worst. By focusing on his headaches, the patient realized that he resented having to get out of bed in the morning. This realization prompted a flurry of revealing images.

The young man first recalled an incident from his own prenatal life. He re-experienced an incident when his mother was seven months pregnant and woke one morning with a headache. His brusque father refused to be sympathetic and angrily ordered her out of bed to fix breakfast. The patient then recalled how his mother drank coffee in hopes that it would relieve her misery. Dr. Netherton took this recollection as a valid prenatal memory, suggesting that his patient had adopted the same strategy.

This emotional prenatal memory acted as a catalyst for a series of past-life recollections that surfaced with frightening impact. The first setting took place in some woodlands where the patient found himself making love to an Indian girl with whom he was in love. The liaison had apparently been going on for a long time, even though he was not an Indian himself. He explained how the woman's tribesmen caught him during the tryst and killed him by crushing his head. This recollection then led immediately to a different scene in which he now _was_ an Indian and about to be killed by some white men. He heard them accusing him of hunting their buffalo. The patient then lived through the agony of being left on some railroad tracks with an excruciatingly tight metal band wedged around his forehead. A third lifetime surfaced as a fleeting scene in which he found himself running through some woods. He was being pursued by a man on horseback who was trying to shoot him for seducing his daughter. He was finally killed by a bullet that lodged in his head.

Dr. Netherton explains in his report on this case that several common themes crop up in these memory constellations that probably contributed to his patient's present life problems. He points out that "the most significant link here is that all three scenes involve the extreme head pains being accompanied by 'lessons' of some sort." These themes revolved, of course, around such important life experiences as love, maturation, and business (who properly owned the buffalo in the second scene). The failures in each life, the psychologist explains, apparently resulted in death through head injury. Dr. Netherton naturally concluded that it was this pain that the patient was re-experiencing in the face of yet another failure.

These ostensible revelations about the patient's headaches did not alleviate the problem, unfortunately. The subject merely reported one week later that the headaches has shifted from the morning to the afternoon and were now focusing toward the back of his head. So to get to the root of these new developments, Dr. Netherton conducted a second session along the same lines as their previous one. What resulted was a colorful memory in which the patient saw himself as an Indian fighting a rival for the position of chief of his tribe. The story was very dramatic and, even though he suffered a head injury during the fight, he was able to kill his opponent by a blow to the head.

Because Dr. Netherton likes to explore the birth expriences of his patients, he concluded Lask's treatment by asking him to relive his own birth.

There he discovered that Lask could recall the icy sensation of a retractor pulling him by the head reluctantly from his mother's body.

The results of all these remembrances and birth trauma had the desired effect on the patient. His headaches became rarer and rarer and he was finally able to begin picking up the pieces of his marriage.

This case has been summarized from Dr. Netherton's own conceptual standpoint, of course. But just as with the case of his alcoholic patient, there really seems little reason to adopt a reincarnation-oriented interpretation of the case. Remember that migraine is a symptom more than it is an illness. The attacks are often and partially the somaticized result of internal conflicts or social pressure. Dr. Netherton does not explain in his book just when his patient first began complaining about the headaches, but they were obviously occurring before he broke from his family and his work. Now it is apparent from Dr. Netherton's summary of the case that his patient was harboring a great deal of conflict over his marriage and his career. It is also obvious that he did not possess the psychological resources necessary to deal with his problem. This is why he probably chose escape (desertion) as his only solution. His migraines were thus little more than a bodily expression of his guilt and conflict . . . a guilt that was no doubt exacerbated when he walked out on his family and his job.

The dynamics and messages contained within his past-life fantasies, if interpreted along those lines, make considerable sense. The prenatal scene in which his pregnant mother was forced out of bed despite her headache probably reflected the patient's feeling that his family was a burden. The recurring themes of death and sexual transgression probably relate to his poor adjustment to marriage. The fact that he had to kill to become head of his tribe reflected his ambivalence about the cutthroat world of business. The fact that he left his optometry work (to which he, in fact, never returned) suggests that he did not believe himself cut out for this type of work.

But what about the fact that the migraines abated? Dr. Netherton was able to cure his patient, just as many past-life therapists have chalked up some impressive clinical successes. But does the fact that past-life therapy does, on occasion, result in a cure prove the conceptual validity of the reincarnation doctrine? This is the issue to which we will now turn.

The idea that reincarnation may be the cause of at least some phobias and behavioral problems is a notion I resisted for many years. While I could readily acknowledge that specific memories of a past-life could possibly affect our behavior, it seemed unparsimonious to believe that such an unrecognized factor could be at the root of phobias, neuroses, and problems in living. I based this view on the fact that, by and large, psychiatry and psychology have done a commendable job in explaining how most behavioral problems develop. Phobias in particular can be learned responses, symbolized fears, or even inherited. There just doesn't seem to be much room for reincarnation in all this.

But the fact that at least *some* long-lived phobias and neuroses may be linked to previous lives is a possibility that cannot be summarily dismissed. My thinking along these lines was challenged by a case I collected while investigating the "Lenz effect," which I discussed in Chapter Two. One of the cases in my files provided strong evidence that some phobias might be inherited from a past life. This curious piece of evidence was contained in a letter from the woman in Texas who had been haunted by dreams of a catwalk bridge. This letter appears earlier in this book, but since it is such a short account, no harm will be done by citing it again:

> There was a suspension bridge high above a wide expanse of water. It was a narrow walkway, swaying in the wind, with nothing to hold on to and floor boards spaced so one could see the water below the cracks. The bridge was reached by a ladder. Here my dreams varied: sometimes I would mount the ladder and turn back as soon as I reached the top; other times I would creep out onto the bridge on hands and knees and a few other times I would go out onto it a short distance walking erect. Never did I reach the other side.
>
> About 25 or 30 years ago I picked up a copy of _Life_ magazine, and what should I find in it but a half page picture of _my_ bridge. And what is more, it was taken from the same angle that I always approached the bridge in my dreams. The article accompanying the picture identified it as the first catwalk thrown across the East River preparatory to building the Brooklyn Bridge in the 1870s; it also stated that a number of persons, both men and women, had fallen to their deaths from the bridge.
>
> I am convinced that I was one of those because I have never had that particular dream again.

The upshot of this memory is pertinent to the whole issue of past-life therapy. Here is the rest of the letter, which was _not_ cited before:

> I am convinced that I was one of those because I have never had that particular dream again and because a lifelong fear that I would meet my death falling from a great height was dispelled with the recognition of the bridge.

So here we have a case in which a phobia or obsession was instantly cured by understanding the nature and causation of the problem.

What is also so strange about this cure is how sudden it was. Despite what you may have picked up from such popular movies as _The Three Faces of Eve_ and _The Snake Pit,_ you can't necessarily cure a mental problem merely by helping a person understand its nature and cause. Most phobias must be treated by desensitizing the patient so that the focus of the phobia (high places in the above case) no longer provokes any anxiety for the patient.* I am sure that every reader of this book suffers from his or her own little phobias and

---

*The main exception to this rule is a form of treatment called abreactive therapy, in which the patient is forced to dramatically relive the trauma that produced the fear while in a drug-induced trance. This approach to therapy will be discussed later in this section.

even knows where they were learned or picked up. Knowing *why* you are frightened of something doesn't make the anxiety any less real. So the fact that this woman was instantly and permanently cured of her long-term obsession is nothing short of miraculous. I know of no principle in psychology or psychiatry that can account for it.

Cases such as the above suggest that many common problems in living may indeed be rooted in our previous lives.

Despite this fact, the general success of past-life therapy cannot really serve as very strong evidence supporting the rebirth doctrine. Those therapists and writers who promote such cures as proof of reincarnation must have a very naive understanding of the psychotherapeutic process and why it works.

Yes, past-life therapists certainly produce their share of cures. But remember that orthodox psychoanalysts produce cures; behavioral psychologists produce cures; Christian science practitioners produce cures; faith healers produce cures; and witch doctors produce cures. So the issue is not really whether past-life therapy actually works some of the time. The real issue is whether it works better or more consistently than any other form of therapy. The answer sems to be no. Very few responsible past-life therapists claim one hundred percent success in their work, and these professionals certainly have their failures as well. Detailed case studies in which past-life therapy failed have even been placed in the literature. The story of one such failure is given by R. Macready's autobiographical *The Reincarnations of Robert Macready*. Macready was an unhappy man living in Toronto who was suffering from all sorts of problems, including (though only implied in the book) impotency. He had not responded to conventional therapy. Reincarnation-oriented treatment didn't fare any better. He walked away from the therapy as unhappy as he entered it.

So even though past-life therapy does work in some instances, reincarnation is probably not the reason why.

Psychiatrists and clinical psychologists have been arguing for years over why therapy works. Most therapists will tell you it works because of the validity of the conceptual framework from which they work as well as the therapeutic tools they use. So past-life therapists are on common ground when they claim their techniques work for the simple reason that reincarnation is a fact. But this assumption cannot explain why two different psychologists, working with different tools and from opposing theories about the nature of mental problems, will often be equally successful in their practice. So there must be something more to the art of psychotherapy than the validity of the concepts, theories, and tools used by the various factions presently schismatizing orthodox psychiatry.

It was just this controversy that led an innovative and somewhat iconclastic young psychiatrist-turned-anthropologist to wonder why shamans, witch doctors, and faith healers are able to produce cures as astounding as his psychiatric colleagues often report. This observation led Dr. E. Fuller Torrey, who is now a practicing psychiatrist in Washington, D.C., to travel around the world examining how folk healers deal with mental illness. By comparing what he witnessed in many different cultures, Dr. Torrey came to the conclusion that _any_ form of psychological therapy will work if four factors are present: (1) When the patient and the therapist entertain the same world view; (2) when the patient firmly expects to get well; (3) when the therapist possesses certain qualities that promote trust and confidence; and (4) when the therapist employs certain basic medical or behavioral change strategies.

Dr. Torrey's work has often been cited by researchers interested in why therapy both succeeds and fails. It is especially quoted by opponents of psychiatry who are eager to pull the rug from under the psychological establishment.

By and large, though, most psychologists will readily admit that the four factors Dr. Torrey has identified are at least partially critical to successful therapy. Past-life therapy probably succeeds for the same reasons. In fact, by applying these four principles to the way past-life therapy is usually conducted, it should become clear why this form of treatment _should_ result in a good many cures:

1. _Both past-life therapists and their patients entertain similar world views._ A person who seeks out a past-life therapist probably believes in reincarnation in the first place. That would seem self-evident. So in this regard, both the therapist and his client share a crucial set of beliefs—not only about reincarnation, but in the idea that some mental problems are inherited from a past life. Now there are some past-life therapists who claim that they have successfully treated patients who were resistant to the notion. This statement should be taken with a grain of salt. The fact that the patient initially consented to undergo this unconventional form of therapy suggests that he or she wasn't as resistant to it as the therapist may have thought. Successful past-life therapy may also entail a phenomenon called _internalization_. This is a term used in developmental psychology to describe how a child eventually adopts his parents' values and takes them as his own. A similar process may occur during the course of past-life therapy, in which at some unconscious level the patient may also adopt the therapist's world view. Such a phenomenon occurs in patients undergoing Freudian psychoanalysis and Jungian depth psychology, so it probably occurs during reincarnation therapy as well.

2. _The patient firmly expects to get well._ If we assume that the therapist and the patient share the same beliefs about the cause of at least some behavioral problems, it is not too difficult to assume that the patient also expects to be cured by past-life therapy. It is well known that positive expectancy can act as a strong placebo in therapy as well as in medicine. Drs. Norman Sundberg and Leona E. Tyler even state in their widely used textbook, _Clinical Psychology,_ that "it is evident that any kind of psychotherapy may also have a placebo effect. In fact, it is the most plausible explanation for the often-noted

fact that almost all techniques, even though they are diametrically opposed to one another, chock up therapeutic successes." There is simply no reason to exempt past-life therapy from this principle as well.

Now the past-life therapist could counter by noting that he or she has been successful with patients who have failed to respond to more conventional treatment. This finding may not seem consistent with the views outlined above. In these rare cases, however, it appears likely that the patient was a believer in reincarnation who sought out past-life therapy as a last resort. These factors may have simply produced a greater motivation on the part of the patient to get well. A great deal of evidence has been amassed that clinical success is directly related to the level of the patient's initial expectancy and motivation.

3. *Past-life therapists probably possess personal qualities that make them especially good clinicians.* One of the most curious and humorous findings ever made in clinical psychology came about some years ago when a team of researchers decided to find out why behavior modification techniques work so well. (These techniques seek to cure an unwanted behavior by coupling it with an unpleasant experience. For example, a smoker will be shocked every time he touches a cigarette until he no longer wishes to smoke.) Most psychologists they questioned adamantly maintained that behavior modifications work because of the strength and validity of the procedures used. Yet most of the patients they spoke with denied that the techniques to which they had been subjected resulted in their cures. They preferred to believe that it was the personal qualities of their therapists that had prompted the changes.

This little finding highlights the fact that psychotherapy is an exercise in human relations. Psychotherapy is more of an art than a science. And just as in the world of art and music you will find many therapists who are mediocre, many who are inept, but a few who are true geniuses. These are those rare clinicians who can work wonders with just about any client they treat.

There appear to be many factors that go into the making of a successful therapist. Not only must he be the master of several psychological skills, but he must also bring to the therapy a number of personality qualities that encourage the patient to get better. Research into just what these qualities entail has recently come to the forefront of psychology. The evidence points to three specific traits that consistently characterize good therapists. These include the abilities to accurately empathize with the patient, to exhibit nonpossessive warmth, and to display a certain amount of personal genuineness.* In commenting on why therapy works, Dr. E. Fuller Torrey has even gone so far as to argue that the importance of the therapist's own personality is " . . . perhaps the most striking thing that has emerged from recent research in psychotherapy."

---

*For more details on this research, the reader should consult D. B. Truax and R. R. Arkhuff, *Towards Effective Counseling and Psychotherapy:* (Chicago; Aldine, 1967).

There is no doubt that therapists who engage in past-life treatment are dedicated people who are fiercely and humanitarianly devoted to alleviating human suffering. Their approach to treatment is not only an outcome of their professional training. It is also a result of their metaphysical approach to life. The combination of these two factors probably makes them exemplary therapists. They are successful in helping their patients because of the type of people they are, not necessarily because of the premises from which they work.

4. _Past-life therapists often employ treatment strategies that are unintentionally adopted from conventional psychology._ It is the fourth of Dr. Torrey's principles that may be the underlying reason past-life therapy works. For despite all their talk about reincarnation and karma, past-life therapists may be unintentionally using some tried-and-true procedures adopted from conventional psychology.

The specific technique they chanced upon seems based on an effective procedure called systematic desensitization. This technique is based, in turn, on principles derived from behavioral psychology. It was first proposed by J. Wolpe, a South African psychiatrist, in 1958 and has been standardly used by behavioral therapists ever since. It is very effective for curing phobias and some neuroses. It is also the basis from which many of the inroads in treating sexual dysfunctions have originated. Wolpe's system works from the assumption that most phobias are learned reactions that are debilitating because they set up a vicious cycle—you see a spider and tense up from fright, which makes you even more frightened, which causes more anxiety, and so on _ad nauseum_. The goal of the procedure is to break the cycle.

The practice of systematic desensitization begins when the therapist receives a list from the patient cataloging what makes him frightened or anxious. The clinician then either relaxes or hypnotizes the patient and asks him to visualize the least threatening situation possible involving the object of his fears. (If the patient is afraid of death, for instance, he may be asked to visualize an ambulance.) By using this technique, the patient is taught to experience the focus of his fear while remaining relaxed. The therapist then has the subject visualize potentially more anxiety-provoking scenes (such as visualizing a funeral) while making sure that he stays as relaxed as possible. Gradually the patient learns to confront the source of his fears without tensing up. This, in turn, results in the virtual disappearance of the original and aberrant behavior.

This form of therapy can also be used in real-life settings. The pioneering sex therapy of W. H. Masters and V. E. Johnson uses similar behavior modification techniques, though in this case a sexually dysfunctional couple actually engages in nonanxiety activity until they are comfortable enough to resume sexual relations.

Notice how this basic procedure seems to have been adopted by many past-life therapists. They, too, begin by asking the clients to relax or by hypnotizing them. The patient is then instructed to visualize and relive traumas from his or her past while remaining passive and relaxed. The patient probably really is re-experiencing *something* but probably not memories from a past life. He or she is more likely visualizing subconsciously created fantasies symbolizing the source or nature of the current life problem. The client is then instructed to reconfront these events session after session. By learning how to confront these problems in such a non-threatening way, the patient probably succeeds in overcoming the behavior that has brought him or her to therapy. The client has learned to confront the source of the problem without buckling under to it.

Another technique that many past-life therapists are using is a form of abreactive therapy. I mentioned in an earlier footnote that reliving a past trauma under certain special conditions can result in a cure. The use of abreactive treatment was developed during the Second World War by British psychiatrists who discovered that it was a successful strategy for the treatment of battle neurosis, or "shell shock." Many soldiers simply broke down under the horrors of war. To get them functioning again, the psychiatrists took the soldiers, drugged them, and then recreated events that led to their breakdowns. Soldiers subjected to this treatment (which was used as a plot device on one M*A*S*H* episode) usually collapsed into unconsciousness after reliving the crisis, but they usually woke up cured. This emotional crisis somehow wiped out the aberrant response to the original trauma.

A related technique used by some psychologists is called flooding, during which the patient is exposed to the source of his fears or obsessions in the most frightening way possible. Cures often result from this use of emotional shock.

Some of the procedures used in past-life therapy probably entail a form of flooding and/or abreaction. The hypnotized subject is commonly instructed to relive his past-life trauma and sometimes will have a violent reaction to this suggestion. The patient is most likely responding, however, to a symbolized version of an event he or she suffered during the present life, but this is inconsequential. The stress caused by this response may produce a curative abreaction.

Taking all the above considerations into account, can normal psychological dynamics therefore be found for *all* cases in which past-life therapy has succeeded?

The answer is probably yes for most cases, but there remains a residue of cases for which such explanations do not seem to apply. Some cures reported by past-life therapists deal with problems that do not respond well to *any* form of treatment. The instantaneous nature of some of these cures is also puzzling. Remember that systematic desensitization is a very long and drawn-out procedure, while abreactive therapy works best to erase only recently learned behavior. So the ideas presented in this section should not be used as a pat explanation for all cures produced through past-life therapy. Reincarnation might possibly be a factor in such cases, but the skeptic could hardly be blamed for rejecting the notion.

But I can't forget about that woman who was cured of her obsession when she simply saw the bridge of her dreams. Nor about Dr. Kelsey's patient who reversed his twenty-five year sexual orientation after only one session. These are mysteries that may well go beyond conventional psychiatry.

Conclusions

Most psychologists and psychiatrists who practice past-life therapy are not really interested in confirming the historical accuracy of their patients' stories. So from a strictly evidential standpoint, these past-life accounts do not offer very strong support for the reincarnation doctrine. The critical issue at stake is whether reincarnation therapy actually works. There seems to be little doubt that it does, but the reason may be because of simple psychological factors. On the other hand, evidence that our present behavior may reflect responses learned or inherited from a previous life is not nonexistent. Some cures implemented by past-life therapy are also astonishing enough to keep the issue at least open, but this body of evidence must be considered inferential and cannot serve as direct support for reincarnation.

10

Drugs, Consciousness, and Rebirth

The psychedelic revolution of the 1960s brought about many changes in our society and culture. A greater awareness of altered states of consciousness, a revitalized interest in Eastern religion, and a new respect for the age-old doctrine of reincarnation were just a few of them. However, few people realize that the psychedelic revolution also brought with it new evidence *for* reincarnation as well. Researchers exploring these drugs and the sometimes bizarre states of mind that accompanied their ingestion soon learned that psychedelic "trips" occasionally ignited the recollection of past lives. It was a sobering thought for many researchers who had been reared within a conservative and mechanistic medical and/or psychiatric tradition. Dr. Lester Grinspoon and John R. Bakalar, two experts on psychedelic drugs at Harvard University, point out in their authoritative *Psychedelic Drugs Reconsidered* how past-life memory was one of many phenomena seen during the heyday of psychedelic drug research. They specifically note that these experiences often had a strong impact on those who recounted them.

"Even sophisticated persons who had previously considered reincarnation a superstition find these experiences hard to dismiss," they write. "And even when they reject reincarnation as an explanation, the strangely compelling quality of the memories may make them unwilling to accept more conventional interpretations."

Oddly enough, the greatest inroads in the study of drug-induced past-life recall did not occur in the United States, where psychedelic drug-taking soon became a popular recreational pastime, as well as a new technique for psychotherapy, when it exploded onto the cultural scene. It was actually in eastern Europe, partially blocked from the West by the ever-present weight of the Iron Curtain, that the discovery of psychedelically induced reincarnation recall was most intensely studied. A young psychiatrist working in Prague, Czechoslovakia, was exploring how LSD could be used in intensive psychotherapy when he discovered the mystical nature of some psychedelic voyages. He wasn't too surprised that his patients relived early traumas and even their own birth experiences while under the influences of the drugs. But it came as a shock to him when some of his subjects began reliving their past lives as well.

Dr. Stanislav Grof is now one of our own country's leading transpersonal psychiatrists as well as a scholar-in-residence at the Esalen Institute in Big Sur, California. It was through the auspices of the Institute that Dr. Grof began publishing the results of his Czech research. *Realms of the Human Unconscious—Observations from LSD Research* appeared in 1975. It was to be the first of (now) three books the psychiatrist has written about the therapeutic potentials of LSD use; and in it Dr. Grof makes no bones about discussing how he became fascinated with the doctrine of reincarnation as a result of his early research. In fact, he describes past-life memories as "probably the most interesting and enigmatic category of transpersonal phenomena" he encountered as a byproduct of his study.

What he found was that past-life revivications can manifest in a variety of ways during the psychedelic experience. "Past-incarnation experiences consist of fragments of scenes, individual events, or entire, rather clear and logical sequences occurring at another time and history," he explains. Grof remains, however, far from sure whether such experiences necessarily relate to the actual rebirth of the soul or whether they constitute the emergence of some form of genetic memory lodged deep within the brain. This is the inevitable problem that many students of the reincarnation controversy ultimately confront. "The events involved, however, are very dramatic," he goes on to say, "and are accompanied by an unusually intense emotional charge of a distinctly positive or negative quality. . . . The subject participating in these dramatic sequences maintains his ego identity; although he experiences himself in another form, another place and time, and another context, he feels that he is basically the same individual as in his present existence. He also has a keen sense of being confronted with a *memory,* of reliving something that he has already seen and experienced."

Most interesting of all is the fact that many of Grof's LSD patients had no familiarity, belief, or interest in reincarnation before reporting their experiences. And sometimes the information these surprised patients came up with turned out to be factual and beyond the scope of anything they might have learned during the course of their regular schooling.

One of the most intriguing cases Dr. Grof came across concerned an unhappy thirty-two-year-old housewife whom he identified only as Renata, a disturbed woman with a history of suicidal attempts, obsessive-compulsive preoccupations, deep depressions, and tendencies toward self-destruction. Her sexual history was also disturbed. She had been the victim of an attempted rape and found normal relationships with men extremely threatening. She had been directed to Grof in Prague after she had developed a neurotic and overwhelming obsessive fear of developing cancer. LSD therapy ultimately helped her to recall an alleged sexual encounter with, and subsequent beating by, her stepfather when she was a child. A traumatic birth experience was uncovered as well. The recollection of these events helped her deal with her problems but did not actually cure them.

During the late stages of Renata's therapy reincarnation memories began to emerge. During four consecutive sessions her mental experiences focused almost exclusively on scenes from seventeenth-century Prague. This was a critical time in Czech history during which the country lost its national identity to the invading Austro-Hungarian armies. One of the worst atrocities of the struggle came when the leaders of the invasion rounded up the heads of the Czech nobility and had them publicly beheaded in Prague. The measure was meant to destroy national pride and make the population submit to defeat.

Renata seemed to be transported back in time to this era and horror during her LSD therapy. She was overwhelmed by scenes depicting the architecture, apparel, weapons, and even minor utensils employed during this period. Despite the fact that she had never made any in-depth study of the era, she also seemed familiar with the interclass dynamics between the seventeenth-century aristocracy and the lower classes. She even began tuning in on the life of a young nobleman beheaded by the Hapsburgs, which included dramatically reliving his execution in agonizing detail. Renata was prone to believe that these memories had somehow been genetically coded into her brain through some type of genetic inheritance, while Dr. Grof remained totally baffled by the recollections.

He writes in his book:

> On one hand, I spent a considerable amount of time in an effort to verify the historical information involved and was increasingly impressed by its accuracy. On the other hand, I tried to apply a psychoanalytical approach to the contents of Renata's stories in the hope that I would be able to understand them in psychodynamic terms as a symbolic disguise for her childhood experiences or elements of her present life situation. No matter how hard I tried, the experiential sequences did not make sense from this point of view, and I finally gave up . . .

It wasn't until two years later that Grof learned of the surprising climax to the case. He had emigrated to the United States by this time and was surprised when he received a startling letter from his former patient. It seems that Renata had run into her estranged father, whom she had not seen since her parents' divorce when she was three years old. She then learned that her father had conducted some extensive genealogical research during the war years to satisfy the Nazis that there was no Jewish blood in his family line. His research necessitated a five-generation search, but, fascinated by the project, he had traced his ancestry all the way back to the seventeenth century. At that point he learned that his family had descended from the nobility—in particular, a nobleman beheaded by the Hapsburgs.

This information only reaffirmed Renata's feeling that her memories arose from genetically inherited information. Grof, however, has long accepted a more reincarnation-oriented explanation for the case, although he has drawn no firm conclusions about it. Grof tends to reject Renata's own genetic memory explanation because it contains a logical inconsistency. He points out that during one of her sessions, Renata actually relived the nobleman's death. This information, he explains, could not possibly have been passed on genetically to any descendents: "A dead person cannot procreate and 'genetically' pass the memory of his terminal anguish to future generations."

Unfortunately, Dr. Grof does not cope with the possibility that perhaps the nobleman's wife and children witnessed the execution and shared in the young man's horror. They could have passed on this information to their descendents. Grof's main point, however, is that Renata actually relived the personal experience of the nobleman's execution and did not merely offer an impersonal depiction of the crime.

Reincarnation? Genetic memory? Or unconscious memory? These are the only possible explanation for the incident. So which one can best account for the case?

Unconscious memory seems unlikely because, even had Renata studied but forgotten all about seventeenth-century Czech history, the tie-in between her mentation and her ancestry is too strong to be coincidental. Nor should the fact that there actually existed a genetic link between Renata and the beheaded nobleman argue conclusively for an ancestral memory theory for the revivications. Dr. Ian Stevenson of the University of Virginia has uncoverd many cases of Asian and Alaskan children who have recalled living their past lives as members of their own present families. These cases do not differ appreciably nor in pattern from those veridical cases in which a genetic link cannot be established or obviously does not exist. Yet adopting a pure reincarnation explanation for the case is not a clear-cut option either, because Dr. Grof has indeed come across cases in which genetic memory _is_ the most likely explanation for some of his patients' experiences. One of his subjects in Prague even recalled a scene from his mother's childhood, which was later verified.

Lester Grinspoon and John B. Bakalar cite this case in their authoritative review of the literature on psychedelic drugs. They, too, admit that they prefer a genetic information theory to a reincarnation-oriented one. They suggest, though, that this case may have actually been one of cryptomnesia, because Renata could have picked up this information as a child from her father while he was working on the genealogy. It may only have resurfaced during the LSD session.

This theory doesn't seem plausible. Dr. Grof made his arrangements to move to the United States in 1966. Because Renata was thirty-two years old when she underwent her LSD therapy, she couldn't have been born any later than 1934. She specifically notes in her account that she had not seen her father since her parents' divorce when she was three. Her father began his genealogical research to show the Nazis that there was no Jewish blood in his family, and the Germans only annexed Czechoslovakia in 1938. This would have been a year *after* he had presumably lost contact with his daughter.

Very few of Dr. Grof's cases contain this much detail, so it is hard to draw many conclusions from his work. He has, however, attempted to explain a little about the dynamics of reincarnation recall and how they relate to both LSD and human consciousness. In his subsequent book *The Human Encounter with Death* (co-authored with Dr. Joan Halifax, who was then his wife), he notes that such transpersonal phenomena were most often seen when subjects were given repeated doses of LSD. The transpersonal elements of the LSD experience apparently grew as the subjects became more comfortable with the experiences. So it seems that reincarnation-linked recollections are not a "surface" aspect of the LSD experience but can only be contacted with time and patience.

While at the Maryland Psychiatric Center in Catonsville (just outside of Baltimore), Dr. Grof was able to partially extend his European research by administering LSD to the dying. Reincarnation memories surfaced during this research as well, although not in such detail as he had previously seen. (Remember that the particulars of the Renata case came toward the end of long-term therapy and were spread over four sessions.) A typical case reported in *The Human Encounter with Death* concerns a sixty-year-old cancer patient identified only as Catherine, who recalled two past lives during a single LSD session. (A very large dose was used in this case.) The patient initially reported a kaleidoscope of color, which she imbued with spiritual meaning. She then began contemplating her childhood frustrations, her sexual and religious conflicts, and her failed marriage. These memories had a purging effect on her. As she withdrew deeper and deeper into the experience, the entire session took on cosmic dimensions. She felt herself being sucked into a whirlpool in which she was hacked apart before being lifted up and immersed in a golden light. During these experiences she felt that all the religions of the world were vying for her attention. The vision of the golden light unified her by cradling her in feelings of divine love.

Later that evening, Catherine told Dr. Grof she felt that she had been given a special grace during her session. This was the privilege of seeing two of her past lives. She had lived once as a Greek scholar bondaged in Rome as a tutor for some children. In the other she had been an Oriental monk. No other details had apparently been forthcoming.

"Catherine saw this session as a very important event in her life," Grof notes. "Prior to her experiences she had been severely depressed and had made several attempts to produce an effective poison for herself. Her preoccupation with suicide now disappeared completely." Unfortunately, Dr. Grof does not attempt to explore a psychodynamic meaning for her past-life recall. He merely cites them as another extraordinary aspect of an extraordinary session.

As a result of his work both in Europe and the United States, Dr. Grof believes that some of his cases point to reincarnation, although he has been reluctant about publishing specific details about them. He has been especially intrigued with how some of the material he has collected seems to bear out the whole concept of "karma," a metaphysical doctrine that has become quite popular in our culture since its importation from the East. Grof explains in his earlier book how many reincarnation-type exprinces help the patient to better understand his or her present life. Often LSD-linked reincarnation memories are bound to past relationships and how the dynamics of these interactions are affecting the quality of the present life. Other memory constellations are more negative in nature and the patient will experience or relive a past-life trauma that has carried over emotionally to the present. "The experiences belonging in this group," the psychiatrist explains, "cast subjects into past-life situations characterized by agonizing physical pain, bitterness, hatred, and murderous aggression, inhuman terror and anguish, lustful passion, insane jealousy, or morbid greed and avarice."

The result of this type of experience, Grof believes, is to help the patient transcend the karmic debt and improve the quality of the present life. Reliving the experience isn't enough, he explains. One must understand and work through the problems on a deep transpersonal level.

"The resolution of a karmic pattern and liberation from the bonds it represents are associated with a sense of paramount accomplishment and triumph," he concludes. "Frequently, an individual feels that he has waited for and worked toward this event for many centuries; and that, even if he achieves nothing else in this lifetime, it has been fruitful and successful because in its course one of the karmic bonds was finally broken. The resolution of a single karmic pattern can thus result in feelings of indescribable bliss . . ."

Stanislav Grof is not the only researcher who has encountered such cases while using psychoactive drugs in his practice, although he is probably the only one who has adopted a mystical interpretation of these episodes. At least one similar case has been encountered by Dr. Claudio Naranjo, a psychiatrist in Chile who has also worked with drug-enhanced therapy. Dr. Naranjo has worked primarily with "mood enhancing" drugs, such as MDA, MMDA, ibogaine, and harmaline, which create deep alterations in emotions and self-image more than visual or hallucinogenic experiences. With the exception of MDA (3,4 methylene-dioxy-amphetamine), which has become popular as a street drug because of its intense aphrodisiac qualities when taken in large doses, few of these drugs are very well known in the United States. Dr. Naranjo reports on his research in his book _The Healing Journey,_ which includes a report on the case.

The episode surfaced while Dr. Naranjo was guiding a young man through an MDA trip at the University of Chile. MDA trips are characterized by extreme euphoria during which the mind tends to wander rapidly from one subject to another. Normal psychological defenses tend to break down almost completely, but the drug is so relaxing that no anxiety arises as a result of this state of psychological vulnerability. Naranjo was using this psychically open state to explore his patient's emotional responses to the experiences of his youth. He was proceeding by showing him photos from his childhood. The reincarnation recall began to emerge when the young man asked the therapist to leave the room so that he could work out a deeply personal emotion and memory that was arising from the depths of his mind. It turned out that this experience was the reliving of his own conception.

This part of his experience ignited the purported recollection from his past life. He suddenly cried out, fell to the floor, and raised his hands to his chest. He explained to the startled psychiatrist that he had just relived his death in his past life. "For the first time," writes Naranjo, "he began to get restless, anxious, and uncomfortable. He expressed the feeling that he shouldn't go any further, but kept hesitating." MDA can be a powerful drug, and soon the young man found himself reliving his past life as a Nazi. He even began speaking in a strange voice and in fluent German. Then he relived a scene in which he was crossing a countryside. He came back to reality with the feeling that, in his present life, he had to take responsibility for the cruelties he had committed in his previous one.

Dr. Naranjo was puzzled by the incident but has not adopted a metaphysical explanation for the episode. He has accepted a more formal psychoanalytical explanation for the reincarnation memories. He notes in his book that the patient's German-speaking grandfather had lived in the boy's home until the lad was four. This perhaps explains how he could have picked up the German he spoke during the session. The psychiatrist also learned that as a child, his patient had taken delight in persecuting and terrorizing his young brothers. This led Naranjo to conclude that his patient's reincarnation drama was nothing more than a symbolic way of dealing with his own guilt over his childhood "atrocities" . . . a deep-seated guilt that had emerged as a result of the MDA.

No one would argue that this explanation is, by all psychiatric criteria, "correct." But if one accepts the possibility that we have lived many lives before and can recall them, such an explanation is just as valid and no less speculative than Dr. Naranjo's. It is also hard to see how the patient could have spoken *fluent* German (in the psychiatrist's own words) from his exposure to a language that he probably couldn't even have understood.

People undergoing the mind-altering effects of LSD, mescaline, psilocybin, and other psychedelic drugs report a wide range of transpersonal phenomena. Not only do they sometimes re-experience their own past lives, they also often enter into and share more impersonal memories of times past.

Dr. Grof cites several such cases in his _Realms of the Human Unconscious_. These cases also bear on the reincarnation issue, although it is hard to tell whether the reports are due to past-life recall, ancestral memory, some sort of experience of the universal unconscious, or merely fantasy engendered role-playing. Some of these cases do contain a curious sort of reincarnation "air" about them, however. Nor was Dr. Grof the only researcher to confront these enigmatic incidents.

Robert Masters and Dr. Jean Houston were at the forefront of psychedelic drug research during the 1960s. They, too, often came across instances where their subjects became transported in time. One of their most impressive sets of observations were made when a young man with only a high school education was given a rather small (one hundred micrograms) dose of LSD. The researcher guiding the session suggested that the subject go back to ancient Greece and relive the rites of Dionysus. These were the famous Eleusinian mysteries and were considered very holy. We don't know too much about them because the actual rituals were never placed on record, but we do have a basic gist of what they entailed.

The subject responded first by describing a wild and savage phantasmagoria of images that culminated in the sacrifice of live animals. He then became calmer and began focusing on a strange stage performance rich with mythopoetic features:

> The scene changed and S found himself in a large amphitheater witnessing some figures performing a rite or play. This changed into a scene of white-robed figures moving in the night towards an open cavern. In spite of her intention to give further clues, the guide found herself asking the subject at this point: "Are you at Eleusis?" S seemed to nod "yes," whereupon the guide suggested that he go into the great hall and witness the mystery. He responded: "I can't. It is forbidden . . . I must confess . . . I must confess . . ." (The candidate at Eleusis was rejected if he came with sinful hands to seek enlightenment. He must first confess, make reparation, and be absolved. Then he received his instruction and then finally had his experience of enlightenment and was allowed to witness the mystery. How it happened that ths subject was aware of the stages of the mystery seemed itself to be a mystery.) S then began to go through the motions of kneading and washing his hands and appeared to be in deep conversation with someone. Later, he told the guide that he had seemed to be standing before a priestly figure and had made a confession. The guide now urged the subject to go into the hall and witness the drama. This he did and described seeing a "story" performed about a mother who looks the world over for her lost daughter and finally finds her in the world of the underground (The Demeter-Kore story, which, in all likelihood, was performed at Eleusis). This sequence dissolved, and the subject spoke of seeing a kaleidoscopic pattern of many rites of the death and resurrection of a god who appeared to be bound up in some way with the processes of nature. S described several of the rites he was viewing, and from his descriptions the guide was able to recognize remarkable similarities to rites of Osiris, Attis, and Adonis. S

was uncertain as to whether these rites occurred in a rapid succession or all at the same time.

This re-enactment eventually faded and the subject next reported experiencing a Roman Catholic Mass.

Masters and Houston were impressed by their subject's experiences because the information he reported seemed much more sophisticated than could be reasonably expected. They knew that their subject's reading over the years " . . . rarely extended beyond the daily newspapers and an occasional popular magazine." Under these circumstances they didn't think that cryptomnesia was the answer. They were impressed not only by the details of the revivication but also by the common themes that reappeared throughout the course of the session. These invariably revolved around the concepts of death and rebirth. The subject had apparently traced his theme from primitive man to modern Christianity. While the two researchers do not specifically adopt a reincarnation-oriented explanation for the subject's memories, they do feel that some sort of transpersonal explanation must be posited to account for them.

It really doesn't matter how we choose to interpret this case, though. The critical point is that it proves how, under the right conditions, the mind is capable of tuning in on past events and people. This is why the study of drug-induced past-life recall is so important. While such incidents may not serve as ultimate proof of reincarnation, they do contribute one more line of evidence that the human mind is somehow linked with the past. This discovery has a critical bearing on the validity of the reincarnation hypothesis . . . and may even account for how this curious doctrine arose as a religious doctrine in the first place.

One of the newest psychedelic drugs on the human potentials scene is ketamine hydrochloride, which was first marketed in 1969 and had a brief "street life" as a recreational drug in the late 1970s. Ketamine is a relatively safe dissociative anesthetic. When taken in small doses it catalyzes a short-lived psychedelic trip that often takes on religious overtones. Marcia Moore and her husband, Dr. Howard Alltounian, who is an anesthesiologist, became interested in the drug's spiritual dimensions in the mid-1970s and experimented with it prolifically in northern California. They, and some of the professional physicians to whom they introduced it, found that the emergence of reincarnation memories was a sometime byproduct of the experience.

Ms. Moore claimed in particular that the drug helped her get to the root of a curious physical ailment from which she had long suffered. This manifested as a crippling ache in her right hip joint, which caused her to walk with a limp. She suffered from this disability for six months before a ketamine "trip" helped her solve the mystery. During a relaxing psychedelic journey, she envisioned herself back in ancient Egypt where she, her husband, and a friend of theirs were rebels against the state. She recalled how they were captured, enslaved, and forced to oar at the galleys of the Egyptian fleet. A spike was driven through each of their hip joints to insure that they would not try to escape.

This emergent memory also helped Ms. Moore explain the curious "coincidence" that both her husband and their friend also suffered from hip problems. But what most amazed her was her physical response to the memory. Soon after the session, she realized that her hip problem was completely healed—a fact that her husband, a trained physician, likewise found astonishing. It is a moot point, though, whether Ms. Moore's problem was organic or psychogenic, in which latter case the ketamine experience may have simply been psychologically purgative. There is no indication in her account that her problem was ever medically diagnosed as an organic one.

Why ketamine should give rise to reincarnation-type experiences is quite puzzling. Unlike most of the major psychedelic drugs, ketamine is not known for catalyzing the emergence of repressed unconscious material. The drug actually short-circuits the brain by overstimulating it. It also apparently disturbs the relay centers in the brain that process sensory and inner-body experiences. So in a way, the drug acts as a chemical analogue to sensory deprivation. It might be suggested that a person in this state of mind might find himself strongly focusing on his inner thoughts, which might (in turn) be a way of tapping into past-life memories. On the other hand, ketamine trips are strongly influenced by expectancy and setting. Ms. Moore was interested in reincarnation long before her ketamine experiments, and this could have prompted the experience to take on spurious past-life overtones.

In the long run, whether drug-induced past-life recall can serve as evidence for reincarnation, like the whole issue of past-life therapy, can be reduced to two central issues. Does the information that has emerged from these sessions point to reincarnation? And perhaps just as important, do the positive effects these experiences have had on the lives of the subjects and patients indicate that they are more than just psychological phenomena?

It can't be denied that in the cases cited above, the past-life memories had a transforming effect on the patients' lives. The past-life recollections seemed to have acted as emotional catharses during which the patients were able to purify their minds of a lot of psychological "garbage" and go on to lead healthier and more actualized lives. Despite this self-evident fact, it is a moot point whether these cases serve as _particularly_ strong evidence for reincarnation. The informational aspects could be caused by cryptomnesia or possibly genetic memory. While the cases outlined in this chapter do suggest that some forms of past-life recall can carry therapeutic benefits along with them, the transformational effects taken alone cannot be cited as any sort of proof of the reincarnation doctrine. These therapeutic benefits may have simply come from the deeply altered and cathartic states induced by the drugs and may not have resulted from the memories that were prompted into consciousness. It is also notable that thousands of LSD and other drug-related therapy sessions were run during the heyday of the psychedelic revolution, but very few cases of spontaneous reincarnation recall emerged from them.

Even Robert Masters and Jean Houston, who conducted hundreds of sessions, cite no *specific* cases of past-life recall in their report s. It was also apparent that most of Dr. Grof's cases were too nonspecific to corroborate. This fact perhaps indicates that the few cases that did arise during the 1960s, when drug research was so popular, are psychological anomalies and not genuine psychic phenomena.

It would be gratuitously dismissive to adopt this view, though. Psychedelic drugs may well be a potential tool by which reincarnation and the distant past may be explored, and it is a shame that legal restrictions have curtailed so much research into these chemicals. But the rarity of such incidents within the published literature indicates that we should be cautious about any conclusions we may wish to draw from them.

Conclusions

A few cases of past-life recall were reported during the 1960s by researchers actively studying the properties of several major psychoactive drugs. These cases were apparently rare, and few of them contained veridical details. The subjects who underwent these revivications were often transformed by their experiences, even when they had previously rejected the notion of reincarnation. But in these instances it is difficult to tell whether these reactions were caused by the past-life memories or merely by the severe altered state of consciousness induced by the drugs. So while these cases and observations contribute to the case for reincarnation, they do not constitute a very compelling line of evidence.

11

Reconceptualizing Reincarnation

Throughout this book, I have constantly emphasized that our Westernized concept of reincarnation is naive and simplistic. This is, in fact, the primary problem we face when trying to make any sense out of the evidence. For if our understanding of this ancient doctrine is basically flawed, it is no wonder that the evidence seems so contradictory and puzzling. Reincarnation is a doctrine that has different meanings to different peoples in various cultures. We here in the West, who are unaccustomed to the subtleties and depth of Oriental philosophy, tend to interpret reincarnation as a simple and lateral cosmic progression: each of us is gifted with a soul; it departs the body at death; it floats about in a state of limbo for a while, and it attaches itself to a new body or embryo as it prepares for rebirth. The goal of the process is to work out the negative influences (or karmic debts) we have picked up in the past.

What is so fascinating is that no sophisticated religion or culture in the world today teaches such a simple concept. The doctrine of reincarnation is a much more complex one in Asian and Oriental thought. So by understanding the true philosophical doctrines of reincarnation, we may be able to make sense of the evidence. Most students of religion know that both Hinduism and Buddhism teach opposing doctrines about the rebirth process, but even this basic dichotomy is an oversimplification. Hinduism is schismatized by competing philosophical systems, and the interpretation of the reincarnation doctrine depends on whether it is approached from a monistic or theistic standpoint.

It is essential to understand the difference between these various conceptualizations before trying to determine how to interpret the empirical evidence for reincarnation.

Vedantic philosophy lies within the mainstream of Hindu monism and was imported and popularized in the west by Swami Vivekananda in the 1890s. The primary teachings of Vedantic philosophy are based on the premise that Brahma, or the Godhead, is merely pure undifferentiated consciousness, whose creative power is expressed through the existence of the Universe. We are all united in a oneness with this consciousness, but because of our illusions, we experience ourselves as separate from it. Each of us is actually a *jiva,* or emanation of Brahma, and we fail to perceive our unity with the divine because of cosmic ignorance. This unfortunate existential state can be rectified, however. If we can remove our veils of ignorance, this illusion would be destroyed and we would become one with the Universe. The concept of reincarnation is integrally linked with the process by which human ignorance is purged. Through the reincarnation of the self, the soul strives for the enlightenment that will reunite it with the Universe. Reincarnation is therefore a form of spiritual progression.

It should be obvious that our Western understanding of reincarnation is actually based on Vedantic philosophy. Vedanta became fixed in the West through the writings of such thinkers as Aldous Huxley, Gerald Heard, Christopher Isherwood, and other intellectuals. This exposition of Vivekananda's teachings spread even wider when these writers became the heralds of the consciousness explosion of the 1960s and early 1970s.

Theistic thought within Hinduism takes a different approach to these same philosophical issues, however. Hindu theism teaches that a personal force lies at the seat of ultimate reality, which deliberately creates the *jivas* (which we perceive as ourselves) through its divine "spirit" or energy. The cycle of rebirth is therefore not a directed or purposeful activity but constitutes an end within itself. It has no beginning or end, and while some of us will reach ultimate enlightenment, the Universe will never become fulfilled in a great oneness. Reincarnation in this light is considered as a simple metaphysical truth, and carries with it no teleological implications. Note how alien this idea is to our Western concept of reincarnation, yet this interpretation is no less valid than monistic ideas.

Probably the most important point to remember is that in Hindu monism, the individual self is considered an illusion. Theistic thinking accepts the ultimate individuality of the soul; therefore, little stress is placed on the "purging" nature of reincarnation.

If all this weren't confusing enough, Buddhistic thinking contributes even other ways of looking at the nature of reincarnation.

Buddhist philosophy is also schismatized by competing philosophical tradition, but it essentially teaches that the empirical self—our conscious personality—exists phenomenologically but is nonetheless a convenient fiction. Any idea that the self contains a soul-entity at its core is firmly rejected. The mind is seen as the ultimate seat of the self, and Buddhism teaches that the mind is no more than a successive stream of thought lacking any true permanence. This stream of thought gives us only the illusion of a permanent self. Some schools of Buddhist thought suggest a somewhat alternate view—that our concept of self is a reality but only a temporary one. The empirical self therefore represents a "process" composed only of a complex of behavioral dispositions.

Because traditional Buddhism does not teach the existence of a finite soul, its concept of reincarnation differs radically from those proposed by Hinduism. Buddhism doesn't even talk about reincarnation, only about rebirth. The concept of rebirth stems from the Buddhist idea that each of us is a temporary and changing conjunction of elements consisting of our body, feelings, perceptions, moral will, and consciousness. These elements gradually disintegrate after death, and what survives is a constellation of character dispositions prevailing in a state of craving for existence and expression. This personality complex is not a stable or uniquely conscious self but merely a formation of psychic elements that are bonded together through the laws of karma. Rebirth occurs because this constellation of character traits and memories ultimately expresses itself by reappearing on earth as a new empirical self. This cycle of rebirth will continue until each constellation of character dispositions learns to extinguish all craving and earthly attachment.

A commonly cited metaphor for the Buddhist process of rebirth is that of one candle lighting another. The second candle does not become the first candle, but it somehow carries on its heritage.

The concepts that I have been summarizing are somewhat obscure and their subtleties are difficult to fully appreciate. The main point to remember is that the term reincarnation is only a blanket designation that subsumes a variety of ideas, interpretations, and philosophical systems. People who talk without qualifying what they mean by "reincarnation," "karma," and "past lives" are really speaking nonspecifically and meaninglessly. It's all like the old cocktail party ploy we've learned to use when someone asks whether we believe in God. The only proper (and rather disarming) reply is to ask the questioner what he or she means by "God." Perhaps we should learn to adopt this same strategy when we are asked whether we believe in reincarnation. The issue is no less complex. We all entertain our private conceptualization about the fundamental truths that lie behind the operation of the Universe, whether we are talking about God, heaven, hell, karma, or rebirth. Because we were all raised in the same culture and share a common language, we too often assume that everyone with whom we come into contact shares these same basic conceptualizations. This is a dangerous supposition to make. It becomes even more dangerous when we are discussing imported cosmological systems, of which reincarnation is probably the most popular. We tend to talk about a _concept_ of reincarnation that simply doesn't exist anywhere within the living traditions of the world's great religions.

In light of the foregoing comments, the only way to make any discussion of the reincarnation question meaningful is to break it down into two parts. We should be talking about the *manifestation* of reincarnation as well as the *process* of reincarnation. Confusion between these two aspects of the rebirth issue lies at the root of the reincarnation mystery.

By the *manifestation* of reincarnation, we are simply asking if we can sometimes manifest the memories and behavioral dispositions of people who have lived and died before us.

By the *process* of reincarnation, we are asking whether each of us inherits another individual's soul or merely inherits his memories and whether it is the donor person or the nearly born who initiates the process. These are the more crucial aspects of the reincarnation question.

Most serious students of the literature would probably agree that the basic manifestation of reincarnation is a real, vital, and psychodynamically active process in the world. The evidence presented in this book, even with all its problems, fully supports the idea that each of us is born with a psychic heritage within our makeup. This heritage sometimes expresses itself through the memories and the adoption of behavioral traits inherited from people who died before our births. What the evidence does not tell us is what mechanism controls this "process of inheritance."

Do we inherit the "soul" of another individual, which expresses itself dynamically (though tacitly) through the formation of our individual personalities and behaviors? Or do we inherit a simple constellation of memories and behavioral dispositions that, while in a sense alien to our individual selves, *influence* us by the very fact of their attachments?

The first idea is somewhat in keeping with traditional Hindu thought. The second notion, which perhaps strikes you as rather more esoteric, would be somewhat of a Buddhistic derivative. There is really only one way to settle this matter, and that is to see which theory best explains the empirical evidence. This is the evidence that was presented in the earlier sections of this book. Since cases of extracerebral memory represent the strongest expression of the *manifestation* of reincarnation, perhaps we should begin with them.

Instead of arguing the relative merits of applying a Hindu versus Buddhist explanation for cases of extracerebral memory, I would like to approach this issue by summarizing a fascinating debate that Dr. Ian Stevenson and the late Dr. Gardner Murphy conducted in 1973. This friendly confrontation appeared in the pages of the *Journal* of the American Society for Psychical Research. The cause of this debate was the former's *Twenty Cases Suggestive of Reincarnation*. Dr. Stevenson has long maintained that his case studies serve as strong evidence (though not proof) for reincarnation. Although Stevenson has never defined what he means by reincarnation, there are tacit suggestions in his writings that he is primarily adopting some form of popular Hindu conceptualization. He has been critical of all other interpretations of his data. Dr. Murphy was less sure just what conclusions should be drawn from his colleague's work. He was intrigued by Dr. Stevenson's case studies but set out to see if he could account for all of his colleague's findings by adopting some sort of telepathy/memory theory. When he challenged the validity of the reincarnation interpretation, Dr. Stevenson was quick to reply.

While never couched in cosmological or theological terms, their debate actually resolved into one of Hindu versus Buddhist interpretation of extracerebral memory cases. It is doubtful whether either participant ever fully realized the fundamentally philosophical nature of their debate. Stevenson, however, eventually realized that Dr. Murphy was adopting a rather Buddhistic approach to the concept of human personality.

Dr. Murphy approached the phenomenon of extracerebral memory by drawing on a philosophy of mind first presented by Whately Carington, a noted British philosopher and parapsychologist. Carington argued that the mind consists of nothing more than a system of images and sense data held in conjunction by associative linkages. He called this network a "psychon" system. He also maintained that these linkages are composed of common ideas, which he called "K" ideas. Thus the mind was merely, in his view, a collection of ideas and experiences with only a tenuous cohesion at best. This is, of course, a very Buddhistic concept. The virtue of this theory is that it leaves open the possibility that one psychon system might integrate with another under certain prescribed conditions. For example, two minds could link together (telepathically) if at a certain time they share a number of associated ideas.

The pure Buddhism of this conceptualization becomes more apparent when we look at Carington's views on life after death. He conceived survival as the continued existence of the psychon system (or "mind"), still held together by the individual's sensory experiences and imagery data. But he also believed that these surviving systems might include within their structure images that " . . . may have become linked with them, notably by telepathic interactions with other minds." In other words, our individual personalities will survive death but not purely as unique structures divorced from the field of interactions in which we participated during the course of our lives and even after death. What survives is a system of ideas and associations somewhat contaminated by other influences we have "picked up" from other people.

"Of special interest to psychical research," Murphy explains, "is the fact that barriers between components of the psychon systems are frequently softened, modulated, or removed so that new conglomerate wholes are formed. We see this process within the individual mind, and we also find that in everything from falling in love to collective group thinking . . . there are processes of clustering and amalgamation." The point I think Murphy was trying to make is that after death, our "minds" can actually fuse with other minds to form collective or "group" identities.

Each hypothetical psychon system would probably gradually extinguish after death, as its associations weaken and dissolve. A psychon system held together by especially strong associations might survive longer before dissolving and/or becoming amalgamated with other psychon systems. (Once again it should be pointed out that little in this conceptualization contradicts Buddhist theories of mind.)

This is, of course, all very abstract and I am far from sure that I understand exactly what Carington was trying to say. But Murphy felt that these concepts could be specifically applied to the phenomenon of extracerebral memory.

Murphy first pointed out that the most evidential cases of extracerebral memory arise when a "reincarnated" child and the donor personality share the same culture. This phenomenon suggested to him that the process of "reincarnation" is an associational one, by which the self (or the "psychon" system) attaches itself to another person or developing consciousness with which it shares common (such as cultural) idea patterns. People who live within the same culture and in close geographical proximity share similar thought processes and life experiences. Dr. Murphy suggested that a psychon system would feasibly be attracted to an embryo developing in its own culture, especially in a neighboring village, and become attached to it because of their mutual or "associational" affinities. He also thought that this process of psychic assimilation (which is not exactly "reincarnation") could explain why anomalous cases of extracerebral memory exist in the literature—cases in which the "reincarnated" child is already born and maturing when the donor personality dies. He especially felt that this process could explain such oddities as the Imad Elawar case, where it appears that the boy's memories were an amalgamation of associated ideas drawn from the terrestrial lives of two related individuals. A psychon system could also become attached to a child after his or her birth as well as before and would carry with it memories and associations from other people known to it in life.

A specific issue Murphy raised against a conventional reincarnationist approach to extracerebral memory was the motivational aspects of these cases. Many of them struck him as devoid of any sense of purpose, as though they were the result of a psychic "residue" rather than of a striving and living presence now reappearing on the earth.

Dr. Murphy was aware that birthmark cases probably constitute the strongest evidence for reincarnation, but he suggested that these markings result from the psychophysiological impact of the psychon system on the developing infant. What confused him was why so-called "reincarnation" could carry such a graphic physical impact but not a corresponding psychological impact. This point led him right back to the problem of purpose. He asks:

> Why doesn't this impact also bring a cluster of personal and unrealized purposes, the characteristic 'unfinished business' of life? It may be replied that it does indeed bring all these, the earnest wishes of an earlier period. But it is odd on this basis that they begin to fade when adolescence approaches and disappears as adulthood begins. And there is another paradox here: the fact that memories of the previous life fade out as the child grows up seems to

mean that the *well-structured* memories of an earlier life are harder to hang on to than the more *fluid* memories of childhood.

My interpretation of what Murphy was saying is that reincarnation memories should affect the maturing child more dynamically than they, in fact, usually do. Being more integrated than the child's own first life experience, they should have a permanent and dramatic effect. They shouldn't manifest in the form of disorganized and often vague recollections that simply die out as the child grows older.

The virtue of Murphy's conceptual model is that it makes the rebirth process a two-way street. It allows for the donor personality's surviving self to seek expression by infiltrating into a newly developing personality. But it also suggests that the embryo or infant could initiate the process by seeking out and tapping into a free-floating psychon system. "We would expect both of these things to happen," Murphy writes, "and that the strength of such interactions would depend not only upon the number of [common associations] available, but also upon other . . . factors which are for the most part the classical factors of association theory—contiguity in space and time, vividness, recency, and frequency . . . "

To sum up: It was Murphy's theory that cases of extracerebral memory do not derive from literal reincarnation but occur when a living psyche amalgamates a network of memories and behavioral patterns released by the donor person at death. To Murphy, extracerebral memory is the psychic assimilation of a memory network and not the rebirth of the soul.

Dr. Stevenson published an extensive reply to Murphy in which he tried to show that all of Murphy's points could be explained by adopting a more traditional reincarnation theory. The fact that people tend to be reborn within their own culture, he suggested, could be the result of conscious decisions on the part of the surviving personalities. As he succinctly puts it, "the deceased person does not think that he could be reborn anywhere else except in the next village, and so he is." He goes on to posit that the whole process of reincarnation might be guided by the newly deceased's cultural expectations. Stevenson also argued that normal psychological principles can account for the reason a child's reincarnation memories will tend to fade in time. "The fading of memories of the previous life when it occurs in later childhood," he writes, "is perhaps not any different in process from the fading of memories in childhood and adolescence when this occurs in adulthood." Stevenson goes on to point out that many factors complicate our ability to preserve early memories, adding that "I think all students of memory agree that one of the most important factors in the loss of conscious memories is the occurrence of later experiences which somehow 'interfere' with the ability to recall memories of earlier experiences."

This process (which is technically called retroactive inhibition) may occur, the University of Virginia psychiatrist suggests, when the child enters school, which forces new life experiences upon him.

Dr. Stevenson also took strong exception to Dr. Murphy's criticism about the "purposelessness" of most extracerebral memory cases. He actually countered this argument by drawing on two lines of reasoning. His first was that the sense of psychological craving Murphy found lacking in his cases may subtly exist. Children born with extracerebral memory often express the personal idiosyncrasies of the donor personalities, including (sometimes) their social snobbery and preoccupations. These are often behavioral features alien to the child's culture or social status. Stevenson believes that these features may be repesenting the actualization of the donor's psychological cravings. But he qualified his response by pointing out that the sense of purpose Murphy cites is a sort of existential striving alien to most people confronting life in the world today. Most people are geared more toward day-to-day concerns, he suggests, than any great far-reaching goals that might be interrupted by the sting of death. It is also possible that a child might be conditioned away from the expression of any past-life strivings by his or her parents. Only the child's raw memories would escape this social conditioning.

Dr. Stevenson specifically counterattacked Murphy's application of Carington's psychon theory by pointing to the long intervals between the time of the donor's death and subsequent rebirth exhibited in some of his cases. While sometimes the rebirth process is undertaken quickly, some cases were found in which up to eighteen years passed between incarnations. If psychon systems tend to dissolve after the death of the donor, he argued, we should not see such cases arising.

To sum up: Dr. Stevenson feels that some of Murphy's criticisms are actually non-issues and that principles drawn from developmental psychology and social learning theory can explain some of the features of his cases.

When I first read the Murphy-Stevenson debate in 1973, I felt that Dr. Stevenson probably made the better case. He countered Dr. Murphy's points reasonably well, and I was especially impressed by how easily principles drawn from conventional psychology could explain some of the idiosyncrasies in his cases. In rereading this debate today, my reaction is somewhat different. The main appeal of Dr. Stevenson's reply was that it constitutes a very lucid and organized reply to an essay that is, frankly, rather rambling, disorganized, and obscurantist. Murphy was never a good writer and was a theoretician of questionable clarity. Some of his genuinely creative insights were often camouflaged in excessively protracted prose. This is especially true of his writings on extracerebral memory. Stevenson seems to make a good case against his colleague only because of his ability to communicate better. If we can bypass this form of literary seduction, it becomes clear that Murphy raised certain criticisms to which Dr. Stevenson simply could not reply.

Murphy especially emphasized that problems often manifest within the memory clusters "reincarnated" children seem to recall. The recollections don't seem to be composed of tightly knit memory networks, the very type of memories a "reincarnated" child would be expected to entertain. Yet this is the very feature a Caringtonian theory *can* explain, since psychon systems would be rather tenuously bonded. Dr. Murphy's adaptation of this theory of mind can also explain some of Dr. Stevenson's anomalous cases much better than simple reincarnation can. Murphy came to realize, just as I did when studying Stevenson's cases, that these anomalous cases might be providing us with important clues about the nature of extracerebral memory. He, too, especially focused on the case of Jasbir Lal Jat, who was three years old when he "recalled" his previous life as a man who had just died. While Stevenson admitted in his reply that he had two additional cases of this same type in his files, he never attempted to explicate how this oddity could be explained according to any conventional reincarnation theory.

So in a way, perhaps Dr. Murphy won this debate by default.

Recent thinking within parapsychology has, I think, sided with Dr. Murphy as well. Stevenson has fallen behind the times with his lateral views about reincarnation. Many students of the psychic field who have seriously studied Dr. Stevenson's work are inclined to reject it as evidence for literal reincarnation. W. G. Roll, who was the first contemporary parapsychologist to specialize in survival research, has never been sympathetic to Stevenson's viewpoints. As I pointed out in Chapter 4, Roll believes that extracerebral memory cases "suggest not so much the survival of any unitary personality of self as the continuation of clusters of associated memories." Roll was primarily disturbed by the fact that some children appear to remember their past lives inaccurately but with relevant associations. (For instance, he cites one case in which a child correctly recalled a past life as the mother of two children, but she named them incorrectly. These names actually designated two _other_ relatives.)

W. G. Roll is not alone in his thinking. Dr. Ruth Reyna, who was educated both in the United States and in India, takes a similar critical approach to the phenomenon of extracerebral memory. In her critical (and often incomprehensible) book _Reincarnation and Science,_ she rejects over and over again Stevenson's cases as evidence for literal reincarnation. She specifically denies "that an entity called 'soul' is reset in total consciousness into a new body with its former accoutrements intact so that it can be recognized as a reincarnation of its former self." She maintains instead, "that certain atomic 'residue' of deceased persons may be absorbed by a new foetus. This 'residue' or undissipated energy, while appearing to be reincarnation in toto is, at best, only a fragmentary rebirth."

Dr. Reyna's theory may sound a little more novel than it really is, since some systems of Asian philosophy recognize that reincarnation sometimes entails the rebirth of only one element of the total personality.

Dr. C. T. K. Chari is a little more agnostic about the interpretation of extracerebral memory cases but proposes that the child may be tapping into a psi-informational complex released at the time of death. This tuning-in process is only interpreted by the child as personal "reincarnation" because of his cultural conditioning.

Even some popular self-help practitioners who espouse the reincarnation doctrine are beginning to re-evaluate their stance. Dick Sutphen, despite his commercial interest in the reincarnation doctrine, has suggested that "maybe we're not tapping in on past lives. It could be that, when we die, we pass on our 'cumulative essence' to a new soul, who attempts to clear up the essence before passing it on again." Sutphen has good cause to question traditional concepts of reincarnation. When he was in his thirties, he developed the overwhelming feeling that he was the reincarnation of Ed Morrell, the celebrated prison reformer and out-of-body traveler made famous by Jack London in his novel *The Star Rover*. It was only in 1981, after he carried out some prodigious research on Morrell's life, that he confronted a peculiar irony. Morrell died in Los Angeles in 1943, years after Sutphen's own birth in 1937. (It is to his credit that while he teaches reincarnation, Sutphen has never hidden this personal idiosyncracy.)*

Several of these same ideas appear in the writings of John H. Hick, an eminent theologian based at Clairmont College in California. Hick is an authority on the doctrine of immortality. Although he approaches the subject primarily from a philosophical and theological perspective, he has long acknowledged the importance of studying the contributions psychical research has made to the issue. Because of his interest in Oriental philosophy, Hick has also studied the reincarnation doctrine—it was inevitable that this line of study would lead him to Dr. Stevenson's work. His book *Death and Eternal Life* includes a ninety-page critical examination of the reincarnation belief, and he discusses the phenomenon of extracerebral memory in surprising depth.

Hick has come to adopt a theory about the nature of these cases that is suspiciously close to Dr. Murphy's. He bases his theory on the supposition that "after bodily death a mental 'husk' or 'mask' of the deceased person is left behind and is telepathically accessible under certain conditions to living persons." This process is probably unconscious, he suggests. It only manifests itself when information absorbed through this telepathic bond begins to intrude on the living person's conscious thoughts and experiences. This may lead the child to adopt some of these alien memories as his or her own and may especially manifest in the child's ability to recognize former relatives and acquaintances. These recognitions come about when the child "is exorcizing fragments of memory-dispositions which are elements of the psychic factors with which he is in contact."

Hick goes on to write:

> With such a theory the idea of reincarnation becomes in effect a matter of degree. There is no rebirth of the full living personality. But there is a kind of reincarnation of parts or aspects of the personality, such attenuated reincar-

_____

*Many students of the psychic field may distrust Sutphen's claims and views on reincarnation because of the commercial nature of his enterprise. However, I met with Sutphen in October 1983 and found him to be a serious and well-read student of the subject. I was also continually impressed by his openness to competing ideas.

nation being equally compatible with the extinction of the personality as a whole or with its continued life in some other sphere, leaving behind only a mental "husk" which becomes entangled in the mind of a living child with whom it has perhaps some kind of affinity and through whom its remaining quantum of psychic energy is discharged. This would seem, at any rate in the present state of the scientific investigation of spontaneous "memories" of former lives, to be one more possible non- or semi-reincarnationist explanation of them.

The specific virtue of the scheme is that it allows us to believe in personal immortality *and* reincarnation at the same time. It suggests that our "psychon system" may be reborn in a sense, while the immortal soul is basking in everlasting life. The only problem with Hick's model is a rather obvious one. Birthmark cases cannot be explained on the theory that extracerebral memory results from a form of telepathic bonding. So this theory would have to be revised. This bonding process would have to come into existence while the infant is still *in utero,* and I see nothing in Hick's writings that would prohibit such an extension to this theory.*

Please note once again that none of the theoreticians I have been quoting actually deny the *manifestation* of reincarnation. They are only arguing about the *process* of rebirth or what aspect of the total personality is being expressed through it.

Before going on to explain my own feelings about the nature of reincarnation, perhaps one last question should be asked: Are there any cases in the literature that really do point to *literal* reincarnation? Throughout the course of this book, emphasis has been placed on imperfect and anomalous cases. My basic point is that the exceptions within the evidence are probably more revealing that the laws. The "true believer" could rightly argue that I haven't been able to see the forest for the trees. In other words, my approach might be artificially weakening the case for literal reincarnation. So before concluding this chapter, can we point to any cases in the literature that look like virtual reincarnation of the soul? Can any alternate theory account for them?

The best single case I have been able to find is contained in two books by Dr. Arthur Guirdham, a retired British psychiatrist in Bath who is a staunch supporter of the reincarnation doctrine. He believes that he is the reincarnation of a Cathar priest, a member of a twelfth- and thirteenth-century heretical cult that flourished in Italy and France. He further believes that, through a series of synchronistic events, he has come into contact with other reincar-

---

*Another attempt to explain extracerebral memory cases is offered by science writer John Gribben in his book *Timewarps* (New York: Delacourt Press, 1979). He posits that extracerebral memory occurs when a child telepathically tunes in and views scenes and people from the past and makes contact with a time stream from that era. This theory cannot account for birthmark cases, either, so will not be considered further.

nated members of the band. The story of how he came to these realizations is contained in his book, *The Cathars and Reincarnation,* and in its sequel, *We Are One Another.* The story is immensely complex, so it can only be briefly summarized.

Dr. Guirdham admits that he has always been attracted to the Cathars, who taught that good and evil are equal forces in the world, which serves as its cosmic battleground. They despised the world, and they believed in reincarnation. These beliefs were considered heretical by the Catholic church, which spearheaded a movement to wipe out the Cathars at the beginning of the thirteenth century. Thousands of cult members were subsequently slaughtered. The end came in 1242, when the last members of the sect were besieged at a mountain fortress in Montségur, France. They finally surrendered and scores of their numbers were burnt in a huge *auto-de-fé.*

Dr. Guirdham apparently knew little of this history when he first started responding to his past-life memories. Throughout his life he suffered from a peculiar nightmare in which a man approached him as he slept. The dream seemed innocuous enough, but he inevitably awoke screaming in terror. The dream defied analysis until 1962, when the psychiatrist met a new patient, whom he calls Mrs. Smith in his book. She was suffering from a similar nightmare and was referred to Dr. Guirdham for psychiatric treatment by her doctor. The woman immediately recognized Guirdham as a man she had often seen in her dreams, and her nightmares suddenly ceased. She entered therapy nonetheless, during which she gradually spoke about her unusual childhood. She claimed to possess psychic abilities and maintained that she had nurtured them from early childhood. She also suffered attacks of unconsciousness and headaches in her youth. These episodes heralded the onset of particularly vivid dreams of living back in the thirteenth century near Toulouse, France. (This town was, in fact, a Cathar stronghold.) Some of these dreams revolved around a man who arrived at her house asking for shelter. They became friends, and he took her as his mistress. Later she recalled his imprisonment while she was burned at the stake. The odd thing about this sequence of dreams was the number of proper names communicated through them. Gradually and through painstaking historical searches, Dr. Guirdham was able to verify that these names designated real people and members of the Cathar sect who lived in the thirteenth century. What was even more impressive was that Mrs. Smith had kept notebooks chronicling her youthful experiences. Contained in them were emblems, poems, and information about the Cathars that all proved historically accurate. Some of her "poems" even seemed to be based on medieval French verses she could hardly have learned normally.

Of course, the close identification between the man in Mrs. Smith's dreams and her therapist led Dr. Guirdham to believe that he was the Cathar with whom his patient had fallen in love. This conclusion also helped Dr. Guirdham explain his own nightmares, and he gradually began to remember more about his own Cathar life.

This whole involved story becomes even more complex in _We Are One Another_. Dr. Guirdham opens the book by explaining how he was approached by an acquaintance in Bath one day, who wondered whether two odd names meant anything to him. (Both names alluded to thirteenth-century Cathar history.) "Miss Mills," the pseudonym employed to protect the woman's identity, then proceeded to tell Guirdham about some of her childhood nightmares. She experienced one recurrent dream in which she was fleeing from a castle, though she ultimately found herself being led to a burning pyre. She could make no sense of the dream, but it made a lasting impression on her. Even as a child she couldn't stand to watch anyone building a fire. She, too, could recall a number of curious names that came to her in childhood. All of them referred to historical Cathars, some of whom perished at Montségur.

The upshot of this chance meeting was even more dramatic than the discovery of Mrs. Smith's poems and notebooks. Dr. Guirdham now learned that in October 1971 Miss Mills had struck up a peculiar friendship with a woman from the Midlands. This woman, whom Guirdham calls "Betty," was recovering from her husband's death and wanted to visit the French Pyrenées to recuperate, so she asked Miss Mills' advice about any places worth seeing. Her trip included more than just sightseeing, for it ignited some vestigial memories of her own past life in the mountains and several Cathar names began intruding themselves into _her_ waking thoughts. Before Dr. Guirdham could meet Betty, however, a stroke ended her life. But he was able to make a significant discovery about her childhood. Through his contacts with her mother, Dr. Guirdham gathered some doodlings Betty had made during an illness she suffered when she was seven years old. Within these doodles were not only references to the siege of Montségur, but even the names of several prominent Cathar figures. These were apparently written out by the girl while she was delirious.

If this weren't enough, _We Are One Another_ ends as Dr. Guirdham explains how two other acquaintances in England also began independently remembering dreams of their Cathar incarnations. When one of Miss Mills' business associates died unexpectedly during the unwinding of the plot summarized above, the name of a twelfth-century Cathar was on _her_ lips. This woman was apparently unaware of Miss Mills' own reincarnation memories, and the story only surfaced later when her husband mentioned it to his wife's former friend.

This brief summary cannot do justice to the information contained in Dr. Guirdham's two books nor to the painstaking historical research the psychiatrist undertook to verify it. This has led him to conclude that a group of Cathars deliberately planned a group reincarnation to present-day England after their deaths, which is only now coming to light via a series of meaningful coincidences.

The case looks, in fact, almost too good to be true. This has caused some skeptics to suggest that Dr. Guirdham is pulling a huge joke on the reading public. I was initially impressed when I read Dr. Guirdham's seminal work in 1973 but had to reconsider my opinion when I read all of his subsequent works. It is peculiar that as his books progress, his views and claims become wilder and wilder. The assertions he makes in *The Cathars and Reincarnation* are astounding but certainly credible. The clockwork synchronicities that serve as the focal point for *We Are One Another* are certainly not beyond the realms of possibility but begin to tax our credibility a bit. But when we read the books that follow, the whole story becomes rather suspect. Dr. Guirdham and his friends are now recalling an entire series of group reincarnations going back in time all the way to Roman-occupied England. Dr. Guirdham talks about the ghosts of deceased Cathars who come to him in sleep, call him on the phone, and momentarily possess his friends. And the reader begins to wonder if he is dealing with a psychiatrist or an ambulatory psychotic.

The second cause for concern is Dr. Guirdham's curious response to criticism, since he refuses to document his claims in any way. Ian Wilson attempted to document them when he was working on his *All in the Mind?* and even visited the doctor in Bath. The aging psychiatrist wouldn't provide Wilson with the real names of the key players in his reincarnation dramas. This struck Wilson as suspicious because some of these people were now dead and their privacy no longer had to be protected. The only documentation Dr. Guirdham provided was the old sheet of paper containing the childhood scribblings "Betty" made during her illness. (This is also reproduced in his second reincarnation book.) Wilson readily acknowledged that the paper looked old, but this one item hardly constitutes evidence for the entire Cathar story. Dr. Guirdham has refused to answer any of Wilson's subsequent requests for documentation.

I have to side with Wilson, who is now very skeptical of Dr. Guirdham's claims. His refusal to reply to Wilson's requests certainly looks suspicious. If the psychiatrist has genuinely stumbled across evidence supporting the great cosmic truth of reincarnation, it seems to me that he would be eager to prove his claim in any way possible. By refusing to cooperate with those interested in exploring his assertions, he has rendered his investigations worthless.

The strange story of Dr. Arthur Guirdham and his past-life Cathar priesthood is certainly an entertaining and absorbing one. It is also probably the single most important case placed in the literature. But too many questions remain unanswered about it. To cite it as scientific evidence supporting the reincarnation doctrine would, therefore, be rash.

Even if it ultimately turns out that Dr. Guirdham's claims are true, the story of his group reincarnation may represent some sort of cosmic anomaly. I doubt whether the process that possibly guided the reincarnation of his Cathar band is the same as the process that underlies most cases of extracerebral memory or hypnotic past-life recall. On the other hand, even if I were convinced that Dr. Guirdham's story is literally true, I would have no problem applying the Murphy/Carington theory to it. The Cathar band, of which Dr. Guirdham claims to be a part, believed firmly in reincarnation during their lives. They were therefore strongly bonded together by their religious associations, belief systems, and deaths. The personality constellations or the psychon systems they released at death probably strove for rebirth. Their inability to disengage from one another may have led these individual (yet bonded) psychic systems to become reborn at the same general time and in the same general area—twentieth-century England.

This is, of course, stretching the psychon theory a bit. But I am suggesting it only to show that these types of theories can be stretched to account for even the best cases of the reincarnation type.

So with all this in mind, I think it is high time for me to explain my own theories about the nature of reincarnation cases.

Coming to grips with the reincarnation problem is not easy. The student is ultimately confronted by a network of intertwining lines of evidence. We have to take into account that some people remember their past lives from birth, while others make contact with them through hypnosis or during LSD sessions. Some people only remember single scenes from their karmic pasts, while others exhibit more cohesive memories. Some individuals consciously recollect their past lives, while others only display phobias or bizarre behavioral dispositions inherited from ages long since past. The problem with most of the theories I presented earlier in this chapter is that they only address a single line of evidence. They were only proposed to account for cases of extracerebral memory. A truly comprehensive theory for the phenomenon of past-life recall would have to encompass evidence drawn from several sources. So my plan is not really to present a radically new theory about the nature of reincarnation. I think we can best proceed by drawing upon the insights of the many thinkers I quoted earlier and by expanding them to encompass those avenues of evidence ignored in their writings.

To begin with, I adopt a somewhat Buddhistic theory about the nature of the self. I believe that the human personality survives death, but this is not the same as positing the existence of an immortal soul. (If we are each gifted with a soul, I doubt if it would be imbued with any sort of individual personality.) My view is not primarily a religious one but one developed through my study of psychic phenomena and the survival issue. But just what is this "personality" that survives? We cannot really speak about personality without also speaking about our memory, for personality is simply the sum of our memories and our (partially genetically determined) behavioral dispositions. Even most textbooks on psychology refer to personality as an "organization" rather than an entity. So what really survives death is a personalized network of memories. It is a moot point whether any spark of divinity (a "soul") lies within this network.

Following along the lines of Carington's theory of mind, I don't believe that this personality network is concrete or impermeable. It probably retains its individuality and consciousness but could readily share in the experiences of other memory systems shed at death. In other words, after death we will exist as a "personality" but also as part of a larger network or "group mind." This group mind is formed by the many people who share our own cultural views and expectations. During our lives after death we would probably be linked to our deceased relatives and friends in a huge interpersonal matrix. I would also expect that, in time, we shed our individuality and merge totally into this more impersonal field, thereby experiencing a blissful annihilation.

This general conception of the afterlife ties in mutually with the whole concept of reincarnation. I simply believe that, for some cosmic reason, a developing embryo can become linked with one or more of these surviving personality constellations and with the whole network of which it is a part. Either the craving of the constellation for existence drives it to attach itself to a new life, or the developing consciousness latches onto one or more of these personalities of its own accord. A case of the former might express itself in those cases that look like "possession," in which the personality of the living person will temporarily transform into that of the donor. We saw this process at work in the case of Uttara Huddar, and to a lesser degree during the strange trances to which Kumkum Verma was prone. The outcome of the second process might be a more passive expression, in which the child merely assimilates some of the memories of the donor personality. Of course, we may not actually be dealing with an either/or situation. This process of psychic attachment may result from the craving of the surviving personality constellation *coupled* with the desire of the developing life to initiate such contact. How each case expresses itself may be the result of which aspect of the process is dominant.

This linkage is not really reincarnation, since the developing life is only *tapping* the resources of the donor personality's surviving memories and dispositions. The infant's own spiritual essence is not being taken over by, or emerging from, the donor in any real sense. Now just why such a process should exist is a puzzle. I have no definitive answer to this cosmic question. My own personal speculation would be that the process may serve the survival needs of the unborn child. Latching onto the memories and behavioral dispositions of a surviving personality may in some way help prepare the child for its coming birth. Perhaps it provides some sort of psychological energy that will help it survive the shock of birth and cope with life outside the womb. So we might sum this all up by saying that at birth, an infant is complete with its own burgeoning personality. But it is born with a psychic heritage based on its prenatal contact with "the dead." The donor personality is not a living presence within the child but remains as a blueprint underlying his or her memories, responses, and behavior. The past-life heritage serves as a resource and does not constitute a dynamic presence.

This theory can account for birthmark cases as well as for the emergence of past-life memories and phobias. Because an unborn child has few psychological resources of its own, any surviving personality constellation with which it comes into contact is bound to exert a strong influence. This influence may become a physical as well as a mental one. We should *expect* to see a "reincarnated" child possessing birthmarks, behavioral idiosyncracies, memories, and phobias that relate to the terrestrial life of the donor.

What exactly happens to the surviving personality at the time of the child's birth? Conceivably the psychic contact with the unborn child causes the constellation to dissolve, thereby leaving behind only a series of marks on the personality and subsequent behavior of the child. "Reincarnation" memories would then be the result of these marks. It is also possible that the surviving personality might maintain its own structural integrity while not remaining permanently linked to the developing life. It may "depart," so to speak, after making its imprint.

I also think that this general theory can explain anomalous cases of the reincarnation type. When the child or fetus establishes psychic contact with a surviving memory constellation, he or she may get more than was bargained for. Coming into contact and symbiotically drawing from a surviving personality would also place the child in contact with a whole network of other personalities. These comprise the "group" mind to which the surviving personality cluster is a part. Memories and behavioral dispositions derived from these sources would be weaker than those adopted from the primary donor but could exert some sort of presence as well. This process could explain why some "reincarnated" children recall information derived from two previously living people. It can also explain why a once-living person can apparently reincarnate more than once . . . granting that a surviving personality does not dissolve once it comes into contact with a newly developing life.

This general framework also helps explain why so many "reincarnated" children recall violent past-life deaths. It may be that people who die violently shed particularly dynamic or tightly integrated memory constellations. They might especially strive for existence and might more readily attach themselves to a newly developing life or hold out a greater attraction to the developing infant.

I might also add that this linkage phenomenon may occur at times _other_ than when the child is yet unborn. It is conceivable that the same process might occur after the child's birth. A close brush with death, such as Jasbir Lal Jat suffered during his illness, may somehow cause such a linkage to occur.

Nor does it take too much expansion to show how this theoretical model can be applied to other forms of reincarnation experience.

It is likely that we all harbor memories of our psychic heritage deep within our subconscious minds, even if they seek expression only rarely. They may especially seek expression in those cultures in which the doctrine of reincarnation is taught and generally accepted. Perhaps these cultures set up some sort of psychological or even genetic dispositions in the personality that allows reincarnation memories to emerge more readily than in other cultures. Because each of us is born with this peculiar sort of psychic heritage, it is not unthinkable that we can make contact with memory traces left by these links by digging deeply into the subconscious. This is why such traces would tend to emerge during hypnosis, as a result of an LSD session, or during intensive psychotherapy. Any procedure that temporarily places the conscious mind in abeyance could allow these memory traces to surface or to be tapped.

Under these circumstances, the same patterns that emerge in cases of extracerebral memory would appear in cases of hypnotic past-life recall, LSD-evoked memory, and so forth. This is probably why some cases of hypnotically elicited past-life memory mimic the features that emerge in anomalous cases of extracerebral memory. (This was an issue we examined in Chapter 6.)

I might add that if the traces left by these prenatal psychic contacts are able to form into a subsystem within the living person's mind, he or she would be endowed with some amazing abilities. He or she might be able to speak a foreign language he never learned or display precocious artistic and mechanistic skills and other talents. Of course, the skeptic might object that my whole scheme is inconsistent with all that neurology and psychology have learned about the structure of human memory. But my response would be that neurology and psychology really *don't* know very much about memory. It is an embarrassing fact that modern science simply has no understanding of human memory. We have no idea how information is coded, processed, or stored within the brain. The fact that no neurological seat for memory has ever been discovered has led some psychologists to suggest that memory may not be a physical or biochemical process at all. In fact, *nothing* I have been saying can be rejected as inconsistent with modern psychology and science.

Perhaps the idea of reincarnation was a theory by which primitive peoples attempted to explain how some people could experience the memories of other people long since dead. But these memories may not have been a "part" of them anymore than reading a book about Abraham Lincoln makes this long-deceased gentleman a part of us. We probably all retain many memories of the past within us, but even though they are with us from birth, they are nevertheless alien.

So, in conclusion, do I "believe" in reincarnation?

Based on the evidence, I suppose that I should say that I do: but not in the reincarnation of the soul, but in the fact that certain apparently vanished memories and traits of personality *can* actually be born again.

12

References

Chapter 1

BERNSTEIN, MOREY. *The Search for Bridey Murphy.* Garden City, N.Y.: Doubleday, 1956.

CAMPBELL PRAED, MRS. *The Soul of Nyria.* London: Rider, n.d.

CHARI, C. T. K. "Recent research into Hélène Smith's 'Hindoo cycle.'" Appendix to the reprint of *From India to the Planet Mars* by Theodore Flournoy, New Hyde Park, N.Y.: University Books, 1963.

DUCASSE, C. J. *A Critical Examination of the Belief in a Life After Death.* Springfield, Ill.: Charles C. Thomas, 1961.

FLOURNOY, THEODORE. *From India to the Planet Mars.* Reprint. New Hyde Park, N.Y.: University Books, 1963.

HAYNES, RENÉE. "Historian looks at past lives." *Fate* 34 (1981) 85–90.

HILL, J. ARTHUR. "Some reincarnationist automatic scripts." *Proceedings* of the Society for Psychical Research 38 (1929).

MYERS, F. W. H. *Human Personality and Its Survival of Bodily Death.* London: Longmans, 1903.

ROCHAS, ALBERT DE. *Les vies successives.* Paris: Charcornal, 1911.

———. "The regression of memory—case of Mayo." *Annals of Psychical Science* 2 (1905), 1–52.

RYALL, EDWARD, *Second Time Round.* Jersey, Channel Islands, Great Britain: Neville Spearman, 1974.

SHIRLEY, RALPH. *The Problem of Rebirth.* London: Rider, n.d.

STEVENSON, IAN. "Cryptomnesia and parapsychology." *Journal* of the Society for Psychical Research 52, (1975), 1–30.

———. "The evidence for survival from claimed memories of former incarnations." *Journal* of the American Society for Psychical Research 54 (1960) 51–71; 95–117.

WILSON, IAN. *All in the Mind.* Garden City, N.Y.: Doubleday, 1981.

Chapter 2

BANERJEE, H. N. *Americans Who Have Been Reincarnated.* New York: Macmillan, 1980.

LENZ, FREDERICK. *Lifetimes.* New York: Bobbs-Merrill, 1979.

NEPPE, VERNON. *The Psychology of Déjà-Vu.* Johannesberg, South Africa: Witwantersrand University Press, 1983.

RESTAK, RICHARD. *The Brain—the last frontier.* Garden City, N.Y.: Doubleday, 1979.

Chapter 3

GUPTA, L. D., et al. *An Enquiry into the Case of Shanti Devi.* Delhi: International Aryan League, 1936.

SAHAY, K. K. N. *Reincarnation: Verified cases of rebirth after death.* Bareilly, India: Gupton, n.d.

SHIRLEY. *The Problem of Rebirth.* London: Rider, n.d.

SPRAGGETT, ALLEN. "Have you died before? An interview with Dr. Ian Stevenson." In *Probing the Unexplained* by Allen Spraggett. New York: World, 1971.

STEVENSON, IAN. "The 'perfect' reincarnation case." In *Research in Parapsychology-1972.* Metuchen, N.J.: Scarecrow Press, 1973.

———. "The search for the less than perfect case of the reincarnation type." *Journal of Indian Psychology* 2 (1979) 30–34.

———. "The case of Jagdish Chandar." In *Cases of the Reincarnation Type Vol. I. Ten cases in India* by Ian Stevenson. Charlottesville, Va.: University Press of Virginia, 1975.

———. "The case of Kumkum Verma." Ibid.

———. "Some new cases suggestive of reincarnation. V. The case of Indika Guneratne." *Journal* of the American Society for Psychical Research 68 (1974) 58–90.

———. "The case of Mounzer Haîdar." In *Cases of the Reincarnation Type, Vol III. Twelve Cases in Lebanon and Turkey,* by Ian Stevenson. Charlottesville, Va.: University Press of Virginia, 1980.

——. *Twenty Cases Suggestive of Reincarnation.* Rev. ed. Charlottesville, Va.: University Press of Virginia, 1974.
——. "The case of Sujith Lakmal Jayaratne." In *Cases of the Reincarnation Type Vol. II. Ten Cases in Sri Lanka* by Ian Stevenson. Charlottesville, Va.: University Press of Virginia, 1977.

Chapter 4

BARKER, DAVID R. Letter to the editor. *Journal of Parapsychology* 43 (1979) 268–9.
CHARI, C. T. K.. "Reincarnation research: method and interpretation." In *Signet Handbook of Parapsychology*, Martin Ebon ed. New York: New American Library, 1978.
COOK, EMILY WILLIAMS. "Research in reincarnation-type cases: present status and suggestions for future research." In *Case Studies in Parapsychology*, edited by K. R. Rao. Jefferson, N. C.: McFarland & Co., in press.
PASRICHA, S. K., AND D. R. BARKER. "A case of the reincarnation type in India. The case of Rakesh Gaur." *European Journal of Parapsychology* 3 (1981) 381–408.
ROLL, W. G. "The changing perspectives on life after death." In *Advances in Parapsychological Research, Vol. 3*, Stanley Krippner, ed. New York: Plenum, 1982.
STEVENSON. "The case of Mounzer Haîdar," *Cases, Vol. III.*
——. *Twenty Cases Suggestive.*
——. "Characteristics of cases of the reincarnation type in Turkey and their comparison with cases in two other cultures." *International Journal of Comparative Sociology"* II (1970) 1–17.
WILSON. *All in the Mind.*

Chapter 5

BARKER, WILLIAM. "The case for Bridey Murphy in Ireland," in *The Search for Bridey Murphy* by Morey Bernstein. New York: Lancer, 1965.
——. "Bridey's debunkers debunked." Ibid.
BERNSTEIN. *The Search for Bridey Murphy.*
DEVEREUX, GEORGE. "Bridey Murphy: a psychoanalytic view." *Tomorrow* 4 (no. 4) 15–24.
HILGARD, ERNEST. *The Experience of Hypnosis.* New York: Harcourt Brace & World, 1965.
IVERSON, JEFFREY. *More Lives than One?* New York: Warner, 1976.
JUSSEK, EUGENE. *"The Puzzle of Charles: Many Lives?"* Unpublished ms.

MOSS, PETER AND JOE KEETON. *Encounters with the Past.* Garden City, N.Y.: Doubleday, 1980.

REIFF, R. AND M. SCHERER. *Memory and Hypnotic Age Regression: Developmental Aspects of Cognitive Functions Explored through Hypnosis.* New York: International University Press.

STEIGER, BRAD AND LORING G. WILLIAMS. *Other Lives.* Cottonwood, Ariz: Esoteric Publications, 1969.

SUPLEE, ZELDA. "In the wake of the Titanic." *Reincarnation Report* 1, (no. 7) 18–21.

TARAZI, LINDA. "The Reincarnation of Antonia." *Fate,* 37 (4), 1984, 50-6.

VAN OVER, RAYMOND AND LAURA OTERI, eds. *William McDougall—Explorer of the Mind.* New York: Garrett, 1967.

ZUSNE, LEONARD AND WARREN H. JONES. *Anomalistic Psychology.* Hillsdale, N.J.: Lawrence Erlbaum, 1982.

Chapter 6

KAMPMAN, REIMA. "Hypnotically induced multiple personality." *Acta Universitatis Ouluensis* (1973) Series D, psychiatrica 3

———. "Hypnotically induced multiple personality: an experimental study." *International Journal of Clinical and Experimental Hypnosis* 24 (1976) 215–27.

———. "The dynamic relation of the secondary personality induced by hypnosis to the present personality." *Psychiatria Fennici* (1975) 169–72.

KAMPMAN, REIMA, REIJO HIRVENOJA, AND OLLI IHALAINEN. "Hypno-analytic therapy of hysteric hemiphegia by means of secondary personalities." *Hypnosis* (1979) 121–6.

MOSS AND KEETON, *Encounters with the Past.*

RICHET, CHARLES. "Xenoglossie: L'ecriture automatique en langues etrangères." *Proceedings* of the Society for Psychical Research, 1905, 19, 162–94

STEARN, JESS. *The Search for the Girl with the Blue Eyes.* Garden City, N.Y.: Doubleday, 1968.

STEVENSON. "Cryptomnesia and parapsychology."

WALKER, BENJAMIN. *Masks of the Soul.* Wellingborough, Northampstonshire: Aquarian Press, 1981.

ZOLIK, EDWIN. "An experimental investigation of the psychodynamic implications of the hypnotic previous existence fantasy." *Journal of Clinical Psychology* 14 (1958), 179–83.

Chapter 7

DUCASSE, C. J. *A Critical Examination of the Belief in a Life After Death.* Springfield, Ill: Charles C. Thomas, 1961.

HULME, A. J. HOWARD, AND WOOD, FREDERICK H.*Ancient Egypt Speaks*. London: Rider, n.d.
KAUTZ, WILLIAM. "The Rosemary case of Egyptian xenoglossy." *Theta* 10 (1982) 26–30.
STEVENSON. "Xenoglossy: a review and report of a case." *Proceedings* of the American Society for Psychical Research 31 (1974) 1–268.
WILSON. *All in the Mind*.
WOOD, F. H.. *After Thirty Centuries*. London: Spiritualist Book Society, n.d.
———. *This Egyptian Miracle*. Philadelphia: David McKay, n.d.

Chapter 8

AKOLKAR, V. V. *Search for Sharada—summary of a case and its investigation*. Poona, India: Unpublished ms. circulated by the author.
DETHLEFSEN, T. *Voices from Other Lives*. New York: Evans, 1977.
FIORE, EDITH. *You Have Been Here Before*. New York: Coward, McCann, Geoghegan, 1978.
PLAYFAIR, GUY. *The Unknown Power*. New York: Pocket Books, 1975.
STEVENSON. *Twenty Cases Suggestive*.
———. "Xenoglossy: a review and report of a case." *Proceedings*.
STEVENSON, IAN, AND PASRICHA, SATWANT. "A case of secondary personality with xenoglossy." *American Journal of Psychiatry* 136 (1979) 1591–2.
———. "A preliminary report on an unusual case of the reincarnation type with xenoglossy." *Journal* of the American Society for Psychical Research 74 (1980) 331–48.
WHITTON, JOEL. "Xenoglossia: a subject with two possible instances." *New Horizons* 2 (1978) 18–26.

Chapter 9

EDELSTEIN, M. GERALD. *Trauma, Trance and Transformation*. New York: Brunner/Mazel, 1981.
KELSEY, DENYS AND JOAN GRANT. *Many Lifetimes*. Garden City, New York: Doubleday, 1967.
MACREADY, R. *The Reincarnations of Robert Macready*. New York: Zebra Books, 1980.
NETHERTON, MORRIS AND NANCY SHIFFRIN. *Past Lives Therapy*. New York: Morrow, 1978.
SARGENT, WILLIAM. *The Mind Possessed*. Philadelphia: Lippincott, 1974.
STEVENSON, IAN. "The southeast Asian interpretation of gender dysphoria: an illustrative case report." *Journal of Nervous and Mental Disease* 165 (1977) 210–8.

———. "The explanatory value of the idea of reincarnation." *Journal of Nervous and Mental Disease* 164 (1977) 305–26.
SUNDBERG, NORMAN AND LEONA E. TYLER. *Clinical Psychology*. New York: Appleton-Century-Crofts, 1962.
TORREY, E. FULLER. *The Mind Game*. New York: Emerson Hall, 1972.
WOLBERG, LEWIS R. *Hypnosis—Is It for You?* New York: Dembner Books, 1982.

Chapter 10

GRINSPOON, LESTER, AND JAMES BAKALAR. *Psychedelic Drugs Reconsidered*. New York: Basic Books, 1979.
GROF, STANISLAV. *Realms of the Human Unconscious*. New York: Viking, 1975.
GROF, STANISLAV AND JOAN HALIFAX. *The Human Encounter with Death*. New York: Dutton, 1977.
MASTERS, R. E. L. AND JEAN HOUSTON. *The Varieties of Psychedelic Experience*. New York: Holt, Rinehart and Winston, 1966.
MOORE, MARCIA AND HOWARD ALLTOUNIAN. *Journeys into the Bright World*. Rockport, Mass.: Para Research, 1978.
NARANJO, CLAUDIO. *The Healing Journey*. New York: Random House, 1973.

Chapter 11

CHARI. "Reincarnation research."
GUIRDHAM, ARTHUR. *The Cathars and Reincarnation*. London: Neville Spearman, 1970.
——— *We Are One Another*. Jersey, Channel Islands: Neville Spearman, 1974.
HICK, JOHN H. *Death and Eternal Life*. New York: Harper & Row, 1976.
MURPHY, GARDNER. "A Caringtonian approach to Ian Stevenson's *Twenty Cases Suggestive of Reincarnation*." *Journal* of the American Society for Psychical Research 67 (1973) 117–30.
REYNA, RUTH. *Reincarnation and Science*. New Dehli: Sterling, 1973.
ROLL. "Changing perspectives on life after death."
STEVENSON. "Carington's psychon theory as applied to cases of the reincarnation type: a reply to Gardner Murphy." *Journal* of the American Society for Psychical Research 67 (1973) 130–45.
SUTPHEN, DICK AND LAUREN LEIGH TAYLOR. *Past-Life Therapy in Action*. Malibu, Calif.: Valley of the Sun Publishing, 1983.

Annotated Bibliography

There are a number of books on the market that deal with the reincarnation *belief,* but that do not discuss the evidence. Chief among these are *Reincarnation: A Study of Forgotten Truth,* edited by E. D. Walker (New Hyde Park, N.Y.: University Books, 1965); *Reincarnation: The Ring of Return,* compiled by Eva Martin (reprinted by University Books [ibid], 1963); and *Reincarnation: An East-West Anthology,* edited by Joseph Head and S. L. Cranston (New York: Julian Press, 1961). The entries below have been chosen because they deal with the empirical evidence for reincarnation. This list is not exhaustive but is meant to serve as a guide to the popular and scientific literature on the subject. Obscure or historical books have not, with a few exceptions, been included.

BANERJEE, H. N. *The Once and Future Life.* New York: Dell, 1979. Although subtitled "an astonishing twenty-five year study on reincarnation," this short book is actually a credulously written and flimsy evaluation of a few cases of dubious distinction. It is also heavily padded wth extraneous information.

——————— . *Americans Who Have Been Reincarnated.* New York: Macmillan, 1980. The theme of this book is that some people in the United States recall their past lives and that past-life recall is not purely an Asian phenomenon. This is an interesting theme, but once again the author's uncritical approach and lack of both parapsychological and psychological sophistication ruin any value the book may have had for the serious student of reincarnation.

BERNSTEIN, MOREY. *The Search for Bridey Murphy.* New York: Lancer, 1965. This is the latest reprint of a case that will probably never be resolved. This edition includes chapters on the search for Bridey Murphy in Ireland that help substantiate the author's claim that Virginia Tighe's memories were not caused by cryptomnesia.

BLOXHAM, DULCIE. *Who was Ann Ockenden?* London: Neville Spearman, 1958. Drawn from the records of the late Arnall Bloxham, who specialized in the art and practice of regression, Dulcie Bloxham's book is a full-length treatment of one of his most interesting cases. The volume should be read as a study in how complex this phenomenon can become.

BLYTHE, HENRY. *The Three Lives of Naomi Henry.* New York: Citadel, 1957. This book rode on the coattails of the Bernstein volume, which originally appeared in 1956. It reports on the successful regression of a young woman in England, but because no attempt was made to verify any of her memories, the case is worthless as evidence for reincarnation.

DETHLEFSEN, THORNWALD. *Voices from Other Lives.* New York: Evans, 1977. This is one of the more refreshing volumes on past-life therapy, written by a German therapist who draws on his own case work. The book is much more sophisticated than most devoted to the same subject. The only problem is that sometimes the author isn't too clear about how or when his subjects' memories were occasionally verified.

EBON, MARTIN, ed. *Reincarnation in the Twentieth Century.* New York: New American Library, 1969. As a quick reference guide to several of the classic cases in the literature, Ebon's volume is hard to beat. Though very popular in style and presentation, it is enjoyable and thoughtfully edited.

FIORE, EDITH. *You Have Been Here Before.* New York: Coward, McCann, Geoghegan, 1978. Of all the books on the virtues of reincarnation therapy, Dr. Fiore's is probably the worst. The author focuses chiefly on the cures she has obtained but offers no critical evaluation of the many alternative explanations for her (apparent) success.

GLASKIN, G. M. *Windows of the Mind: The Christos Experiment.* London: Wildwood House, 1974. The focus of the Christos technique is on helping a person explore his or her past lives through guided imagery *cum* massage *cum* out-of-body travel. Interesting, but not very evidential.

GRAHAM, DAVID. *The Practical Side of Reincarnation.* Englewood Cliffs, N.J.: Prentice-Hall, 1976. This is a very popular and somewhat junky book on the subject. It contains several popularly presented cases, interviews, and metaphysical discussions. The author's uncritical approach toward the subject becomes unbearable at times.

GUIRDHAM, ARTHUR. *The Cathars and Reincarnation.* London: Neville Spearman, 1970. As an engrossing case study in reincarnation, Dr.

Guirdham's book would be hard to beat. It revolves around the author's discovery that one of his psychiatric patient's problems
stemmed from her past life as a Cathar heretic in which he, too,
played a role. Despite the fact that this is potentially one of the most
important cases ever documented, the author has undermined his
own case by his refusal to provide any documentation of the case to
outside investigators. (For more on this problem see Ian Wilson's
book cited below.)

_____. *We Are One Another*. Jersey, Channel Islands: Neville Spear-
man, 1974. This sequel to *The Cathars and Reincarnation* presents
evidence that the author and many of his friends *all* lived their previous lives as Cathars. Just as engrossing as the first of Dr. Guirdham's
reincarnation books, it suffers from the same fault.

IVERSON, JEFFREY. *More Lives than One?* New York: Warner Books, 1976.
Probably one of the more solid books on past-life regression, this book
is a journalistic investigation into the work of the late Arnall Bloxham,
who was active in England until his recent death. Several of these
cases are provocative because of the wealth of historical detail his subjects tended to come up with. Although some doubt has been cast on
the validity of some of these cases by Ian Wilson (see below), this is
one of the more sober books on a much-maligned approach to the reincarnation issue.

JAY, CARROLL. *Gretchen, I Am*. New York: Wyder, 1977. Dr. Ian Stevenson actively supported this case, which revolved around an Ohio housewife
who spontaneously began remembering a past life in Germany while
under hypnosis. The most significant factor of the case was the subject's ability to speak in German during her past life "spells." The case
has all the earmarks of a hoax, despite Dr. Stevenson's whole-hearted
endorsement.

KLINE, MILTON V. *A Scientific Report on "The Search for Bridey Murphy."* New
York: Julian Press, 1956. The publication of this book was a backlash
to the success of the publicity over the Bridey Murphy case. Whether it
is truly "scientific" is a matter of opinion, but it does contain some
excellent information on the problems inherent in the use of hypnotic
regression.

KELSEY, DENYS AND JOAN GRANT. *Many Lifetimes*. Garden City, N.Y.:
Doubleday, 1967. Joan Grant is a British psychic who recalls several of
her previous lives. Dr. Kelsey is her psychiatrist husband. Most of the
book consists of personal statements about the psychic sense, written
by Joan Grant; while Dr. Kelsey contributes a fascinating chapter on
his own work with past-life therapy. This chapter is more sober than
most material on the subject.

LENZ, FREDERICK. *Lifetimes*. New York: Bobbs-Merrill, 1979. This book takes a
refreshing look at cases of spontaneous past-life recall. The author

feels that the cases follow a predictable pattern, although research conducted by the present author did not bear it out. The case material is provocative, nonetheless.

LEONARDI, DELL. *The Reincarnation of John Wilkes Booth.* Old Greenwich, Conn.: Devin-Adair, 1975. Many people are turned off by those who claim to remember having been famous people. Dr. Leonardi's book is devoted to a case in which a subject relived his life as John Wilkes Booth and was able to recall much accurate information about the famous assassin. It is hard to tell whether it was a case of cryptomnesia or paranormal recall. The author takes a critical attitude to the material, so the book is much better than it might strike the reader at first glance.

MACREADY, R. *The Reincarnation of Robert Macready.* New York: Zebra Books, 1980. This three-hundred page paperback offers the complete inside story of the author's attempt to trace his sexual problems through past-life therapy. The case is disappointing because his problems were never cured, but the book will be of value as a psychological study on this form of treatment. Interesting, but basically inconsequential.

MOSS, PETER AND JOE KEETON. *Encounters with the Past.* Garden City, N.Y.: Doubleday, 1981. If you have been put off by most of the drivel written on past-life regression, this book will be an eye-opener. It is an analysis of several cases Joe Keeton has uncovered in his practice. The authors carefully chose their cases so that each of them point to a *different* source for hypnotically elicited past-life memory. A truly fine analytical work, though it could have used a comprehensive synthesis or discussion chapter at the end.

NETHERTON, MORRIS WITH NANCY SHIFFRIN. *Past Lives Therapy.* New York: Ace, 1978. This book appeared on the market during a time when reincarnation was all the rage. The emphasis is on the therapeutic virtues of past-life therapy. While I feel the tone of the book is psychologically naive, at least the author realizes that there are alternate explanations for his success, so he doesn't "push" reincarnation. Worthwhile to some degree.

REYNA, RUTH. *Reincarnation and Science.* New Delhi: Sterling Publishers, 1973. Talk about books that promise more than they deliver. Dr. Reyna's book is actually an almost incomprehensible compilation of metaphysics, badly understood physics, and parapsychology. The reader will probably put down this book with little idea of just *what* points the author was trying to make.

RYALL, EDWARD. *Twice Born.* New York: Harper & Row, 1974. Originally published in Great Britain as *Second Time Round,* the book and the author's claims are discussed in the first chapter of this present book. Although earnestly written, the case seems to be more one of cryptomnesia than anything else.

STEARN, JESS. *The Search for the Girl with the Blue Eyes.* Garden City, N.Y.: Doubleday, 1968. Jess Stearn has made a name for himself as the author of several books on the paranormal. This was his tenth book and it is primarily an investigative report into the memories of a young woman in Canada who recalled a past life under hypnosis. Though many of her memories were not verified, it is hard to dismiss the case as a result of cryptomnesia. In general the case is more important than many writers and scholars on reincarnation have considered it.

STEIGER, BRAD. *You Will Live Again.* New York: Dell/Confucian Press, 1978. As a popular rehash of the evidence and teachings of the reincarnation belief, this book will be of some limited use. Some of the case material is interesting, but the whole approach adopted by the author is naive and very unsophisticated.

——————— . *The Enigma of Reincarnation—We Have Lived Before.* New York: Ace, 1967. The same comments made above apply to this earlier work as well, although *The Enigma of Reincarnation* is somewhat worse and much of the material is drawn from questionable sources.

STEIGER, BRAD AND LORING G. WILLIAMS. *Other Lives.* Cottonwood, Ariz.: Esoteric Publication, 1969. This book, which was eventually reissued by Hawthorn Books, is a genuinely interesting account of the work of the late Loring Williams, who successfully regressed several gifted subjects. Some of his cases are very hard to explain away, and the whole tone of the volume is more sophisticated than one usually finds in Mr. Steiger's more popular books.

STEVENSON, IAN. *Twenty Cases Suggestive of Reincarnation.* Charlottesville, Va.: University Press of Virginia, 1974. Dr. Stevenson's seminal volume has become a classic and still remains his most readable treatment on cases of the reincarnation type.

——————— . *Cases of the Reincarnation Type, Vol. I: Ten Cases in India.* Ibid, 1975. Although the cases in this volume are more extensively analyzed then in his earlier volume, the presentation comes off a little drier.

——————— . *Cases of the Reincarnation Type, Vol. II: Ten Cases in Sri Lanka.* Ibid, 1977. The same comments apply.

——————— . *Cases of the Reincarnation Type, Vol. III: Twelve Cases in Lebanon and Turkey.* Ibid, 1980.

WALKER, BENJAMIN. *Masks of the Soul.* Wellingborough, Northamptonshire: Aquarian Press, 1981. As a book that attempts to critically evaluate the evidence for reincarnation, this volume is a total failure. The author's negative appraisal is based on weak and often superficial criticisms of some of the classic cases in the literature.

WAMBAUGH, HELEN. *Reliving Past Lives.* New York: Harper & Row, 1978. The author of this book eventually became somewhat of a cult figure with her techniques for "group" past-life hypnosis. Her evidence is not very strong and some of the discussions are not very compelling, but it is at least an interesting book. The author's description of her early work and how she became interested in reincarnation is alone worth reading.

_____ . *Life Before Life.* New York: Bantam, 1979. This sequal to the author's previous book is a not-very-interesting account of her hypnotic explorations into the actual process of reincarnation, especially the soul's fate in between incarnations. It is all rather tedious but to quote Abraham Lincoln, "For those who like this sort of thing, this is just the sort of thing they'll like."

WILLISTON, GLENN AND JUDITH JOHNSTONE. *Soul Search.* Wellingborough, Northamptonshire: Turnstone Press, 1983. Subtitled "spiritual growth through a knowledge of past lifetimes," *Soul Search* subjects readers to nothing more than a boring, naive, and annoyingly bombastic argument for belief in reincarnation and karma. Most of the "evidence" used to promote the author's viewpoints are based on hypnotic regression sessions.

WILSON, IAN. *All in the Mind.* Garden City, N.Y.: Doubleday, 1981. Mr. Wilson's volume is probably the most important critique ever attempted of the reincarnation question—apart from the present book, of course! Some of his criticisms are extremely valuable, especially his analyses of some hypnotic regression cases. Unfortunately, the book is marred by the author's snow-job approach to many cases and his equally questionable treatment of Ian Stevenson's work. His attempts to "explain" reincarnation memories as constructed by an element of the unconscious will be superficially appealing to readers unfamiliar with the research on which he improperly builds his arguments. Nonetheless, it is one of the few serious books on reincarnation available and should be read by students of the controversy. The author's bias is usually so transparent that the critical reader will have little trouble spotting it and taking some aspects of the book with a grain of salt.

The following books contain chapters on reincarnation that offer capsulated summaries of the evidence. They do not usually include in-depth treatments of the issue but can serve as introductory surveys:

BEARD, PAUL. *Living On.* New York: Continuum, 1981. A short chapter is included on spiritualist beliefs and psychic communications relevant to the reincarnation doctrine. No summary of the evidence is included.

CHRISTOPHER, MILBOURNE. *Search for the Soul.* New York: Crowell, 1979. The book's final chapter is a generally non-committal yet skeptical account of some of Dr. Stevenson's cases, the Bridey Murphy case, and Helen Wambaugh's work. The treatment is superficial and hackneyed.

DUCASSE, C. J. *A Critical Examination of the Belief in a Life After Death.* Ducasse devoted about one-hundred pages of his book to evaluating and summarizing all the evidence then available on the reincarnation question. His analysis of the Bridey Murphy case is especially good, and he includes a brief summary of de Rochas' research. A very intelligent handling of the subject and well worth reading.

GAULD, ALAN. *Mediumship and Survival.* London: Heinemann, 1982. Although the author's chapter on reincarnation is unfortunately short, Dr. Gauld presents an intelligent and analytical treatment of several lines of evidence. The focus is on Ian Stevenson's research, which he analyzes both pro and con.

JACOBSON, NILS. *Life Without Death?* New York: Delacorte, 1973. This book was translated from the Swedish and the chapter on reincarnation is rather novel. The author focuses on several cases of spontaneous past-life recall as well as on some of Stevenson's cases. Most of the original case material included is not very compelling, but at least it is fresh information. The treatment given this material is also fairly sophisticated.

SIBLEY, MULFORD A. *Life after Death.* Minneapolis: Dillon, 1975. Since this book was written basically for teenagers, its chapter on reincarnation is brief and simple. But the author does a fine job of summarizing some of the classic cases from the literature.

SPRAGGETT, ALLEN. *The Case for Immortality.* New York: New American Library, 1974. The author's chapter on reincarnation covers a wide range of case material and draws upon Stevenson's work, Joan Grant's writings, and some critical material on reincarnation. All this information is set against the philosophical and religious issues that arise from belief in reincarnation.

_____ . *Probing the Unexplained.* New York: World, 1971. This volume includes an interview with Ian Stevenson, who has long been reticent about presenting his research via the popular press. The introductory remarks concentrate chiefly on the Corliss Chotkin Jr. case and a few others. The interview is very interesting since Dr. Stevenson discusses a few cases he has not yet formally written up.

TABORI, PAUL. *Beyond the Senses.* New York: Taplinger, 1972. Mostly just a rehash of Stevenson, Ducasse, and Bridey Murphy.

Index